START AND RUN A PROFITABLE CATERING BUSINESS

START AND RUN A PROFITABLE CATERING BUSINESS

From thyme to timing:
Your step-by-step business plan

George Erdosh

Self-Counsel Press
(a division of)
International Self-Counsel Press Ltd.
Canada U.S.A.

First edition: March, 1994

Canadian Cataloguing in Publication Data

Erdosh, George, 1935–
Start and run a profitable catering business
(Self-Counsel business series)
ISBN 0-88908-772-5

1. Caterers and catering — Management. I. Title. II. Series.
TX911.3.M27E72 1994   642'.4'068   C94-910071-4

Cover photography courtesy of Gary Ritchie
Drawings by Janette Lush
"Blondie" cartoons reproduced with special permission of King Features Syndicate.

Self-Counsel Press
(a division of)
International Self-Counsel Press Ltd.

Head and Editorial Office	*U.S. Address*
1481 Charlotte Road	1704 N. State Street
North Vancouver, B.C. V7J lHl	Bellingham, Washington 98225

Contents

Samples

Acknowledgments

"Too many cooks spoil the broth" goes the proverb; this is true for commercial and domestic kitchens. By choice, I am the cook both in my catering kitchen and in our home kitchen, and I like it that way. One cook is enough in a family.

One writer is enough in a family, and that was true for some time in ours. My wife is professional writer. Because of this, I was surrounded by writers as several of our friends are writers, too. Writers' groups meet at our house and writing and editing successes and failures are frequent topics of conversations.

I thought I was immune to the writing bug and was quite happy to be the king of my kitchen. But eventually I caught the infection and once I got into it, I could see what keeps writers going. I could feel all the excitement of transmitting information to others who may benefit.

That's how this book was born. From the beginning, my wife, Marj Stuart, kept me going through the frustrating and doubtful phases. By default she became the editor and she even gave me a family rate. The book was my idea, but it would have succumbed to infant mortality at a very early age without her help and constant encouragement. I would like to thank her for that and apologize for intruding into her territory as the only writer in the family.

I would also like to thank Nicky Major of Major, The Gourmet, a catering company in Vancouver, British Columbia, for helping me with the legal aspects of catering on the Canadian scene. Finally, I would like to acknowledge Mike Roman of CaterSource in Chicago, a selling/marketing and catering guru, for the information I obtained from his seminars.

Introduction:
The Appetizer

Catering — the business of preparing, presenting, and serving great food (and tasting it along the way), then graciously but modestly accepting the compliments at the end of an event. Every guest wants to know who the caterer is and they all take a business card. The reputation of the caterer spreads at once (since word-of-mouth is the best advertisement of all) and the telephone rings all the time. People beg the caterer to reserve dates for them. Sounds like a truly lucrative business.

Is it really that easy? To an outsider who has had no inside contact with the catering business before, this scenario sounds ideal, a perfect way of making a good living while having fun. This is the main reason so many people turn to catering as a possible source for a new business venture, part- or full-time.

Many caterers jump into their new profession from completely different fields. My own experience is a good example, having been a mineral exploration geologist for some 25 years prior to establishing myself as a caterer. You don't need to be afraid of a complete career change; it really is not that uncommon.

Opening a restaurant seems to have an equally high appeal, though restaurants and their workings are a little more visible to the public. The failure rate in both businesses is extremely high, showing that the lucrative appeal is illusionary. No matter where you live, restaurants are

opening and closing constantly. Some of them cannot stay in business even for a year. This is equally true for catering except that business is much less visible. Most caterers don't want walk-in clients, so the public is often unaware of their presence.

However, the business of food catering is not quite as gloomy if you know what you are getting into from the very beginning; it can be fun and a pleasure to run a profitable catering business.

This book is written for people who either have already started catering on a very small scale and are struggling to establish themselves and their businesses, or who think they might enjoy opening a catering business but have little or no concept of what to expect. This book is also for those who already have the knowledge, experience, and financial backing to start a business right away. For those of you who think of catering as a possible future career — perhaps in retirement or once the children are raised, this book shows you how to get yourself ready.

It tells you what to expect, what you are risking, what skills are essential to have even before you consider getting into catering, and what skills are desirable though you can succeed without them.

Other books on catering are written from the point of view of large catering establishments, hotels, and banquet halls. But very few, if any, caterers ever started large. Most start tiny and grow as they succeed. This book is written by a small caterer for entrepreneurs who want to start small and become successful as small caterers.

This book is also for those who want to start with minimal financial backing and equipment, minimum staff, and for those wanting to know what to learn, how to gain experience, and when to apply for a business license.

The dream of being a professional caterer is appealing to many: the lure may be the pleasures of cookery, creating, or altering recipes and dishes; presenting them with an artistic touch that instantly stops the most stimulating conversation around the table; serving and pleasing guests; or simply the mistaken belief that catering is an easy way of earning a living.

Many people have considered catering a profession; few have acted on that wish seriously. First of all, once you stop and think about all the logistics of starting a complex business like catering, you may quickly lose your belief that it is easy. But if you follow the advice and steps given in this book, you may realize your dream and enjoy the varied life of a successful caterer.

1
Entrée: The Ifs And Whys Of It

a. *Before you decide to start a catering business*

Before you embark on your new catering business, you should realize that there are essential skills and knowledge that every caterer must have. Your chances of succeeding without these prerequisite skills are slim indeed. To succeed as a caterer, you've got to be an organizer, a planner, a problem-solver, an excellent cook, and an artist with a flair for presentation. Some catering skills are relatively easy to learn; all you need is practice. Others you have to be born with.

The knowledge and skill considered essential for catering is discussed in more detail in chapter 3. You must decide for yourself how many of those skills you already have, where your weaknesses lie, and how you can overcome any problem areas.

When you operate a reasonably large catering business, you won't need to know how to do everything; someone else on the team may have the skills you lack. But if you want to start a small operation, often doing all the work by yourself, be sure there is no weak spot in your business: you need to have all the required skills and knowledge.

By the time you are ready to spread the word about your new catering service, you should be fully confident about your abilities. Of course, you'll learn through trial and error and through the day-to-day experience of running your business, but it will take years before you can call yourself an expert.

Even if you have employees or a partner who complements your weak areas, you should not neglect those skills. After all, when your part-time food preparer with an artistic touch in food presentation cannot make it into the kitchen for a last minute lunch order, you will have to take his or her place and attempt an almost equally glamorous presentation.

Even if your business is large enough to employ workers who can take over the various tasks required to successfully execute an elaborate wedding, your expertise in the different fields will make you a better manager, a better judge of your employees' work, and a better person to coordinate the event.

If you look at the list of essentials and find you're lacking several that won't be easy to acquire, perhaps it is time to reconsider. Maybe this avocation is not meant to be your next career. Can you learn to be extremely organized and efficient or have these always been alien concepts to you?

Since you're now considering catering as a profession, chances are good that you already have a number of skills you'll need.

For now, let's presume that you consider yourself an excellent potential caterer and proceed to the next step.

b. *Types of catering*

There are at least a dozen different types of catering niches or styles. Some are not exactly catering (e.g., preparing and serving food to clients) but they are closely related. All of them deal with food and food preparation. Decide which type of catering best fits your personality, skill level, interest, and expectations, and focus on that. As you learn more, you can expand into other areas without much effort, either slowly, gradually, or all at once.

First of all, catering services have two broad areas: corporate and social catering. Corporate catering is fairly routine concentrating on breakfasts, luncheons, and occasional dinners. Corporate receptions, however, are not routine at all — they are often very lavish — and they let you express your full artistic creativity with food presentation.

Social catering (i.e., catering for private clients) calls for every type of food service imaginable. Most of these events are receptions, breakfasts, luncheons, and dinners. The number of guests for full meals are relatively small, and receptions are not as large as corporate receptions. The difference is in the budget. Most corporations can be more lavish with their budgets. However, large private parties, like weddings and bar mitzvahs, may also have substantial budgets and a large number of guests.

There is another area that is not so easy to classify: institutional catering. It includes off-premise catering for any institution, or for government agencies that really are not corporations, but the type of catering requested by them is similar. This includes schools, hospitals, various other public institutions, and government offices. In fact, many of these catering jobs are done in-house, but if the requirement is for better quality catering or the in-house staff cannot accommodate catering needs, an outside contractor is called in.

The main difference between institutional and corporate catering is the budget. The budget for institutional catering is usually lower, sometimes far lower, than for corporate catering. It is a catering niche in the low-end or medium-quality sector.

Nearly all caterers do both corporate and social catering, but how much of each varies widely from business to business. Even if a caterer attempts to work in corporate catering entirely, never marketing to social clients, he or she will find that guests attending the corporate events may call to request catering for social events. This kind of solicitation is hard to refuse. The same applies if you try to restrict your business to private parties. However, the two types of groups make a pleasant blend. Both require a different approach and different types of service, and both pose different problems. They complement each other on your calendar, too. Corporate events are generally scheduled on weekdays, social events on weekends.

What separates caterers most from each other, however, is what class of catering they choose to do. The field varies from low-end to high-end (or low-budget to

Reprinted with special permission of King Features Syndicate.

high-budget) with a complete spectrum in between. Decide where you want to be, but never attempt to span the complete spectrum. That is simply not good business philosophy. Large caterers may have a low-budget division along with their medium-budget business. Small caterers, however, should stick to a narrow band of the spectrum.

In low-budget catering, expect much more business, much higher volume, more competition, more production-line food preparation, and little leeway for creativity. Your business will be more in demand (though it also depends on the state of the economy), and you can expect lower profit margins, higher volume, better overall profits, and longer working hours.

In high-budget catering, you will have much more fun, less competition, possibly less work, more exacting demands, and more tension. Your clients will be much more particular and expect more from you, but will pay to have those demands met. Your business will be vulnerable to economic problems because high-end catering is slashed quickly from both corporate and social budgets. Events are less frequent, but if you price them right and watch your costs, they can still be very profitable.

In addition to the broad catering areas outlined above, here are niches that are possible for a small caterer:

- Picnics
- Barbecues
- Kosher catering
- Subcontracting to large caterers
- Selling to retail outlets
- Subcontracting to hotels, banquet halls
- Corporate gifts
- Coffee breaks, meeting breaks
- Breakfasts and brunches
- Food styling
- Fundraising
- Catering for small groups only
- Last-minute catering
- Producing private-label food items

The last item, producing private-label food, is not strictly catering, but if you find the right food item, it could be very profitable. Thousands of new food items hit the market every year, but only a small number make it to long-term profits. The other niches are fairly obvious and can be profitable. Food styling is not exactly catering, but is an artistic niche you may consider. Some caterers hire food stylists on a consulting basis to present their food displays for particularly fancy events.

Two areas are in great demand: catering for small groups and last-minute catering. Few caterers want to do either. Small groups are simply not profitable unless this is your niche and you are set up specifically to do those events. Caterers get many calls for small events, such as lunch or dinner for five to ten guests, but are reluctant to take them unless they are for good, steady clients.

Similarly, there are many last-minute calls, mainly from corporations, when unexpected events call for a meal in the boardroom. Those are also hard for caterers and many take them reluctantly or refuse them. If you decide to market yourself as a last-minute caterer, you may find another niche here. Advertising in the Yellow Pages and letting other caterers know your niche will help in getting small and last-minute events.

c. What to expect in catering

You can expect long hours and little profit, at least in the beginning. As you establish your business, the profits will slowly creep up and the number of working hours will slide down. Don't expect catering to be a get-rich-fast business. However, if you find just the right niche for yourself and you are

3

good at what you do, there is no reason not to expect a very handsome profit.

Be warned that the burnout rate in the food business is very high, in both restaurants and catering. If you put all your energy into the business for several years, you are likely to feel the symptoms. In the beginning, the business will demand all your energy and enthusiasm, but eventually you have to balance your life in other directions as well or burnout will come even sooner.

In spite of these gloomy warnings, there are bright aspects to catering. If there weren't, the business would not have any interested followers. It can be a glamorous, show business-type world if you are in medium- to high-end catering. It is varied, rarely monotonous, and whenever there is a lot of long routine work to do, it means you have a large party that will bring in a good profit if you priced your event right. That prospect surely brightens the hours of messing with unruly phyllo dough.

And here is one more bright aspect: very few small businesses in today's aggressive markets can compete successfully with large corporations. Small farms, small grocers, even small law offices cannot compete with the large firms and chains. Catering begs to differ. The industry is characterized by small- and medium-sized businesses with very few large ones. Large caterers mainly offer mass-produced, airline-type food; the quality suffers thanks to the huge volume produced. Few large caterers are able to maintain reasonably good quality. A good example is hotel and banquet catering. Have you ever had high-quality catered food from these establishments? There might be some, but so far I have not heard of them.

Your small operation *can* successfully compete with any large caterer in your area. You can offer competitive prices and far better quality than they can.

2
How To Become A Caterer

There are three ways for you to get into the catering business:

(a) start from scratch with nothing and build slowly into a business,

(b) purchase an existing business with a name, client list, and equipment, or

(c) buy into an existing business as a partner or work for an existing caterer to earn equity as a partner.

The first method is by far the least expensive way to start, but without a client base, it is a slow rise to the top.

Purchasing an existing business can be quite costly, but you are running a business from day one with a cash flow, presumably a positive one. Often the purchase agreement stipulates that the former owner will assist for several months with the smooth running of the business and perhaps even deal with the clients you inherit. You have all the equipment and staff in place.

Buying into an existing business as a partner may also be costly, but you don't take on all the responsibility and the tremendous tension of running a business all by yourself all at once. Here you can ease into the business and partnership over months or even years. These three methods are discussed in more detail below.

a. Starting out on your own

Most catering businesses start with one individual simply starting from scratch.

Perhaps you are known as a good cook and organizer, have been in charge of several church dinners for 100 to 150 guests, and you pulled each one off beautifully. The dinners were great, on time and plentiful, everyone was served promptly, and you were showered with praise.

Then someone who attended one of the dinners called you and asked if you could cater her daughter's wedding reception for 50 guests. You are stunned with the request and you give a noncommittal answer. You want to think about this for a day. But once you have a chance to consider the idea, it begins to take shape in your mind. What a challenge it would be! An exciting possibility to earn money while having fun at the same time. A career change is on your mind and by pure coincidence, an interesting possibility suggests itself: catering!

So you agree to do the wedding, but before that happens, someone else wants you to cater a classy dinner party for eight guests, which turns out to be a fabulous affair. You are gaining confidence, and by the time you're getting ready for the wedding reception, you've not only earned a little unplanned income, you've also earned a great deal more in self-confidence. You managed to cater two completely different events all by yourself. You may have made a few errors at the wedding reception, but neither the hostess nor the guests noticed anything thanks to your quick thinking in resolving the problems.

This example illustrates how a large number of catering businesses start.

When it is not by chance, it takes deliberate planning to begin a catering service. You may have worked for a caterer and come to the conclusion that you could do it even better. So you decide to go out on your own and perhaps even give yourself a tentative date for when you want to be ready to start.

Virtually all caterers start out part-time from their own home kitchens on a very small scale and generally grow by word-of-mouth. This kind of catering in most, if not all, communities is illegal. Serving the public from a home kitchen is against health department standards; nonetheless it is done all the time. As long as your business remains small, chances are you will not get into trouble with the local authorities.

Many caterers work out of their kitchens for years without a problem. But as your volume increases, you will attract more and more attention. If the local health department finds out about your catering business, an inspector will be ringing your doorbell and asking questions. Under very strict codes, you are allowed a limited number of meals served out of a home kitchen legally, maybe eight meals a day, but this number varies in different municipalities.

The next problem is your competitors. Once you challenge a significant part of their market share and undercut their prices (your overhead is almost nil when working from a home kitchen), they will report you to the health inspector. Zoning laws probably do not allow a commercial operation in your residential neighborhood, so an unfriendly neighbor may report you, too.

Finally, chances are you are operating without insurance to cover your catering activities. Unless you are in commercial, approved facilities, you cannot be underwritten for a policy. It is unwise and dangerous to operate a food service business without substantial liability insurance. In our litigation-prone society, it would not take much provocation for a disgruntled client to sue you. Spoiled food that a guest became sick from, an olive pit inadvertently left in that broke a tooth, or a fish bone someone choked on when you served boneless fish fillets — all of these situations can result in a lawsuit that wipes you out completely. With no permits, no health inspection, no business license, and no paid sales tax, you don't have a leg to stand on. That would be the permanent end to your catering career.

Look into the laws in your area and decide for yourself if you want to start from your home to see if this field is for you. You may realize that the business is not just the pleasure of cooking, presenting, serving, and then waiting for the praise and the client's check. Since you have invested very little money, if any, so far, you can easily and painlessly change your mind. If you make arrangements for a commercial facility, you cannot change your mind without a great loss of investment, not to mention the blow to your ego.

I know a caterer who worked eight years out of her home kitchen before trouble started from her competitors. She managed to escape that long because her business started from a niche that didn't bother the competition or the health authorities. She acquired a reputation for making the most sumptuous holiday fruitcakes.

The business was very seasonal at first, her small operation perfectly legal (though I doubt that her income tax form ever showed profits from the fruitcakes), and her reputation spread in the local community. In a few years the demand was so great that she baked fruitcakes for five to six months a year and froze them for the Christmas season.

Pretty soon calls started coming in to cater little dinner parties, and in no time she was running a full-fledged catering business. The holiday fruitcakes remained a part-time operation. It was then that the competition noticed and called the health inspector. She was told to go legal or close the business.

She found a commercial, approved kitchen, and in a few weeks her operation continued almost uninterrupted, now legally, with higher prices, a bigger staff, substantially expanded space and equipment, and with a great deal more overhead expense and headache.

Soon, however, she grew big enough to hire an office manager/receptionist and a kitchen manager/chef. She spent all her time coordinating events, dealing with clients and marketing her business. She rarely went to functions unless they were exceptionally classy. Instead she played tennis in the morning, dropped into the kitchen mid-morning to have her coffee and taste a little bit of everything that was on the prep tables, and proceeded to deal with clients for a few hours. By mid-afternoon she left the facility in the capable hands of her competent staff.

This is one of the rare, successful catering stories. It illustrates how catering can start from a small niche — in this case, a great fruitcake.

You may find a similar niche for yourself. This is indeed an excellent and legally acceptable way of starting a food service from your home. The right product is very difficult to come up with, however. The market is flooded with every conceivable food product and new products come out by the hundreds every month. Only an extremely small percentage survive. If one of them is yours, you are in business.

Once you have made your decision to be a caterer, work toward your goal with a definite, deliberate plan that includes distinct steps, each of which will give you the required knowledge, skills, and information.

Many would-be caterers want to slip into the business slowly on a part-time basis while holding down another job elsewhere.

This concept sounds feasible, but rarely works in practice. A full-time commitment is necessary. Catering requires your full attention. Potential clients call to ask questions (usually about prices) and an unanswered telephone, telephone answering machine, or even an answering service discourages the caller. Very few will leave a message on your answering machine unless they know you personally. An overloaded answering service puts the caller on hold for minutes and the caller knows that it is not your receptionist. Voice mail is no better. If you cannot answer the telephone personally, hire an employee, preferably one who knows your business reasonably well. Otherwise you lose precious business every time the phone rings.

If you have another occupation that allows you to stay near the telephone where the catering calls can be answered as they come in, then part-time catering is quite acceptable. Call forwarding is an excellent solution, provided that you can answer the telephone with your catering business name, not the company for which you're working, which could be, say, embalming.

Another solution that I discuss below is partnership. If you have a partner who is a friend or a mate, then telephone sitting may be divided up between the two of you, freeing you up for some serious earning. You may need it to support your catering business.

b. Purchasing an existing business

In order to get into catering by purchasing an existing business, you need to have the following prerequisites:

- You must have funds to purchase the business outright or at least secure it with a down payment. You must also have a significant financial cushion left to run the business for many months with a possible negative cash flow and the purchase of additional equipment (see details below).

- You must be an accomplished caterer with significant skill and knowledge related to the business, *every* aspect of the business. You must be able to take over, manage, and run the business by yourself even if the former owner promises to help you in the first three months.

- You must be able to devote up to 16 hours a day to the running of your business for the first five to six months until you know all your clients well and your business intimately. After that initial period, you should be able to relax slowly, reduce your working hours, and resume your social activities.

Restaurants and catering services are often available for purchase, which makes it a buyer's market. In the restaurant business, the hours are very long, in catering the tension is extreme, and in both industries the profit margins are low and the rate of burnout is high.

If you live in a fairly large town, chances are you'll find a catering business for sale. If this is the route you have chosen, write a letter to every genuine catering establishment in town. Even delis with sideline catering or small restaurants may be possibilities. Unless they are located in high-volume, downtown areas where rents are prohibitive, their health department-approved kitchen facilities may be reason enough to consider the purchase. You can always scrap the deli or restaurant part if the purchase price is right. However, if catering is a sideline business, their client base may be too small to be of much use to you.

A fair purchase price is tricky to determine. Larger businesses with good record keeping are easier to qualify, but smaller ones are notoriously poor when it comes to books. You must know the true annual gross and net of the business for several years back to determine the fair price. Good record keeping by the current owner is a must, something as rare as a new client who pays in full in advance for an event three months from now.

Get a lawyer to help you with the purchase and an accountant to decipher just how true those records are. Needless to say, income tax returns are not reliable and the seller isn't likely to show them to a buyer since the reported gross earnings on these returns are often not as high as the true gross earnings.

There are several formulas to help determine the fair price of a running business: one calculated as a percent of the last full year's gross profits, and another based on the average of the last three years' net profits. This topic, however, should be discussed by an expert in that field, and that is why you need a lawyer who can protect your interests. The accountant you hire will thoroughly check all records, verify, if possible, their authenticity, and will tell you his or her opinion of how realistic those records are. Naturally, you should study the records very carefully yourself. Working with the present owner for a while will likely give you a clue to how good the bookkeeping records are.

If the books and record keeping have been maintained by professionals, you'll know they are reasonably accurate and correct. But a bookkeeper can only do as good a job as the records given to him or her allow. You never know if receipts are missing due to neglect or if unrelated receipts have been added. For example, when the owner bought the food mixer for her home use, did she include the receipt as a business expense in order to reduce her net income? Always be suspicious.

Chances are the owner tried to include all realistic expenses connected with the business, all labor and other costs, and every possible income in order to make both the annual gross and net profits as high as possible. The higher the annual gross, the better the business looks in the eye of the buyer, and the more the net profit is, the more the business is going to be worth.

Check the client list carefully and see how often each one uses catering services. Discuss with the owner the style of catering service, the prices charged, the average size of events, minimum and maximum number of guests, suppliers, credit lines, the labor force he or she uses, pay scale, and so on. Other questions to ask yourself: Is this the style of catering I want to do? Can I run the business without the owner's help?

Before you utter even one word expressing serious interest in purchasing the business, ask if you can work in the kitchen for a week or two with the crew and go with them to several events. No charge, of course. Even better, don't ask, demand to do it. You will learn a lot about the business and whether it is for you. Remember, you are likely to be in a buyer's market and the owner will try to bend over backwards to please you. You can do this while the lawyer and accountant are doing their work. You will be totally involved with the business you are trying to purchase.

Remember, this total immersion in every aspect of the business is essential. Do nothing else. Drop your social life to a minimum, try to live in and with the business you are trying to buy. Do your library research on legal and financial aspects, even checking out the suppliers. Whenever you have free time, work on your recipe collection and food preparation techniques. Work on your efficiency as well.

Once you have worked in the business for two to three weeks, attempt to figure out the costs for food, labor, insurance, rent, utilities, taxes, vehicles, and so on. Keep the overhead separate and compare the figures with those reported by the owner. Then estimate the food costs, or even better,

ask for a current monthly food and supplies total and calculate roughly what that current month's gross and net profits (or losses) are. That will certainly give you some indication of the authenticity of the owner's records. Discuss those with your accountant. Remember that catering income is very erratic from month to month and also seasonal. The two and a half weeks of Christmas holiday season could bring you 50% to 70% of your annual gross income!

Then it is time to develop the purchase agreement and haggle over the price. The owner will likely come up with an asking price, and you will, in consultation with your lawyer, give a much lower figure, what you feel the business is worth. No matter how far apart you start, eventually you usually can come to a mutually satisfactory agreement.

How you are going to come up with the dollars is not the subject of this book; it could be cash up front, or payments over a year or two, or there could be conditions attached to your payments regarding the seller's true representation of the business. It will depend on your situation.

Before a purchase agreement is prepared, you and the owner should do a thorough inventory of all equipment and vehicles that are a part of the business. Prepare a complete list of everything, including vehicles, office furniture and equipment, even an approximate number of china, glassware, silver, napkins, and tablecloths. Make a separate list of items that will be excluded from the sale, if any. The owner is likely to have personal items, perhaps a collection of cookbooks, files, pictures, etc. The list of items included with the business should show anything having an approximate value of $50 or more.

The purchase agreement is now the lawyer's territory. It should include the purchase price, the full list of all equipment and vehicles that are part of the purchase price, and any contracts or events in progress. If much work has already been done on an event, the owner could be entitled to some of the net proceeds. That, too, should be outlined and included in the agreement.

If the seller is willing, contract with him or her for a specified period of weeks or months, perhaps setting down a certain number of hours he or she is required to assist you per week. This can be considered "training" for the new owner at no extra cost. Be specific about what the training should include. Perhaps you want the seller to attend all catered events for a month. This may not always be possible.

The agreement should also include a list of clients with addresses, telephone numbers, contact names, a copy of the rental lease, and many other clauses for mutual protection, like goodwill. Goodwill is the client list, the results of years of marketing and selling, word-of-mouth recommendations, the name of the business, client satisfaction that generates future events, and everything else that is part of a profitable business.

The third major piece of the agreement is a covenant not to compete. Insist on this. The owner may have faithful clients he or she served for years who want the same accustomed service, not yours. Without this covenant, the owner could set up another location and keep most of the clients, leaving you sitting by a quiet telephone. The covenant should be for a minimum

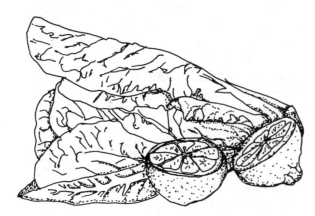

two-year period, preferably more, and it should specify a geographic area of a 30 to 40 mile radius around your kitchen.

Chances are, once you take the business over, you *will* lose some clients, perhaps many. You cannot exactly duplicate your predecessor's style, charm, food, and service. But why would you want to? You have your own style, cuisine, service, and presentation manner to develop. If you suddenly lose many clients, start worrying and ask clients about what changes they would like to see in your service or food.

Another common way to buy a business is through a business broker. Business brokers are like realtors; the best way to find them is through someone's recommendation. Your local Chamber of Commerce is also a good source. The broker will find a buyer and take care of the paperwork. When you use a broker, by contract law he or she represents the seller, because the seller pays the broker's commission. A few brokers are willing to represent the buyer. The broker can also assist in selecting an escrow officer. He or she can help in reassigning the seller's lease to you if there is one on the premises. Their fees are high since most of them don't like to deal with small businesses. Their commission is about 12% and a minimum of about $8,000.

If you are considering purchasing or expanding an existing business and you don't have ready cash, your challenge is to borrow money or equity either by selling shares or stocks, or by bringing in partners with ready cash. Both options have advantages and disadvantages, but it is beyond the scope of this book to delve into a discussion on the subject. I mention it here so you are aware of the possibilities.

c. Buying into an existing business as a partner

If you buy an existing business, make sure you know that business well: the owner, the help, and the style of catering.

Generally, there is only one way to know a business well, and that is to work in it for some time. This usually means a partnership with someone who you feel has common goals, interests, and complementary expertise. The business must be able to run profitably without serious friction between the two of you.

Business partnerships work in some cases and fail in others. It is completely unpredictable. You may get along well with a partner today but you may grow in different directions later. Like marriages, some partnerships succeed, some fail, and some float along without much satisfaction to either partner. If you find a good business partner, you have many advantages such as shared work, responsibility, expenses, and net profits. In a partnership you don't have to be an expert in all aspects of catering. In the best circumstances, your weakness is covered by your partner's strength. It is also pleasant to take some time away from the business without worrying about leaving it in dubious hands. Taking a week or two off for a well-deserved vacation is especially hard when you are the only key person. There is an unwritten law that says that the week you take off for your own pleasure, will be the week every client you have calls about an important event.

You have two choices when buying into a business. You either buy or earn part of the business up to a predetermined share and become a partner, or you work toward becoming a full owner over a period of years. For instance, you may have worked in a catering business for a while and the owner is approaching the age when he or she wants to quit and retire. This is a fairly ideal situation since you have the time to pay for the partnership slowly over time or add the so called "sweat equity" of your own labor toward ownership instead of cash. You work for little or no compensation and the value of your time applies to your equity in the business at a predeter-

mined rate. This is not easy unless you have an income-producing job and your effort into the catering business is part-time. It is also hard to work for something that gives no immediate return. What if you have worked say, 1,000 hours over a year, (averaging 20 hours a week) which earned $10,000 equity in the business (at a rate of $10 per hour) and all of a sudden business drops off significantly because of an unexpected crisis. Since you have not earned much equity yet, you have no control. You may have to see your equity slowly losing its value as the business suffers from neglect. At this point your only choice is to borrow money from Aunt Mabel or the local loan shark and buy the business outright to save the equity you already have.

Look out for diminishing personal interest in the business by the current owner. Once the end is in sight, enthusiasm weakens and you may find yourself taking the brunt of the responsibility, worries, and workload, though the owner takes much of the profit.

Whatever way you approach this, you must be sure that there is a crystal clear understanding between you and the owner. Everything, of course, must be on paper and legally binding. The help of a lawyer familiar with partnerships is essential.

Resolve critical issues before a partnership deal is finalized. For instance, define contributions to the partnership (cash, expertise, property) and the percentage of ownership granted to each partner at the inception of the deal. Arrange for a method of obtaining additional funds in the event of operating cash deficits. Define the responsibilities and remuneration for each partner. Also define when and in what order of priority cash will be distributed. And finally, make sure there are adequate provisions for buying out or removing a partner in the event of unexpected problems and procedures, or if a partner wishes to terminate the venture or if the partner dies.

Before making the decision to get involved in a business, here are some sobering statistics to consider:

• According to the National Federation of Independent Business, owners who worked with the same products or services in prior jobs have a 10% better chance of surviving over owners who have not.

• A study conducted by the same organization and American Express states that 80% of people who worked between 60 and 69 hours a week remained in business after three years.

• The same survey found that companies emphasizing good service had a higher survival rate than those offering low prices to promote business.

• Of the firms surveyed, 84% that started with $50,000 or more investment had a 10% better chance of making it than those who started with less than $20,000.

In the late 1980s, a survey on small business failures conducted by the United States Small Business Administration (SBA) over a six-year period produced these gloomy statistics shown in the chart below. Another survey by the SBA found that 65% of all new businesses fail within the first five years.

Years in business	Failure in all businesses	Failure in growing businesses	Failure in non-growing businesses
In 2nd year	23.7%	8.0%	29.5%
In 4th year	51.7%	19.1%	65.5%
In 6th year	62.7%	33.7%	72.5%

3
Personal Ingredients

a. *Essential skills and knowledge*

As briefly discussed in chapter 1, certain essential skills are a must for running a catering service. You are starting small and you must be able to run the business without help from time to time, when your helper is sick, when no one is available on such short notice, or when that small business luncheon is only profitable if you do it yourself. Whatever the reason, you don't want the extra worry of not being able to execute every piece of the event competently.

Here are the essential skills and knowledge you must have:

- Competency in cooking and food preparation

- The highest degree of planning and organizational skill

- A high degree of efficiency

- Ability to work well under pressure

- Skill in problem solving and crisis management

- An artistic touch in food presentation

- Ability to deal with clients confidently and successfully

Let's discuss each of these essentials individually.

1. Cooking and food preparation

A high degree of skill in cooking, as well as ease, efficiency, and speed in food preparation are by far the most important prerequisites for a successful small caterer. Many would-be caterers start as good home cooks with a moderate-sized repertoire and better-than-average food preparation skills. Some are knowledgeable about cookery, its chemistry and physics, while others have done a lot of food research and experimentation. Still others are professionally and formally trained food professionals, especially chefs who are tired of working for someone else with low pay, long hours, and difficult conditions in tiny, poorly equipped, inefficient, overcrowded, and hellishly hot kitchens.

Your cooking skill should be far better than a good gourmet cook, and you should have a sizable repertoire of well-tried recipes. Also, you need to be well-versed in most aspects of cooking, including the preparation of hors d'oeuvres, entrées, side dishes, salads, desserts, breads, and beverages. You not only have to know how to prepare all these items, but you must also be able to present them in an appetizing, appealing way.

If you haven't had any formal training in cookery, get some. It can be done, and you can have a great deal of pleasure and fun doing it. You don't need the entire curriculum of a cooking school, or even the majority of it. A small fraction will be quite sufficient for your catering business; which fraction will depend on what type of catering you choose. It is hardly necessary to learn the dozens of French sauces when you have no intention of using any more than a few basic ones (they are out of date anyway). And if a demanding client insists on having boulettes of beef with sauce financière, don't worry. Just look it up in your extensive reference collection and prepare it. If it is a complicated sauce, you may not get it right on the first try. Do it again, well before the event of course. With a basic cooking background and some experimenting, you will come up with the perfect dish in no time at all. And you should also have a satisfied, amazed, and impressed client.

How are you going to acquire all that cooking skill and knowledge? Practice, more practice, and plenty of reading and research. The information is available, but you have to find it. You, your friends, and family have to eat daily; the place to practice is your own kitchen with readily available and eager guinea pigs sitting around your table daily.

Cooking classes may or may not be a good idea for you. Try several offered in your local area. If you are already a good cook, you may not learn anything new, but watch the instructor's techniques. That is where the lessons may pay off for you. Videotapes and television cooking programs can help the same way. There are seminars and cooking camps for experienced chefs, too, on both cooking and presentation, though they don't come cheap. Expect to pay several hundred dollars for a two- or three-day cooking seminar, plus accommodation and related expenses. Sample #1 shows promotional material for a four-day intensive course. When you consider that in those four days you would be exposed to new tips and techniques, new knowledge and resources — things that you might otherwise have learned the hard way — several hundred dollars looks like a wise investment.

No matter how you choose to do it, total immersion in cooking and cooking techniques for an extended period is what you want. Keep on reading books on food and cooking and even simple cookbooks. No matter how poor a cookbook is, chances are there is some useful information in it.

Learn to cook an entire cross section of dishes, but emphasize the ones you want to

A Rare Opportunity!!
Strategies For Successful Catering

Napa Valley College announces a four-day intensive course on tactics and strategies for building a successful catering business. Join two outstanding instructors in the heart of the wine country for lectures and cooking workshops created for those entering the catering business or those who want to make their catering business more profitable.

MIKE ROMAN is the caterer's caterer! After 20 years of "hands-on" experience managing his family's catering business in Chicago, he founded CaterSource, The National Institute for Off Premise Catering, in July of 1984. Since then, Michael has organized, promoted, and taught over 1,600 days of seminars, lectures, conferences, and his "Hands-On" Catering Symposiums, which have brought him great acclaim. In 1988, Michael began teaching at The Culinary Institute of America as an adjunct instructor for their new catering courses, in addition to the courses he does for the CIA's Continuing Education Department. He has also taught seminars for the National Restaurant Association.

SARAH SCOTT founded Sarah Scott Catering in 1984, and the business expanded at an exhilarating pace as she developed a reputation for creating beautifully prepared meals and well-run events. She is a graduate of the School for American Chefs at Beringer Vineyards and has worked with the Great Chefs at Robert Mondavi and Napa Valley Cooking Classes. Sarah is well known as an excellent chef, offering dishes and menus that reflect her southern background, the influences of her travels in Southeast Asia, and her passion for Italian food.

TOPICS TO BE COVERED

- Low-Cost Marketing Ideas That Work
- Pricing: New Ways of Looking at an Old Problem
- Creative Event Design and Menu Planning
- The Food: Cooking Ahead, On-Site Cooking, Transportation
- Staffing and Supervision
- Site Inspections and Logistics
- Selling Corporate Catering
- Writing and Selling More Effective Bids and Proposals

The class will be held daily, Tuesday-Friday, from 9:30 a.m. to 4:30 p.m. in the Chiles House of Inglenook-Napa Valley, 1991 St. Helena Highway, Rutherford. Each day will begin with lecture, discussion, and cooking in the morning, followed by lunch and discussion, and finish with lecture and prep for the following day. Each meal will demonstrate a type of catering event.

We will be happy to assist out-of-town visitors with restaurant and hotel reservations and winery visits.

For additional information, call
Sue Farley, Culinary Arts Program Coordinator at (707) 253-3377 or
the Community Education Office at (707) 253-3070

Registration Information Listed on Reverse

*Used courtesy of Mike Roman, CaterSource, 1-800-932-3632.

prepare in your catering business. Sounds like a formidable task, but it really isn't. Once you get into the rhythm of preparing new and unusual food with unaccustomed kitchen techniques, trying other new items becomes easier and easier.

Mark each of your recipes with significant information you've discovered in preparation — anything you might need to know in the future preparation of this dish. Ingredients should be slightly adjusted to your own taste as well as to current trends. Older recipes use less spices and herbs than today's more sophisticated palates demand. Sugar used to be used more generously, too, producing the over-sweetened desserts that are not much in favor today. Oils and cooking fats were used more generously than our present awareness about good nutrition tolerates. So adjust the recipe accordingly and make sure you've marked the adaptation and results.

You will need a substantial collection of recipe books for yourself as well as reference books on cooking and food. Your choices will be dictated somewhat by the kind of catering you want to do. Of the enormous selection of cookbooks available, most will be useless to you. There are very few books with original recipes, but those are the ones you need, both for their ideas of new things to try and for your own reference.

You will also want to have several good reference books on cookery, basic food chemistry and physics, and nutritional information. These books should be read and reread, studied and restudied. It is very important for you to understand the basics behind food and cooking and to know where to look up the information if you suddenly need it quickly. As Irma Rombauer says, in her classic *Joy of Cooking*, "Knowledge is of two kinds. We know a subject as our own, or we can find information on it."

Joy of Cooking is the best and most comprehensive cookbook ever written in English, a classic since its original publication in 1931. In its revised form, it is still on almost everyone's bookshelf and should definitely be on yours, too. The amount of information and research that went into *Joy of Cooking* is simply incredible and the information is useful and up-to-date on most subjects.

There are two basic ways for cooks and chefs, whether professional or amateur, to work — either following a recipe or free form cooking (i.e., sampling the dish while cooking it until it tastes just right.) In catering, free form cooking is not advisable, particularly in preparing large quantities of food. Food should be consistently prepared from one event to the next and very predictable. If you have an excellent memory, you may be able to do it without using a recipe as a checklist, but it is certainly much safer to use one. This way you never need to taste or adjust ingredient amounts. Most chefs using recipes produce the food and serve it without even tasting it. They check and double-check recipe ingredients, making sure that nothing was left out and the right quantities were used. When the dish is finished, it is ready to be served. The chef knows exactly what it tastes like without sampling it.

Most food preparation techniques involve chopping, dicing, cutting, cleaning, peeling, and preparing at least half a dozen different types of doughs and batters. Even though machines are now used for most of these jobs, you must learn to do all the basic techniques by hand. In a small catering business, the use of a machine, even if it is available, may not be justified for a small job. Knowing how to do jobs by hand also comes in handy if machines are suddenly unavailable.

The same applies to the many doughs, batters, yeast and baking soda breads, muffins, scones, biscuits, crepes, pies, puff and choux pastries you will be preparing; you must know the right technique for each by both hand and machines.

One more hint — use your hands often. Your hands are perfect tools for the job. They accomplish the tasks quickly and are easy to clean. But don't abuse them. Use rubber gloves if you don't want to have your hands in water constantly. Kitchen work is not easy on your skin, so save your hands as much as you can. The restaurant kitchen cook is just fine with rough, red hands, deadened nerve endings (also called asbestos fingers), split skin, and cracked fingernails. But in catering you need pretty hands — they are exposed to the full view of the guests, particularly at full-service meals. In fact, that is the only part of you most guests will ever look at.

2. Planning and organization

Few fields of work require you to have such a high degree of skill in planning and organization as off-premise catering. Some areas of catering demand only a modest amount of these skills: industrial catering with a mobile kitchen, bulk-prepared food you sell to retailers, large-event catering, or even barbecues are relatively simple to conduct. But off-premise catering compels you to plan and organize for each event. However, much of it can be learned on the job if you have a good dose of common sense.

Not everyone was born a good organizer and planner. If you feel that you are poor at doing substantial planning and organization, you should not consider off-premise catering as your next career. There are many other related fields where your interest in the kitchen can be exploited.

In off-premise catering, all food and equipment must be brought to the place of the event. Nothing should be missing and the food must be in prime condition at the time of serving even though several hours may have passed between the crew's departure from the kitchen and the serving of the first guests. The hot food must be hot and the cold food must be icy cold. The facilities at which you are serving may have no kitchen whatsoever or may only have a tiny office kitchen. So you know that your equipment must be complete. Imagine if someone miscounted the silverware and you are short one fork. What can you do? How can you produce a single fork during the next 20 minutes when the crew's every minute is planned for the next three hours? The answer is careful planning so that disaster doesn't happen. If it does, then you quickly switch to your next prerequisite skill as a caterer, solving crises and emergencies.

If you think that you are a reasonably good planner and organizer, you can improve those skills by diligent effort and careful checklists. Review your first few events. Did you remember to take everything? Was planning adequate? Did what you anticipated happening happen? If so, you are capable of organizing and planning progressively larger parties.

Planning for an event must be done well in advance of the date of execution. Even the smallest event demands some thinking four to five days ahead of the date to schedule the various phases of preparation, like defrosting food and ordering supplies. Large events need even more advanced planning because you have to reserve staff time, rental items, and maybe additional subcontracting services.

Advanced planning and organization has five major parts:

- Securing supplies and rental items
- Scheduling food preparation
- Reserving staff time
- Preparing equipment and invoices
- Planning the event

The chapters that follow deal with all these aspects of planning in greater detail.

3. Efficiency

Very few professions do not benefit from efficiency. In some fields, it is an essential skill to ensure success; food service is one of those fields. The food the guests are waiting for must arrive at their table as quickly as possible. Preparation time must be kept to a minimum; only a high degree of efficiency can achieve this.

You quickly discover what you can prepare far in advance of the event and what must be done at the last minute so that staff time is used efficiently. With careful planning, organization, and good efficiency, you'll pull it off with the minimum staff possible to protect your profit margin. Fine tuning allows a small safety factor of time for unexpected problems that notoriously crop up at the last minute. If you're not a very efficient person and are unwilling and incapable of learning how to be one, hire a good catering or kitchen manager who is. Then you can concentrate on other aspects of the business, like selling and marketing, food styling and presentation or, everybody's favorite, loading and unloading.

Efficiency is necessary for several reasons. First, you must be able to shape tons of raw material into gorgeous food in the shortest possible time or you'll never get to the culminating step, feeding people. Second, many items can be prepared only at the last minute. Some foods hold well hot but every extra half hour of standing will lower the peak serving status. Many foods don't like to stay chilled too long either. Salads and fruits lose their crispness. An extra hour makes a noticeable difference. One more hour and even the host or hostess will notice. Such foods must be prepared at the last minute so the end of preparation signals the beginning of serving with no time lag. That requires meticulous preplanning so nothing goes wrong. Some catering tricks you'll learn along the way will help alleviate the last minute rush and tension. Maybe what you'll learn is how to deal with the pressure.

4. Tension: if you can't stand the heat...

To be a caterer, you must be able to live with and work under pressure and not show it. Outwardly you must be cool, smiling, apparently doing your work with ease, without rushing. Inwardly you may have five different things to worry about (e.g., the guest who is back at the buffet table to pile another ten shrimps on his plate when you allowed two-and-a-half per person, whether the sterno under the chafing dishes is going to hold out, plus countless other potential minor disasters). Nothing is predictable during an event. The guests at each one are completely different, they prefer different food, eat different portions, and interact with you and your staff completely differently.

When it is obvious that the guests like your food and ooh and ah at the elegant presentation, then you can relax and quit worrying. Once the guests and host or hostess are pleased, they will overlook any slight problems, like a missing punch ladle. If they are not pleased from the beginning, however, even small errors will grow into gross negligence and there is no forgiveness.

5. Crisis management and problem solving

Off-premise catering, no matter how well-planned and organized, is bound to have unexpected problems. Occasionally, they reach crisis proportions. When so much equipment, food, drink, staff, and peripheral items must be transported and set up for a complex event, problems *will* crop up from time to time. In the best scenario, your event is flawless as far as the client is concerned, though you and your staff know of the little bumps that you successfully overcame.

Just think of the numerous little things that must be on hand for you to prepare an elegant meal for 35 guests at home. Then think of the further complications when a similar meal must be served for 135 at an unfamiliar location. Then add the complication of another crew in your kitchen preparing a reception for 50 at the same time. Everything that goes into the refrigerator is carefully labeled according to which event it belongs to. When loading, you must be really careful that you don't accidentally take the other crew's stuff. No matter how much care is taken, there is a possibility that some things could end up in the wrong vehicle.

Other sources of problems are at the event site. No matter how carefully you

discuss every detail with the client, expect surprises. One of the things you must learn is not to despair or panic, but quickly find a way out of it, preferably before your client notices and, if at all possible, before the guests notice. Some problems can be solved with the help of the host or hostess. If an important piece of equipment or tool or ingredient was left behind, he or she may have something you can use. But usually you are better off solving it yourself without consulting the client, even if it means a quick trip to the store.

To successfully solve problems, you must expect them to happen. Remain cool and rational. Talk with your staff. Someone might come up with a good idea. For some things there is no easy solution. If you left your ice in the freezer back in your kitchen, check the hostess's freezer to see if she has enough to last while you send someone for more ice. If all else fails and you must delay the bar setup, explain the situation to the hostess with apologies and make the delay as short as possible.

Crises are more difficult to solve, but they should be expected occasionally, too. On your way to the event someone pulls in front of you and you have no choice but to hit the brakes hard (something you should never do in a catering truck!) and four lemon cloud pies scoot at high speed against the lip of the shelf. They are now misshapen and can only be served to your staff, their families, and yours. There is no time to get a comparable pie from the local French patisserie, and you have to stop at a nearby supermarket and pick up their flavorless, over-sweetened pies with the artificial topping. It is that or nothing.

Should you mention it to the client and give her a discount on the invoice? The decision is yours. I would be tempted to not say a word about it to anyone and serve them, feeling red-faced and guilty, instead of my own wonderful pies. Chances are, no one will mention the pies provided the rest of the dinner is excellent. Should the hostess tell you later that she was a little disappointed in your "lemon cloud" pie, admit your guilt and apologize. Deduct enough from the invoice to console her and promise to send her two genuine lemon cloud pies.

It is a little scary to be in a profession where you are in the limelight, where everything must go smoothly and there is so much chance for errors. Accept it, learn to live with it, even learn to love it. Eventually, solving the problems and crises will come naturally, and you'll have plenty of anecdotes to share with trusted friends and family.

6. The artistic touch

Food presentation is extremely important in many catering businesses. For high-end upscale catering, the emphasis is heavy. For fundraising projects with minimum budgets, it is much lower. High-class presentation takes time and money and you can only afford to do it if someone is willing to pay for it. That doesn't mean that the low-end caterer can get away with dumping food on aluminum disposable platters. Food can be presented nicely with minimal effort and cost, with small additional garnishes, and with a touch of artistic presentation.

Demand for high-quality food presentation is higher in affluent, sophisticated areas of the country. In some places, and especially for some clients, presentation is so important that they neglect the food quality. As long as it is beautiful, elegant, and artistic, you can serve sawdust on arugula leaves with squash blossoms, drizzled with motor oil.

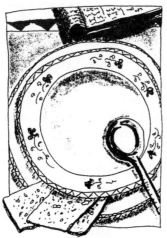

In some circles artistic presentation of food has gone too far, especially in the trendiest areas of California. The kitchen and chef put more emphasis on presentation than flavor. The two should be balanced, but flavor shouldn't suffer because of presentation. I would rather see a few simple but carefully placed garnishes on a plate complementing the entrée rather than the time-consuming creation of a food stylist.

(a) Keep it simple

Even if you are not artistically inclined, you can learn the art of simple and tasteful garnishing. There are many books on garnishes, and you should have at least a couple on your shelf. Read them, pick out a few ideas that appeal to you, and practice using them. Depending on your dexterity, you can try more elaborate garnishes.

A prepared garnish, whether a simple radish rose or scallion flower, takes time. You have to weigh this time spent against the importance of the event and the budget. If you feel the time spent is justified, then do it. But keep it as simple as possible. When the food arrives at the table, it is the entrée that guests' eyes should be focused on and only then should they wander to the side dish and the garnish. If the garnish is too elaborate, that is what guests see first. You don't want the guests to be so dazzled by small details that they miss the main attraction.

(b) Getting ideas

Glance through recent food magazines, and look at food ads and books with beautiful full-page photos. See what the professionals and food stylists are producing. Scale these ideas down, since they tend to be exaggerated in magazines. Copy them and after a while you'll be devising your own. Just look around the supermarket and see what is interesting. Use contrasting textures and colors to complement the food you are serving. For example, if it is a Tex-Mex dinner, a thin round slice of jicama could be the base on top of which you carefully place tiny rounds of red and green chili slices and a sprig of cilantro. All are prepared ahead of time and carried to the job site, ready to be placed on plates. It will take only ten extra seconds per plate once the food is on it.

(c) Decorations and garnishes

Plate garnish can only be done when the meal is full-service. For self-service, the decoration is on the table and on the serving platters. Magazine pictures will give you ideas, but most decoration in those illustrations looks artificial, commercial, and cold.

If you prefer something a little more casual, something a real person and not a computer created, then add your own more personal touch to it. I like to use fruits and vegetables with different shapes, colors, and sizes scattered around the table, encircling the serving platters.

A few unusual eye-catching items are fine but don't overdo it. A good supermarket produce department or your local farmer's market have all kinds of interesting items but you need keen eyes to find them. Look for things like an elephant garlic with its long stem topped with a flower. Or use common items like a fresh, shiny Japanese eggplant, or bright red and green chilis.

Another simple garnish is fresh carrots with the green tops left on. Place them on the table in a loose, wreath-like fashion or create a bouquet in a vase. A bouquet of combined vegetables is simple and effective, not overpowering, and reusable. The next event's guests are going to be seeing them in a different form, on their plates.

A cream pitcher filled with cherry tomatoes, wine goblets with oil-cured olives, a glass vase with a bouquet of two-foot long vermicelli — all are good examples of focal points on the serving table.

(d) Use attractive serving dishes and utensils

Creativity is required for serving pieces, too. There are only a few points to keep in mind. First, whatever the serving piece is, it must not chemically react with or discolor the food. Take special care when presenting acidic foods, like salads, pickles, or marinated vegetables.

The serving piece must also look appealing with food in it or on it. No matter how pretty a porcelain bidet is, or a brass spittoon, they are not suitable containers unless you are short of food and want to make sure you don't run out.

Highly polished silver is not used commonly anymore except for very formal, strictly traditional affairs. Anything rustic and exotic is in: terra-cotta flower pots and saucers, rough wood and baskets, and old baskets. Clay, bricks, and stones all add a certain air to your table for informal catering.

(e) Collect special props for theme parties

For theme parties you are on your own. Look for table decorations in secondhand shops, thrift stores, and at flea markets. You may want to start a collection of special props for catering to corporate clients. If you have several law firms, for instance, use a few old leather-bound law books; for health-related organizations, use a small collection of old medicine bottles or antique health books. To decorate the reception table for a construction company, buy small eye-catching toy tractors and bulldozers or some rusty old tools. Your guests

will remember that your table didn't have the same dull, standard look as dozens of other catered parties. It is a good marketing technique and is worth the extra expenditure and personal time.

7. Dealing with clients

Being a small caterer, you will be dealing with your clients personally most of the time. If you have a sales and marketing person, he or she may be the first contact with a potential new client. From that first contact the deal will be determined mainly by your relationship with that client. It will be your personal interaction that determines whether there will be any future business from that client. This is where your skill in working with people enters the scene. (See chapter 8 for further discussion on dealing with clients.)

Contact with strangers is intimidating to many, while others feel immediately comfortable with anyone. But even the most timid person can learn to be perfectly at ease when meeting potential new clients, introducing the business to them, and letting them know what you have to offer and at what price. Evening courses on public speaking are popular and there are helpful books and audio guides that offer techniques on better communication and presentation skills. See *Effective Speaking for Business Success*, another title in the Self-Counsel series, for further discussion.

Based on an initial introduction, the client will decide if you are the right caterer. If you are, start selling yourself and your business. A great deal of your success depends on how well you can do that. Catering, particularly small catering, is a very personal business. It is *you* and not your company that will be hired. Your reputation and recommendation from satisfied clients will help a great deal, but if *you personally* don't impress your client (and the first impression is always the most important), you may not have a deal. He or she may want to talk to someone else before deciding. If you give the right impression, the client may decide right away with a deposit check.

For a small catered affair, that first contact may be the only face-to-face meeting you and the client have until you arrive on the agreed-upon date with the agreed-upon food. If it is a large wedding, chances are that you will be dealing with the client (or often two or more) several times. Some clients will call you daily, even several times a day for the entire week preceding the wedding. You have to know how to reassure this client so that he or she will relax.

b. *Desirable skills and knowledge*

No one can be so perfectly well-rounded that he or she has *all* the necessary and desirable skills and knowledge for running such a complex business. You are a fortunate person if you have all seven of the essential skills just discussed; if you do, you have a good chance of becoming a successful caterer. However, there are another six skills

Reprinted with special permission of King Features Syndicate.

that are very desirable, although not essential, to have. The following are definitely ingredients for success, too.

(a) Well-developed marketing and selling techniques (networking)

(b) Good record and bookkeeping skills for administrative chores

(c) Ability to deal with staff

(d) Solid financial backing along with good budgeting skills

(e) Financial and emotional stability to deal with seasonal highs and lows

(f) Ability to deal with extreme pressure and stress during the holiday season

Let's look at each of these desirable skills in detail.

1. Marketing and selling

It is a great advantage to have solid marketing and selling skills when you own virtually any business, particularly if you are a sole proprietor. Unless you have few competitors and what you provide is much in demand, you have to think about selling your service.

If you live in a small town with few competing caterers and many social and corporate clients needing catering services, you can probably forget about the extra expense and time for marketing. If, through word-of-mouth and repeat clients, your business is operating at the level of your expectations, marketing is again a waste. But these are rare cases.

You may or may not have the time to do marketing and selling while running a catering business alone. It depends on your volume and the other time requirements the business imposes on you. To properly market your business and sell your services you will need to put in anywhere from 10 to 20 hours a week, possibly 30 to 40 hours if you want to do aggressive marketing. Can you sacrifice that much time from the catering side?

Many caterers who have all the essential skills to run a good catering business, but who also can sell and market, prefer to do the latter and delegate the catering end either partly or entirely. The choice is yours as long as you can find competent, reliable help. Good sales and marketing people are rare. It is often easier and cheaper to find a good catering and kitchen manager.

Networking is an important part of marketing. To be good at networking, you have to have self-confidence and social skills. If you have decided to hire a person to do your marketing, you can either do your own networking or delegate it to your marketing person. Many people love networking and are good at it. Networking will bring business for you, both directly and through referrals.

2. Record and bookkeeping

Many, if not most, small business owners detest the numerous chores that keep popping up at the record keeping end of their business. They consider them unnecessary headaches and procrastinate as long as possible, except when it comes to depositing the checks. Office chores are a necessary headache and the longer they are postponed, the more difficult it will be to do them, not only because of the sheer volume of the work but because you forget the useful little details you didn't record when they were still fresh in your memory.

The best way to approach office chores is to do them daily, keeping up-to-date on every record keeping system you use. There will be some extremely busy periods in your business when you simply cannot get into the office. Fine. Postpone the office stuff, but only until the next opportunity comes, that next free hour or two. Don't let your mind tell you there is no free time. Much of the office work approached this way can be, if not exactly fun, at least tolerable. Adding up your books every month can definitely be fun, provided your cash flow is a healthy positive one.

Without good records you face many potential problems. You don't know how much you owe your staff. You'll have to rely on their record keeping, a very poor practice. You don't know how much to charge clients; you forget a scheduled event because it didn't get on your calendar! You don't know how your business is doing, what your actual expenses and your total receipts are, and what your gross and net profits (or losses) are. Your business is doomed under these conditions, no matter how good your food is.

Your other choice is to hire someone to do all the office chores. But remember, if someone else is doing your book work, you will still have to hand your carefully kept records to him or her, and the bookkeeping won't be any better than your record keeping.

3. Staff management

If you are basically a one-person operation, with on-call staff only, your staff and production control problems will be minimal. If your business is a little larger and you employ part-time or even full-time staff and perhaps a sales representative and marketing person as well, the ability to deal with your staff becomes important.

(a) Good serving staff

One ingredient of a successfully executed event, besides your excellent food, good planning, and timing, is the gracious and superb service your staff provides. How your people present themselves, how they interact with the guests, how much they are interested in serving the food and not just receiving their weekly checks, is what the client perceives as service. Good food with mediocre service will not bring you repeat clients. Good food with poor service gives rise to complaints.

There are two common problems with serving staff. One is their acceptance that being a server puts them in a subservient position. This is often a problem with better-educated staff from middle-class backgrounds who take catering jobs to earn extra income. They resent being treated like servants. A second problem occurs with serving staff being overly friendly with the guests, talking with them and treating them as equals, even engaging them in lengthy discussions while the food is getting cool on the serving tray they are supposed to be passing around.

When hiring your staff, make it clear to them that you are in a service business and their role is to *serve* the invited guests, not just to dispense food as a host or hostess would. (See chapter 7 for further discussion on staffing.)

Determine how to give good service. Choosing and motivating your staff are two essential parts of this. These two items also apply to your kitchen staff. In the kitchen you are dealing with a staff whose duty is plain work, often monotonous and unpleasant, like cleaning 42 pounds of shrimp. Rotating your staff from monotonous to creative work is helpful. Doing the routine work in teams is also a good way of easing the burden.

Your relationship with your sales and marketing staff will probably also be reflected in their performance unless you are lucky enough to find someone who works well without your supervision.

(b) Combatting employee theft

Theft is a serious problem in virtually all food service facilities; the bigger the institution, the bigger the problem. The problem is the staff taking some of your raw material home. This is not easy to deal with and the amounts taken are relatively small since food does not represent large values. This may be part of the reason why the poorly paid staff hardly considers it dishonest to lift a pound of butter or half a dozen chocolate chip cookies. The issue is more serious if half a dozen pieces of filet mignon disappear regularly. Even $20 worth of food a day departing your kitchen with the staff can have an impact on your profit margin, especially if it happens routinely.

To make matters worse, in a small business you don't purchase much extra of anything. If you need 23 steaks for a dinner, you may buy a few extras in case the guest number increases at the last minute or as an insurance against one steak being ruined beyond repair, or being dropped in the dog dish in front of the client. Six steaks taken from the refrigerator can spell disaster.

Theft is usually not much of a problem in a small business with a small staff. You know each other well and your relationship is cordial. Once you and your staff grow and you hire minimum wage dishwashers and extra food prep staff, that is when theft could become a real problem, particularly if you are frequently absent from the kitchen.

Larger restaurants, hotel, and institutional kitchens deal with the problem by daily and weekly inventory control. This does discourage theft since the staff knows about the strict control. If they are taking the butter, it will be limited to one pound instead of four. The disappearance of one pound of butter is hardly noticeable when a lot of food is being prepared; four pounds is. Large kitchens put someone in charge of logging everything coming into the kitchen in raw form and keeping track of each item and quantity being used. (This serves as more than theft prevention; it is also the system for ordering and restocking.)

In your much smaller business, the idea of inventory control is still valid. You have to know what you have in your freezer and refrigerator, on your shelves, and in the bins. You don't need to itemize every last article, but at least keep track of the major items (e.g., how many chicken breasts, how many cans of caviar). Do your best to make your staff understand that you know every ounce of vanilla in that bottle and every pound of flour in the flour bin.

Another way to make the staff less likely to take food behind your back is sharing generously the delicious extra food after a successful party.

4. Financing and budgeting

Records compiled by the Small Business Administration indicate that a significant number of small businesses fail because of undercapitalization. What a waste! Would-be entrepreneurs start their undertakings full of enthusiasm, hope, diligence, skill, and a willingness to put in 80-hour work weeks — without enough money. All their resources are put into the business, the money from a second mortgage on the house, spouses moonlighting for extra funds, just to end up losing it all.

No amount of work and enthusiasm compensates for undercapitalization. You must have sufficient financial backing to start a business, to pay monthly fixed expenses even in negative cash flow months, and a hefty cushion for unexpected expenses that can be large if you need sudden repairs. You shouldn't have to worry about paying your bills even if they turn up unexpectedly. The only thing that should concern you is cash coming in. That is plenty to worry about. You cannot afford to start your business until you are sure that you have enough money to support both your family and the business for at least six months to a year without relying on what you're bringing in from events.

Budgeting skills are also necessary. Once you have a financial cushion, you still can't afford to see it shrinking because of poor budgeting. It is definitely a skill you can learn. You know if you already have it. In our financially complex lifestyles, budgeting skills have to be acquired early if we are to survive financially. Have you survived so far in your personal life by bringing in more than you send out? If so, chances are budgeting in your catering business will not be a problem.

5. Dealing with seasonal highs and lows

Seasonal highs and lows are difficult to deal with in small businesses. The smaller the business, the harder it is hit by a month or two of little income and negative cash flow.

In your catering business, the seasonal highs and lows will vary with the type of catering you do. If much of your business comes from industrial catering, the holiday season will not shoot up; it might even reduce in volume. But most caterers are in great demand around the holiday season with up to one-half of their annual gross income earned in two-and-a-half weeks. Caterers who specialize in weddings will be very busy in May, June, August, and September, the traditional wedding months. But they will have slumps during the early and late months of the year. Corporate catering is fairly even throughout the year, though it tends to dip somewhat during summer vacation months.

These are just broad generalizations to give you a concept of what to expect. In reality, the highs and lows are very difficult to predict from year to year, even by caterers who have been in business for a long time. No one knows why. For example, most caterers expect to have slow months in January and February. But the same months could be very busy if corporations decide to expand their employee training and schedule their classes right after the holiday season in January. They may want you to cater breakfasts and lunches for their classes, and you'll be swamped with work.

If you have planned your financial setup adequately and have a comfortable cash cushion, you can also take the seasonal highs and lows without losing your peace of mind. You will simply have to dip into it during lean months, while keeping your faith in the financially solid future. When money pours in all of a sudden, put some back into the savings account for those future lean months. Rely on your good budgeting skills and spend some on those pieces of costly equipment you've been wanting, but don't spend it all.

Seasonal highs and lows are something you can live with, even enjoy, once you expect them. It is nice to be busy again after a period of being in the maintenance and house-cleaning mode, but it is even nicer to anticipate a few weeks of very little to do after a busy schedule. This is one characteristic of catering that distinguishes it from other food service fields.

6. Beyond a rolling boil: the holiday season

Catering is busiest during the Christmas holiday season, when both individuals and corporations are expected to invite guests and employees to lavish and elegant parties. Many, many catering clients are only going to call you once a year, during this time. Your year-round clients expect to have you cater their holiday affairs, too. This is the time when you have to be very careful with scheduling events. You can schedule up to your maximum capacity of your equipment and staff, but no more, no matter how tempting it becomes to bring in even more income. You will have many more requests for catering than you will be able to take.

The stress and pressures of working at maximum capacity for 16 hours a day for a little over three weeks can be tremendous, emotionally and psychologically. You are in the limelight during your events, sometimes several times a day after an extremely demanding time in the kitchen. It is not uncommon to start in the middle of the night and end late the next night. Then it starts again a few hours later.

If you can take the pressure and stress, you will be handsomely rewarded. If you cannot, schedule just a limited number of events, with reduced stress and income. You cannot afford to fail to deliver whatever you promised to your clients. That will cost you much more than you'll earn from turning down one more event. Just knowing how much you can comfortably take for those three weeks will reduce or even eliminate this problem. You'll learn a lot from your first holiday season and future ones will be much more under your control.

4
From Gravy Boats To Wheels: Essential Equipment

Your major initial investment as a caterer will be in equipment, even if you decide to start slowly from your home kitchen. Should you purchase a substantial business, equipment will most likely come with it and be a major part of the purchase price. Food service equipment keeps its value very well and there is a ready market for its resale provided it has been used properly and kept in good condition. Your investment in kitchen equipment is something you can usually recover when you decide to leave catering.

Even though it is a seller's market on equipment, there is usually a lot available because so many food service establishments go out of business. But since just as many people think that the food service business is so easy, the same number will open new restaurants, so the kitchen equipment remains in circulation.

Buying used equipment makes sense and can save you money. Kitchen equipment is made for heavy duty application.

In most larger cities, restaurant equipment auctions are common. Attend some of these even if you are not in the market for equipment at this moment; it will give you an idea of the condition of equipment being auctioned off and the prices. You will learn, too, that it is hard to find individual smaller items, the type of things you most likely need. Lower-priced items are sold in batches, or in a collection of many small, unrelated things with a single auction number. You may have to buy a box of utensils to get the one spatula that is the shape you've been looking for.

Secondhand restaurant equipment stores are a good source for small equipment. Their prices are more reasonable than auction prices and you can buy a single item no matter how small. If you are searching for specific items, you may have to visit several stores before you find what you want.

You can buy new equipment as well. Weigh the value of your time against the difference in price. Some things, of course, you have to buy new. But in many cases secondhand equipment in good condition will serve the purpose and save you money. Use your best judgment.

Your current domestic kitchen equipment can be used for your initial catering work, provided you start with smaller events. In this initial stage, it is easily possible that you book a larger event that you simply cannot do out of your home kitchen. Your best choice is to rent a large commercial facility for that specific event. You will have to investigate what is available in your area.

Generally, church kitchens are the best bet; churches can use a little extra income and the kitchens are usually only used on weekends. Many caterers start off in church kitchens, sometimes with an agreement that they can use the kitchen with the ongoing use of storage, refrigerator, and freezer space. It is far from ideal, but may work temporarily. Church kitchens are notorious for having equipment and tools disappear. You may be ready to put together an event and discover an essential ingredient or piece of equipment has disappeared, a costly nuisance since you have not scheduled time to replace what is missing.

Let's discuss the specifics of what you will need in a small catering business.

a. Major equipment

1. Kitchen facilities

Let's assume that you are over the initial stages of using your own domestic kitchen and its equipment. Commercial kitchen facilities that are suitable for your purpose are very hard to find. They have to be approved by the health department and regulations governing what is required to approve a kitchen vary depending on where you live. They range from lax to reasonable to overstrict. Local health departments will usually have a pamphlet stating the requirements necessary for the kitchen to be approved. Obtain a copy and be familiar with it before searching for a facility. Anything approved already, such as a former restaurant kitchen, is suitable. Starting a brand new kitchen is by far the most difficult initially, but the most convenient for you in the long run. Old restaurant kitchens, often located in older buildings, are notorious for pest control problems.

Your kitchen facilities need to have three major parts — a kitchen with large work areas and at least one work table, a good-sized storage space, and an office. In addition, the bathroom should be large enough for comfortable cleanup for you and your staff. You'll need it after ten hours of preparation in a hot kitchen, before you depart for your event. A shower is highly desirable, if not essential.

The kitchen must be on the ground level, preferably without steps, for easy loading and unloading. Ideally, the storage room is on the same level. The storage area should have very sturdy commercial shelves to hold your equipment and supplies.

Both gas and 220-volt electric wiring are necessary. In addition, you need an exhaust fan, preferably one that has been built in. Plumbing must conform to health department regulations, and good lights over the work areas are essential. There should be electrical outlets everywhere on enough circuits to prevent frequent blowing of fuses, as well as several telephone jacks.

Even if health codes don't require fresh, light-colored, glossy paint on the walls, it is very desirable. It will look cleaner, stay cleaner longer, and be much easier to keep clean. The floor should be smooth and easily washable. Molding should seal the joint between the floor and the walls to keep bugs out. All doors and windows should be sealed tightly for the same reason, especially the space under doors. (Leave only enough space, marked by an arrow, for clients to slip their checks under the door when you are not there.)

Garbage disposal service is also needed. Liquid waste garbage disposal for a food service business is regulated by the local municipality. Check with them about the legal disposal system. The local health department is also familiar with these regulations. For a small caterer, the smallest dumpster available is sufficient. The dumpster should be located near the kitchen, but not close enough to attract insects. The indoor garbage can must be kept tightly closed when not in use and emptied frequently. All these precautions will help your potential insect problem.

A good, well-equipped first aid kit should be part of your kitchen, but hopefully never needed for more than an occasional aspirin, something you should always keep in good supply.

2. Refrigerators and freezers

You will need at least one refrigerator and one freezer. Both must be of adequate size for your business and only you can determine what that size should be. Try to visualize the minimum you would need to store for a good-sized event, and at least double that capacity for your convenience. If you don't have enough space, you cannot keep adequate supplies and will have to shop for perishables more frequently.

You will need space for usable leftovers in the refrigerator and freezer. Many perishable items are only good for immediate consumption by you and your staff, but many other food items, such as cheese, baked goods, and hors d'oeuvres, keep very well and can be served later or used in future dishes. Cheese can often be used up this way.

A large refrigerator space is needed to store finished platters that need to be chilled. An ordinary household refrigerator is not suitable for such a purpose. Ideally, a much larger commercial refrigerator should be part of your equipment.

The same applies to freezers. You have to keep a lot of food handy in your freezer for short-notice events. Keep a supply of things like butter, bread and rolls, juices, ice, and any other items you use frequently in your freezer. It is a good idea to keep a limited

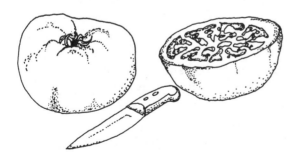

supply of extra meat or chicken on hand, too. All these take extra freezer space but will make your catering life more bearable.

The health department requires a thermometer in both freezer and refrigerator. You must know what the local code is for maximum temperatures for both and adjust your appliances to conform. Once adjusted, they will keep steady temperatures for a long time.

Nevertheless, problems can develop in either your freezer or refrigerator and you should have an emergency plan for such times. Hundreds of dollars worth of food in your freezer may be at stake. Have a smaller household freezer around for emergency use and for an occasional overload (e.g., during the holiday season).

A second refrigerator is also a blessing to have. Consider the size of your utility bill. You can save money by turning off extra appliances for weeks or months. Domestic freezers consume a lot of power. Commercial ones use even more because of their larger capacities and lower temperatures. Refrigerators use less power than freezers. Remember, the more cooling appliances running in your kitchen, the more heat is being generated — something you rarely need when your kitchen is in full swing.

3. Ranges and hot plates

Ranges can be gas or electric, but commercial kitchens favor gas. Gas stoves are expensive but are available secondhand. Since not much can go wrong with a gas range, it is worth your time to investigate the possibilities. You can, however, get away without a range for a long time by relying on commercial hot plates and convection ovens. As a matter of fact, they have a lot of advantages over ranges. Many catering kitchens have no ranges at all. They take up a large amount of your capital and kitchen space. As well, fire codes in most municipalities insist on a hood over any range in a commercial operation. Hoods are very expensive, require an automatic built-in fire extinguisher (for grease fires), and an externally vented system away from anything combustible, which can be costly to install. Fire codes also require range inspections about every six months (depending on your local code).

One way to avoid the huge expenses of a hood and ventilation system is to be licensed as a "cold" kitchen. What defines a cold kitchen varies with health and fire codes. Basically, in a cold kitchen, frying is not allowed, since accumulated grease is the most frequent source of kitchen fires. If you don't have a range or fryer, you presumably cannot fry, and therefore won't accumulate grease in a filter or run the risk of hot oil catching fire. You can use hot plates up to a certain maximum wattage per plate (again, the code varies), and you can use any size of convection oven without a hood or built-in exhaust system. Some localities require that the convection be vented, but that is a fairly simple matter compared to a hood. Large unvented convection ovens are used in many shopping malls, baking chocolate chip cookies. You can smell the chocolate from all over the mall — a deliberate attempt to lure you closer with your salivary glands running — so you know they are unvented. Fire codes in shopping malls are extremely strict.

Almost any catering event can be accomplished with a good-sized convection oven and inexpensive hot plates. When the health inspector asks you what you do with the hot plates, tell him or her that it is for boiling water, blanching and cooking vegetables, sautéing, but never for frying. Hot plates come in all sizes, single and double burner. You'll want to buy the largest allowed by your local code. It will probably be wired for 220 volts with a special plug so you cannot carry it along to sites. However, you should have a second set of hot plates that are wired for 110 volts with conventional electric plugs. The maximum power (wattage) you can get out of a plate that is wired for 110 volts is not very high, but such plates are light, easy to carry, and great for keeping things warm, as well as being ideal for light cooking at sites with no stove.

4. Ovens

If you have a range, you also have a built-in oven. Depending on how large it is, you may or may not need another oven. The additional one should be a half or full convection oven, either gas or electric. If you want to stick with small- to medium-sized events, the built-in range oven may be sufficient.

If you have no range yet, start with a half-sized convection oven, which can accommodate six hotel pans or three fairly large turkeys. You don't even have to rotate them during baking because of the principle of convection heat. A fan distributes heat uniformly throughout the oven. Because of the convective heat, baking temperatures are generally 50°F (10°C) lower and baking time is 15% to 20% shorter than in a standard oven. The only disadvantage is the lack of a broiler, but that problem can be overcome to some extent. Many of the newer and more expensive domestic ranges also include convective heat by turning on a fan.

Convection ovens also come in smaller sizes. They are light, portable, and are great to use where no kitchen facility is available. You should have at least one. Though they are small, you can prepare a fairly large number of hot hors d'oeuvres in them using three shelves, or 20 to 25 boneless chicken breasts at a time. If you use larger pans, you can bake even more.

Domestic ovens and hot plates are not allowed in a commercial kitchen. A health inspector probably will not approve a kitchen for commercial operation as long as there is a domestic stove in it. Small domestic hot plates that are used off-premise are acceptable, but keep them in the storage area, not in the kitchen, so you're not tempted to use them there.

5. Dishwasher

A dishwasher is another essential and expensive piece of equipment that you will need. It is also probably required by your local food service codes. Even the smallest commercial dishwasher is costly, but they are very sturdy and reliable. Even if a domestic dishwasher were acceptable by your local codes, it would not be satisfactory for a catering kitchen unless the operation was restricted to small events.

A commercial dishwasher requires higher water temperatures and chlorine is automatically added to the rinsing cycle to sterilize the load. (The chlorine level in the feed bottle is another item the health inspector invariably checks.) The total cycle is very short compared to a domestic version, one and a half to two minutes. The loads come out very hot and generally dry in minutes by themselves. Dishes are loaded on lift-out trays or racks so as soon as one load is clean, the next one is put in and started. By the time the first rack is unloaded, the second one is clean.

You will need several racks, each made for different types of loads — flat-bottomed for silverware, and racks with spikes for holding glasses or plates. You can manage with two racks, but it saves a great deal of time when you store your glasses on dishwasher trays. You remove the clean glasses from the dishwasher in their rack and put the rack directly on the storage shelf. When the glasses come back from a job site already loaded into the rack, they slide directly into the dishwasher (though you do have to turn them upside down before loading them into the dishwasher since you carry dirty glasses right-side-up in their racks to avoid dripping coffee and wine all over).

The dish washing detergent used is also a high-potency chemical. For a small dishwasher, only one tablespoon per load is used.

6. Holding oven

A holding oven for a catering business is a portable, double-walled warming oven to keep food hot during transportation and setup. They come in different sizes, and your business can get along without one if you don't plan to serve more than 50 people at a time. For a larger event, you must have a way to keep that much food hot (it is a health department requirement) from the moment it leaves your oven until serving time, which is usually at least one hour after you leave your premises but could be much longer.

The holding oven has a thermostat control to keep it barely warm to hot, but it only goes up to about 250°F. It is great for dinner rolls, roasts, turkeys, hundreds of chicken breasts, or any hot food you are transporting to the site.

The most efficient way to use the holding oven is to put it on your truck, plug it in with an extension cord about an hour before departure time to preheat it, load your hot food directly from the kitchen oven, unplug the holding oven, and go. If you need to hold the food for a longer time before serving, plug the oven in again at the event site to keep things warm. Even if it is not plugged in at the job site, it should keep the food quite hot for several hours. A holding oven is ideal in some catering situations, like a Thanksgiving dinner at the hospital for 100 interns, residents, and their families, where dinner is a drop-in affair over a four-hour period, whenever the staff has a free half hour to spare.

7. Transportation equipment

Once you have equipment to prepare and store the food, you will need to transport it to the events. Catering trucks are all different. You and your business will dictate what sort you will need. At the beginning, you may not want to put out the large expenditure (or long-term commitment, if you decide to lease) for transportation that bites heavily into your budget. If the funds are available and you're sure catering is your cup of tea, go ahead and purchase a vehicle. If not, your car will do as a means of transporting equipment and food for smaller affairs, especially if it is a small van or station wagon.

Eventually, however, you will need to commit yourself to a more professional-looking and practical vehicle. Your vehicle should reflect your image. You will be the first one to arrive and one of the last to leave, so your vehicle will be in clear view of the host, hostess, and all the guests. That will be their very first impression of your business. An old, sad-looking vehicle does not radiate an image of elegant food, sparkling-clean serving equipment, and neat staff dressed in impressive, formal uniforms. The familiar proverb, "You cannot judge a book by its cover," simply does not apply in business, particularly in show business, as catering is. A somewhat aged vehicle is acceptable provided it looks very clean and well cared for.

Small businesses need a small delivery truck, either a van (what most small caterers favor), a large station wagon, or a pickup truck with a large camper shell. It depends on the business you are running and the volume to be carried. Always remember that no matter what amount you anticipate carrying, your vehicle is always too small. So if you have to purchase a vehicle to transport your equipment and food, get the largest size possible.

Bear in mind that larger vehicles are harder to park, maneuver, and store on your lot, and your staff should be able to drive your vehicle without problems. Also remember the added cost of insurance, maintenance, upkeep, and gas consumption for a larger vehicle.

If your vehicle cannot carry everything, you have several choices. Your staff members can transport some of the food and equipment that won't fit into the company vehicle. You can reimburse the worker to cover costs. Or you can rent a second vehicle for a day or two. You can also hire someone with a truck for a day just to transport, load, and unload your catering stuff (and don't forget the insurance coverage for that vehicle). Whichever option you choose, your extra cost will be small compared to the income from the event.

The best arrangement inside the vehicle is a set of fixed shelves for small- and medium-sized items and plenty of floor space for large equipment. Your carrying trolley must have brakes on the wheels, so it won't roll around the truck with food stacked on it. Shelving will probably need to be custom-made and fitted into the vehicle. That is a problem you must either solve yourself or rely on a carpenter with a creative touch. For a smaller vehicle, a single shelf across the front part or on one side is the best. It has to be accessible and easily loadable, even when you are balancing a heavy marble board filled with cheeses. The shelves have to be very sturdy and they should have a lip or barrier of several inches all around to prevent anything from sliding and tumbling down in transit.

The interior of the vehicle should be easily cleanable, a requirement of most health departments. Spillage is inevitable, especially on the return trip when loading is less careful and everyone is rather tired. Carpeted floors or walls are completely unacceptable. Surfaces should be kept as clean as your kitchen.

8. Washer and dryer

These are not essential, but very useful to have. If you have space and a little money to invest, I highly recommend them. There are towels, aprons, and uniforms to wash regularly, and the tablecloths and napkins also need to be cleaned. Services to pick up and drop off linens and towels are available, but they don't really want your small business. Many have a minimum charge that doesn't justify your use of them. By far the cheapest solution is on-site laundry facilities, so if possible, budget for a washer and dryer. Ordinary domestic models are fine, but choose the large capacity and heavy-duty models.

You will also need a steam iron for touching up tablecloths and shirts, etc.

b. Kitchen furnishings

As far as kitchen furniture is concerned, there are three important items. First, you need a large, heavy, and very sturdy work table that is solid as a dance floor and preferably just as large. It can be butcher block, solid plank, steel, or any material that is acceptable to the health department and easy to clean. It needs heavy wooden or metal legs that are braced in every direction, and stools around it for you and your staff to sit. In a small catering operation, two work tables are preferable. A foldable banquet table is acceptable for your second table.

Second, you must have two (in some municipalities three) sets of stainless steel sinks with hot and cold water. The vegetable sink has a single tub, the washing-rinsing sink has two or three compartments. The third sink, if required, is the mop sink. The dishwasher must be connected to the washing-rinsing sink. The vegetable sink must have

a floor sink, which is a small additional sink either at or below floor level. It is not directly connected by a drain to the main sink. There is a gap of a few inches in between, with the drain pipe of the main sink hanging over the floor sink. The purpose of this is to eliminate any possibility of sewage water coming up into the vegetable sink and contaminating it. Should sewage water back up for any reason, it will flow out onto the floor and your vegetables will remain uncontaminated.

Third, you'll need as many shelves around the walls as you can fit in, up to the ceiling. Like table space, you can never have too much shelf space. No food material, even though it is in a closed container, can be stored directly on the floor. For larger containers, you need to build a low shelf at least six inches above the floor. This guarantees that when mopping the floor, the mop cannot touch food containers, or serving and cooking equipment.

Finally, you are required to have a proper-sized fire extinguisher, fully charged, inspected and refilled annually, and approved for kitchen fires.

Any other furniture in the kitchen depends on your own needs and space, although chances are there is no space left for even an umbrella stand. It is pleasant to have some decorative items on the walls and on your shelves to soften the image of a dry, plastic commercial operation.

c. Other essential catering gear

Each time you transport your food and equipment to a job site, you and your staff will face the unpleasant task of unloading and transferring everything to the reception or eating area. This can be a considerable distance, especially in office buildings. Downtown areas are usually the worst with parking problems. If the building has a loading dock, use it. Many older, smaller office buildings don't have one, so you will have to park on the street like everyone else. You may be able to pull your truck close, parking temporarily in a restricted zone, just to unload. Unloading can take a full hour if the situation is really bad.

To make the job as easy and quick as possible, you will need a trolley and a handcart. There are many types of trolleys available for the restaurant trade but not many have been designed specifically for catering. Restaurant trolleys have fixed trays. You'll want to change the spacing between trays for different-sized loads. Also, the small rubber wheels on restaurant models won't suit your purpose. Your trolley must be able to roll over rough, decorative cobblestones and bricks in front of office buildings, over deep plush carpets in the corporate boardrooms, and bounce over high thresholds and in and out of elevators that never stop level with the floor. Make sure your trolley has large, good quality rubber wheels with brake levers for all four wheels.

You'll want more than one trolley if you plan to do several simultaneous jobs. The most useful trolleys are stackable. The bottom half has the wheels — the second story has spikes instead of wheels that fit into holes on top of the lower trolley. These can be custom-made. Each cart is just a frame with six lips for sliding trays into. An amazing amount of food can be carried with the two stories stacked, but they must be loaded with care. On the delivery truck they sit separately and double as shelves during transportation. They are made of aluminum, which is lighter than stainless steel but not as easy to clean and keep shiny.

A good, sturdy, collapsible, preferably not very heavy two-wheel hand dolly is also very useful to carry crates of china, glass, convection ovens, and other heavier items in and out. Again, you need fairly large, good quality rubber wheels. This tool will save a lot of backache. Make sure you get one with a long carrying tongue on

the bottom so it is suitable for your large dish racks. The tongue should fold in to save space in your truck, and even better, the handle should telescope down into the body.

There are hand dollies that easily convert into four-wheel push carts. These are heavier and more awkward to use, but once you know your own transportation needs, they may be preferable for your business. Try for the lightest and sturdiest dolly you can find. Expect some drain on your equipment budget; a good one is expensive and rarely available secondhand.

It is usually not a good idea to invest in a large supply of chairs and tables for your clients to rent. They take up a lot of storage space and it is hard work to load and unload them twice. A big catering business is more likely to own a supply of tables and chairs. However, you do need a few folding tables of six- or eight-foot lengths for buffet and bar setups. You'll get requests for them fairly often. Depending on the size of your delivery vehicle, you may not want to keep more than two or three in your kitchen.

You will need equipment to transport both hot and cold food. For hot food transportation, we've already talked about a holding oven, ideal for large events. For smaller luncheons and dinners, smaller-capacity hot boxes are more suitable, though they will not maintain temperature as well as holding ovens. These are meant to be for shorter transportation times. Hot boxes are made of various insulated materials and are fairly expensive. Each should be large enough to accommodate at least two full-sized hotel pans and keep food hot for at least an hour.

You can make your own from a wooden box lined with thick styrofoam insulation and some guide rails inside to hold the covered hotel pans.

Cool items are a little easier to care for. You need several coolers from the largest available to small, family-sized ones. The largest will carry chilled, poached whole salmon while the smaller ones are just right for a bag of ice for the punch. Choose the ones with smooth, easily cleanable outside and inside surfaces.

You will want to have a couple of beverage tubs when you are serving chilled drinks. Depending on your style, they can be fancy or basic. Clean bussing tubs or galvanized steel tubs will serve the purpose. If you want a more elegant presentation, wrap your beverage tub in a clean white sheet or a worn tablecloth no longer suitable for the buffet table. A simple trick is to spread the cloth on the floor, set the tub in the middle and fold all corners into the tub. Now you have a neat-looking beverage container. Add alternating layers of ice and beverage cans, topping with plenty of ice.

You will also need a good-sized carving board for your buffet table. A wooden board will do, but it must have a drain gutter on all four sides to save your tablecloth.

Finally, you will need to keep a good supply of disposable ware for events where china, glass, silver, and linen are not called for. The quality of disposables you use depends on your catering style and your client's budget. Make sure you have an adequate supply of everything you use on a regular basis. It is annoying to run out of disposable plates or cups just before an event.

One or two portable gas stoves, which run on bottled gas, are a nice addition, especially for outdoor events where fresh hot food is to be served. You can do without them to begin with, which allows you time to find secondhand ones at a cheaper price. Make sure they are clean, neat, and in good working order. The same goes for the bottle. Before you use these for an event, try cooking on them either at home or at your kitchen facility. They do not get as hot and heat slower than the hot plates you're used to. Their burners are smaller, so you have to allow extra cooking time.

Portable barbecues are great to have if they are fairly large and you expect to use them often enough. It is up to you to decide whether you want the comfort of bottled gas or the more down-to-earth charcoal with its familiar smell, invoking hunger pangs in the guests soon after you light the fire. A small barbecue is of limited value to a caterer. A barbecue has to be big enough for you to feed at least 20 people. If you don't expect to use it very often, it may not be wise to invest in one. You can rent a large barbecue when you need one; you can pick it up or it can be delivered directly to the site. The client pays the rental fee. A very large one can be towed. If you are expecting to barbecue a lot, it is worthwhile to purchase a large one or even several of varying sizes.

Caterers who specialize in barbecues are often large businesses catering for company picnics and larger outdoor gatherings, often with hundreds or even thousands of guests.

5
Smaller Equipment

a. Small appliances

A catering kitchen doesn't use many small appliances, but two are very useful no matter what kind of cooking you do — a food processor and a mixer. Chances are you already have one of each in your own domestic kitchen and you know how indispensable they are. In a commercial kitchen they can each save a lot of labor. A microwave oven may be another useful appliance.

1. Food processors

Many chefs say that they can do the chopping or grating or slicing just as fast as the machine, if you include the cleaning-up time for the machine in the entire job. That may be true if your food preparation technique is good and you are preparing a dinner for eight or ten guests. You can do a more even, more appealing job by hand than by machine. Certain types of cuts cannot be done with a machine at all. However, in a catering kitchen you are usually chopping for 50 or 100 or more people; cutting up vegetables for that many by hand is a considerable job, no matter how good your technique. It is much easier with a food processor. And the long-term repetitive motion with your knife can eventually hurt your wrist, muscles, or joints, something you cannot afford if you plan to stay in the business. Even for relatively small jobs, it may be better to use your machine.

The most commonly used, most powerful, top-of-the-line food processor in well-equipped domestic kitchens is the Cuisinart. It may do well for a starting business, too, but for commercial operations it is too small and somewhat underpowered.

The next step up in food processors for smaller operations is the Robot Coupe. The smallest Robot Coupe is expensive like all commercial equipment, partly because it is powerful, well made, and not mass-produced like the Cuisinart. You can get along in the beginning with two cutting plates for your machine. Eventually you will want to have at least two more — two slicers with different slicing thicknesses, a grater, and perhaps a julienne cutter. The plates are expensive, so hold off until you need one for a lot of work. Currently there are 14 plates offered for this processor for all kinds of specialized, unusual, and interesting cuts — just what a caterer wants. Before you buy a good food processor, investigate your options.

2. Mixers

The food mixer market for domestic kitchens is dominated by KitchenAid. They are fairly expensive, top-of-the-line, well-built machines with power to spare. The largest one available will do fine for your kitchen for years. KitchenAid also makes a mixer approved by National Sanitation Federation (NSF) for a small commercial operation. It is just a little more powerful than the largest domestic machine, with rating at 350 watts (about two-fifths horsepower), compared to the domestic one at 325 watts (about one-third horsepower). It is also sturdier and can be used in more continuous operation without overheating.

If you are planning to make and mix a lot of dough, the domestic KitchenAid will be too small. You can do the dough in batches, but then your time is wasted. You may have to move up a step to the smallest commercial machine.

3. Microwave ovens

A microwave oven is useful to have but not essential. I personally dislike microwaves and find them useful only for quick defrosting or to heat up your personal lunch. You are probably at a point in developing your kitchen art by now that you can decide for yourself about the usefulness of a microwave. If you have an extra one around somewhere, stick it in your commercial kitchen. If not, decide if you need to buy one.

b. *Miscellaneous electric equipment*

1. Coffeemakers

Coffeemakers are essential in your business. You will need at least two or three with different capacities. The most commonly used ones are percolators, not because they make the best coffee, but because they are convenient for making a large volume with a minimum of trouble.

Fill them up with water, add the coffee, plug it in, and it's ready in 30 minutes to an hour, depending on the size.

Drip coffeemakers make better coffee; that is why they are so much more popular today than 20 years ago. People today prefer stronger, better-flavored, more full-bodied coffee. Portable drip coffeemakers are much less convenient and require constant attention. They are much more versatile because you can make decaffeinated and regular coffee with the same machine, and hot water for tea is also available, but they produce 12 cups at a time at about five-minute intervals and someone must monitor the machine and refill the baskets. This may be slow if you have a large party and it is a prime coffee-drinking time (e.g., breakfast and brunch).

Keep on hand a large, 100-cup percolator, one or two smaller ones with 50-cup capacity, and perhaps one or two 30-cup percolators. (It's nice to have two so one can be used for decaffeinated coffee.) Then you need several drip coffeemakers for smaller events.

Almost every kitchen already has a coffeemaker, but don't count on it even when the hostess says she has one you can use. Take your own. That way you know you will have a reliable machine that is an adequate size for the number of guests. (Most coffeemakers in client kitchens are too small for a party of 12 to 15 guests.)

Although you should have a variety of coffeemakers in your storeroom, for the occasional event when the requirement is beyond your capacity, renting a coffeemaker is no problem.

2. Electric kettles, heating trays, and crock pots

A two-quart electric kettle is nice to have but not essential. It can be used to heat water up quickly for tea and also for supplying hot water for the chafing dishes. The hotter the water, the faster your food will heat; boiling water may not be available on some job sites.

An old-fashioned large electric heating tray with a thermostat control is great to carry along to keep things hot that won't fit in ovens or on chafers. Two or three smaller ones are also useful. Since microwaves came in, these are not used much any more and are readily and cheaply available in secondhand stores.

If it fits into your style of catering, a few crock pots are very useful though not very stylish. They keep food at the right temperature either on or off the buffet table.

c. Kitchen equipment

As you know, there are literally hundreds of pieces of kitchen equipment and gadgets on the market. Most of these are toys and no more. Everyone has his or her concept of the usefulness of kitchen gadgets but most professionals agree that only a few are really needed in the kitchen.

1. Knives

Your single most important tool is your collection of knives. I cannot advise anyone else on how many and what kinds of kitchen knives and gadgets should be part of their equipment. Personal opinions vary a great deal. But you *will* need several "french" (also called "chef's") knives, a carving knife or slicer, a large serrated (notched or toothed on the edge) knife, and several small paring knives. Add a steel knife sharpener and a sharpening stone, and you have the basic collection. You can add more for special purposes as the need arises. For example, a boner and a fillet knife are nice to have if you do either of those tasks. Neither your french knife nor your paring knife will do an easy and good job of boning a chicken or filleting a fish.

It is essential that you know how to sharpen your knives and that you do it often. With a very sharp knife your job is faster, easier, and there is actually less chance of slipping and cutting your finger instead of the food. Insisting on using a sharp knife proves you're a professional in the kitchen. A good chef sharpens his or her knife many times a day — not major sharpening with a stone, but just rehoning the edge for 10 to 15 seconds. Try it and see what a difference it makes in your food preparation. For more on sharpening, see chapter 14.

2. Cutting boards

The second most important item is a cutting board. Actually you should have a number of them. You need at least two little ones and two large ones. How many you need depends on how many people will be preparing food at one time. Most cutting boards are made of either wood or high density polyethylene (HDP), commonly called plastic. Any odor or stain an HDP board picks up can easily be removed with a chlorine soak in five minutes. The only complaint I hear about them is that they dull knives much faster than wood. That may be true, but sharpening your knives a little more often is a small price to pay for a hygienically safer surface. In some municipalities, the health department does not allow wooden cutting boards any more and eventually this may become the general health code. So when you are buying cutting boards, look for the high density polyethylene.

3. Scales, pots and pans, strainers

You will need two or three kitchen scales: a standard, accurate, and sensitive portion-control scale that can weigh a cinnamon stick accurately and anything up to two or three pounds; another, less accurate scale that will weight anything up to five or ten pounds, and a larger scale to weigh at least to 25 pounds.

A few heavy-weight, domestic sauce pans will be useful, but you will also need a good collection of industrial-weight pots of all sizes from two quarts to five gallons. You can start out with four, but as your business grows so should your pot collection. Most should be the regular stock pots, but you also need at least one wide and shallow pot. Your collection should include sauce pans with handles, at least five with two-quart to two-and-a-half gallon capacity, and a few smaller ones down to butter-warmer size. Sauté pans should also range from a couple of very large ones (at least one to start with) down to a tiny one.

You will need four colanders: one huge colander, one large one, and a couple of regular-sized ones. Several strainers, from a tiny fine tea strainer to a tiny but coarser strainer and one or two larger ones, should also be in your collection. You will need at least one deep strainer basket with handles. You'll use it for blanching vegetables, so it

should be fine enough that you don't lose the finely cut vegetables through the mesh.

The food industry favors heavy gauge aluminum pots and pans simply because they are the best available for industrial kitchen work. Don't even think of buying light- or medium-weight aluminum. It won't hold up. Heavy gauge, industrial pans are the only ones suitable and they are expensive compared to domestic pans. You can find them fairly often in a used restaurant equipment stores, but for a complete collection you'll have to buy some new ones as well.

You will also need baking sheets, at least six or eight large ones made of heavy steel or aluminum that will fit in your oven and several smaller ones for baking small amounts and to use on-site because your larger ones won't fit in a standard kitchen oven.

Regular 9" x 13" domestic baking pans and muffin tins are also essential. You will have to determine the number according to your expected need. You will always need more than you think. A good collection of bread pans of different sizes will complete your basic baking pan needs.

Other essential requirements include the standard stainless steel hotel pans or chafing dish pans that fit into chafers, with covers. They can be used for baking, refrigerator storage, and serving on chafer stands. You will want at least six or eight full-sized pans to start with, as well as four half-sized pans with covers (two of these fit in a chafer stand), and perhaps even three one-third size for small parties.

d. Serving equipment

1. Choose attractive serving ware

Unless your catering business serves entirely on disposable platters, you must have a substantial collection of serving platters, baskets, and bowls. You'll want all kinds of shapes and sizes. They can be china, pottery, glass, stainless steel, silver or gold, aluminum or copper, as long as food, especially acidic food, will not chemically react with the material and as long as their appearance fits the image your company wants to create. In addition to price and appearance, consider weight (the lighter the better for you, since you have to carry them around the reception room loaded with food), and their durability (after a 14-hour day you and your staff can get pretty careless packing up the truck to head home). Glass punch bowls are pretty but very difficult to pack and carry. If they break before you get to your event, you have a problem. A false cutglass bowl made of plastic is a nice compromise if it is acceptable to your standard and your event. Sometimes, of course, it is not.

It is entirely up to you to select serving equipment; you know the style you want and the money you can afford. Secondhand platters and bowls are available, but you have to hunt for them in secondhand and antique stores and flea markets.

You will need water pitchers and coffee servers, preferably the thermos type and fairly good-sized. They should look nice as they will be on the buffet table, or your servers will be using from them at the dining tables.

2. China, glassware, and linen

Many times your client wants you to supply china, glass, silver, and linen. You have three choices: have everything supplied by a rental company that bills you and you pass it on to the client, have your own set of everything and charge a rental to the client, or own enough for small events and call a rental company for the larger events. Choose what is most logical to your catering style.

All three choices have advantages and drawbacks. If you have nothing in the way of tableware, you have to run to the rental agency all the time. That may be fine if it is just around the block. If not, it can be time-consuming. On the other hand, at the end of an event you don't have to deal with the dirty dishes or have a large inventory that ties up both capital and storage space.

Even if you choose not to have your own sets, you will still need a nice collection of table linen for your buffet tables. Choose the colors and styles that fit your business image. Be sure that they are easily washable and stain resistant. Sometimes these tablecloths come back from events in sad shape. Do some research on how to get rid of the stains or you will be buying new cloths all the time. Having them drycleaned is just too expensive.

3. Baskets and other decorative items

An extensive collection of baskets from tiny to huge is included in virtually every caterer's store room; the prettier the better. They are inexpensive if you find the right source. You also want pretty napkins in varying colors to use as inserts and covers.

Less essential and more personalized equipment includes candle holders, vases, and decorative table pieces of all sorts. You'll accumulate them as needed. Besides standard table decorations, you may want to collect special items for specific events, so that each client has the impression that the preparation was designed specifically for his or her event.

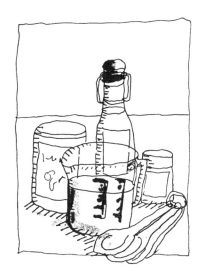

e. Non-essentials and other small tools and equipment

In a small catering business, you are on your own. You equip and furnish the kitchen to suit yourself, the way you feel it serves your purposes best.

However, assuming that you have few tools and equipment at this time and you want a general concept of what an average small caterer might use, here are the non-essential and specialized tools and equipment my catering business uses:

- 2 large polyethylene cutting boards
- 2 small polyethylene cutting boards
- pastry bags (two different sizes) with tubes and tips in assorted sizes and shapes; buy the easily cleanable plastic instead of cloth bags
- 8 tube or bundt pans, several sizes
- 10 quiche pans with removable bottoms (7½" to 11")
- 6 torte pans with removable bottoms (6½" to 10½")
- 6 cake pans (8" to 10")
- cake carriers
- french baguette pans
- 2 sifters: one large, one small
- 5 wire whips, variety of sizes
- 7 icing grates (wire racks), from small to 28"
- rolling pin
- set of stainless steel measuring cups and spoons (flour and sugar bins each have their own that stay in the bins), one 8-cup and one 2-cup glass measuring cup
- 3 kitchen timers
- meat thermometer, oven thermometer, and an accurate digital kitchen thermometer

- 5 brushes, different sizes, the largest 3" (to spread melted butter on phyllo sheets), one reserved for brushing pastry only
- 4 icing spatulas from small (great for spreading sandwiches) to large
- baster
- 3 pairs tongs
- large spoons, both solid and slotted, and carving forks
- skimmer
- 2 mashers, one small, one large
- 5 dishers (like ice cream scoops) with release wires, 0.5, 1, 2, 4, and 6 ounces, respectively
- apple corer
- pineapple corer
- dough cutter and scraper
- pastry blender
- 2 funnels
- cookie cutters
- pastry and pizza roller
- cherry and olive pitter
- vegetable peelers
- kitchen shears
- pruning shears (for flowers and to cut up bunches of grapes)
- zesters
- grapefruit knife
- tiny scoops and ballers
- can and bottle opener
- juicers
- 3 ladles, different sizes
- egg slicer
- butter cutter

- hand chopper
- 2 hand graters, 1 tiny for spices like nutmeg
- 6 wooden spoons
- 3 rubber scrapers
- spaetzle maker
- 1 pair swimming goggles (for cutting onions)
- 16 bowls from tiny to huge
- pizza wheel
- large salt and icing sugar shakers
- mortar and pestle
- spice grinders, small hand and larger electric (formerly coffee grinder)
- 10 bussing tubs
- six 13" rectangular plastic tubs
- 2 electric tea kettles
- 2 electric fans
- fly swatter

6
Menu Ingredients

a. Finding and dealing with suppliers

1. Retail versus wholesale outlets

Suppliers present a formidable problem for a small caterer. Large caterers and restaurants have all types of food and other supplies delivered on a regular basis. If you are a small caterer, the large suppliers are not particularly interested in dealing with you unless they are desperate for business. They usually have a minimum purchase before they deliver — at least $50, and for some $100 or more. Some of them even have a minimum order before you can purchase from them. You can order and do the pick up yourself at many suppliers' "Will Call" department and pay cash until you establish credit with them. This sometimes works out fine, but many suppliers are located out of town where warehousing is cheaper and you sacrifice your time by picking up.

Some large suppliers treat your tiny account fairly well but many don't hide the fact that they would prefer you to go somewhere else. Your purchase of a 15-pound salmon or one case of Roma tomatoes is just not worth the paperwork. Often they will save the top-quality merchandise for their regular clients, so you get second choice.

As for prices, the large suppliers are not cheap. Since you buy so little, you don't get any discount or case prices, so you are paying virtually retail prices. They are unwilling to break cases for many items, for example, produce. They will sell you vegetables by the pound but charge so much that you are better off in the nearest supermarket.

So what can you do? The first step is to decide what quality food you need and then start working out a source for each type. If you live in a large community, there should be a number of choices for you. In small communities, you may be very limited and you may even have to depend on delivery service from central distributors.

Often, your best source for many items is regular retail outlets, while for some things wholesalers are your best bet. You must have your entire line of suppliers worked out before you start booking events seriously. Since you have been cooking for quite a while, presumably seriously (otherwise why read this book?), and assuming that you have lived in your area for some time, you already know many good retail sources for the types of food products you will be using. There are the warehouse-type food stores springing up everywhere which will probably remain a good food source in the future. There are large warehouse discount stores that also have food on their enormous, confusing, and ever-changing shelves. These are here to stay and more than likely will become even more important food sources in the future.

2. Ready-made versus half-ready items

You need to think about how much food you want to buy ready-made or half-ready and what you will prepare from basic ingredients. If you are in low-end or medium-quality catering, you have a wide variety of choices available from ready-made, commercial products that can be served with a bare minimum of preparation on your part. If you are planning to operate a medium-quality or high-end business, ready-to-serve food items of the quality you need are less easy to find.

These are often frozen products, like meatballs, cookies, or cakes that need no more than defrosting and warming up. Partially prepared items include frozen cookie or croissant dough that needs to be baked before serving. Some of these products are poor and some are very good quality, but none are very cheap. You're paying for the labor of preparation, which is what you saved by buying these products in the first place.

There are caterers who buy ready-made products almost exclusively and resell them to their clients. There is minimal kitchen preparation work involved. Other caterers prepare everything, or nearly everything, from basic ingredients. Your best compromise is to try some of the ready-made products and calculate how much profit you can make by buying them versus if you make them yourself, including labor time. Of course, you must compare quality as well.

Here are the main food areas you will have to establish your source of supplies in:

- meat, fish, and poultry, including cold cuts

- dairy products

- fresh produce

- dry and canned goods

- bakery products

- specialty products like vegetarian raw material, gourmet items, unusual and exotic items

- food trade products, like one-gallon cans of sterno

You have two sources for each: retail or wholesale. To buy from a wholesaler, you must have a resale license. Whether you can get any of the above from a wholesaler depends on the quantity and frequency of your purchase. Some things you will have to purchase from a wholesaler, like a large baron of beef, or a case of frozen croissant dough, or four cases of portion-controlled boneless chicken breasts. These items would be hard to obtain through most retail outlets although your butcher may be able to order any meat item for you.

Consider three factors when looking for a source for each of the above categories: price, quality, and reliability. The larger warehouse stores have the lowest prices, often lower than wholesale. However, quality varies in the mid-range area, neither very high or very low. These outlets must turn huge amounts of merchandise through their stores and the only way they can sell at the lowest price is if they buy at low prices themselves. High quality foods are not sold at low prices. This source is also notoriously unreliable. The warehouse people are usually uninterested in your complaints. Regular supermarkets are not a low-priced source but for many items they will have to do.

To buy wholesale, the best bet for a small caterer is a small wholesaler. They appreciate your account even though it is small, and often they don't charge for delivery. They have no minimum order or minimum delivery requirement. They compete with the big food distributors by providing far better service. Once you establish a relationship with them, they tend to treat you well, provided you pay their bills promptly. They need quick cash flow just like you do.

3. Buying produce

For produce you need a source that is not only relatively inexpensive, but also has a good variety for your catering needs, and a quick turnover of food, so you can count on fresh produce. If there is a farmer's market near you, use it regularly. First of all, it is fresh, and sometimes even cheaper. Second, you can find unusual fruits or vegetables that supermarkets won't carry. Small produce wholesalers stay in business to serve small restaurants and food markets. They sell you anything by the pound at near-supermarket prices, and they want your small account. They often have good quality, very fresh produce and a good wholesaler picks the top of the crop from the distributor. These products are often better than those available from an average supermarket. The best of the produce is often reserved for restaurant suppliers: they are the most discriminating.

4. Keep tabs on prices and quality

For finding your sources, you will need to know two things: prices and quality. Keep a complete list of all food prices in your files or in a little book that you can carry with you on all your shopping trips. This is not only for comparison shopping but also to calculate the cost of the final products you are preparing.

You must keep track of prices. Devise your own system if you prefer. I have a small book like an address book with alphabetic markings on its side and I list all food and related items in it. For each item, prices are given per unit, either in ounces, pounds, gallons, or per piece, whatever applies, and the size of the container the item comes in at that price and a code for the supplier where I can purchase the item. In many cases I need to add the brand name so I can compare similar qualities.

Your little price book should list everything you use in your kitchen, from almonds to yogurt. Don't carry this pricing to extremes. Surely you don't want to figure out how much a teaspoon of salt costs! If you feel that keeping track of everything is too much trouble, keep track only of the major ingredients or pricey items. Seasonal items like produce are a little more difficult because their prices vary so much. Nevertheless, you should have some idea of the cost so you can add the corresponding figure when you are pricing your menu.

b. Food quality

Learn how to choose the best quality at your selected price level. Since you are at least a reasonably good cook, you probably already pay attention to the quality of food you buy, much more so than the average shopper. Just watch people shopping at the produce section. Most will pick up the first pineapple that is the easiest to grab and put it in their basket, with no thought given to ripeness, freshness, or quality. Others are more discriminating and take the time to look at the leaves, feel the flesh for soft spots, and smell the pineapple near the stem end to judge its ripeness.

Never take things from the top of the pile because those are the oldest in the bin. Have you ever watched store clerks replenishing produce? They take all the old stuff off the shelf and put it on their cart. Then they pile up the fresh produce on the shelf and on top of the fresh stuff comes yesterday's produce. This is called rotating the stock: "first in, first out." Let other shoppers take the older produce; you want the fresh ones, so dig down for them.

You must make deliberate efforts to be an expert on judging the food items you buy for quality, especially produce, dairy, meat, fish, and poultry products.

And remember the expiration or pull date. Grocers say that the product you buy will be fine for quite a while after the expiration date. Don't believe it. For dairy products, for instance, they say it will be fresh tasting a week after the date. That may be so if the dairy item was stored and transported under ideal conditions; however, this is rarely so. To be on the safe side, consider the expiration date the last day you can still use that aging product.

c. Subcontractors

For most catered events, your business will be the only one that supplies food and services to a client, and no other suppliers are involved. These are the simpler, more routine catering jobs — receptions, grand openings, corporate luncheons, dinners, or breakfasts. But other catered events involve a number of other contractors or subcontractors in providing service and other products. These are the festive, more elegant, lavish events, with substantial budgets to spread among several service businesses.

You can be part of these more elaborate events in two different ways. Either you are one of the subcontractors or you are the main contractor responsible for hiring everyone else. In the first case your responsibility is minimal and your income is less. An event coordinator often hires your services, and he or she is your client rather than the host or hostess. You will be paid by the coordinator who is responsible for the smooth running of the entire event. Menu planning and all details are done with the event coordinator who gets approval from his or her client on your food and prices.

In the second case you run the show. The host or hostess is your direct client and the person who writes out the check. You subcontract for any services you don't provide. You have far more responsibility and work, but your income is larger because each subcontractor pays about 10% of his or her gross to you or you add a 10% surcharge to your bill for the subcontract. This is not free money. You are not only entitled to it — you earn it. It takes many phone calls, much running around, negotiating, and paying of deposits to schedule the whole show.

Some high-budget events have many subcontractors. Here is an example for a birthday dinner party I catered, organized by an event coordinator. The main vendor was the caterer. Other vendors included a florist, ice sculptor, two musicians (one inside, one outside), decorator, chocolate-dipped strawberry supplier, birthday cake baker, rental agency, photographer, limousine service, and magician. When an event is that complex, it is common practice to hire an event coordinator.

However, you should keep a list of all subcontractors available for various services, especially cake bakers, musicians, and florists. Keep track of their prices, the quality of their products, and most of all, their reliability. It is bad business if the baker delivers a mediocre cake, but it is worse if he or she does not show up at all.

Make sure it is understood by both you and the subcontractor what your commission is and how it will be paid. Subcontractors routinely give you a 10% discount and you charge full price to your client, or the subcontractor charges a so-called wholesale price and you add a commission of about 10% to that.

It is important to establish a good relationship with a rental agency whose services you use often. You want to be familiar with everything available for rent, like tents, podiums, dance floors, various outdoor structures, artificial turfs, and so on.

It also pays to forge links with local event and wedding coordinators. If you are providing the type of service and food their clients want, you could be their favored vendor, which can mean good business for you. There is often an association of local wedding coordinators in cities. Think about inviting them to an open house at your facility and provide a lavish food table so they can view your presentation and sample your product. If you have enough space in your facilities, you could offer it as a regular meeting place with a luncheon thrown in. Most hotels, banquet, and reception halls do this routinely, trying to lure these consultants and their clients.

Finally, you should have a list of all reception halls available in your market area that allow outside caterers to provide services. You'll use it and share it with clients once they have committed to using your services. Most clients reserve a hall before booking a caterer, but occasionally there are people who ask your help in finding a place. This is when you need a complete list that gives details of everything about that reception hall, including size, how many it will accommodate for a stand-up and for a sit-down party, what the cost is, whether the kitchen is included, liquor restrictions, security, safety of guests late at night, parking lot size, equipment in the kitchen or staging area, condition, and the upkeep of both the reception hall and kitchen. You can make this list and visit the various possibilities during slow periods when there aren't enough events scheduled to keep you busy 18 hours a day.

7
Too Many Cooks...

a. Selecting your staff

While your business is in its initial, negative cash flow stage, you will not only be the sole proprietor but also the sole employee nearly all the time. If you have a partner, then there will be two of you waiting for phone calls. Unless, of course, you start with a bang when a desperate bride walks through the door and asks you to cater a wedding for 125 guests.

As long as your business is based on relatively small events, you can handle all the work by yourself. By small events I mean meals for 20 to 30 people, or receptions with hors d'oeuvres for up to 50 guests. You can manage these by yourself if they are self-service buffets. For full-service events, you will need help with anything over ten guests. And, initially, with your limited experience, you may feel the need for help even on smaller events, and you will be wise to hire staff.

Whatever the situation, find reliable, good people to help you in your preparation and, especially, in serving.

1. Part-time or full-time staff

Most catering companies, due to the unpredictability of the business and constantly changing workload, rely mainly or entirely on on-call staff rather than permanent part-time or full-time people. The larger companies have a few permanent, full-time staff — a chef, kitchen manager, receptionist, and sales and marketing personnel. The medium-sized companies may

have one or two full-time or part-time permanent people. You and your staff will have irregular hours — 12 to 14 hours one day, off for several days, and work on weekends.

Your motto should be "short list of personnel and long hours of work." The latter part is yours, not the hired helps'. Initially, cash flow dictates that you keep the payroll low. It will eat up your meager profits. Your overhead is likely to be high enough and difficult to trim; your food costs cannot be cut very much without sacrificing quality or quantity. The labor cost is your only flexibility. Once your cash flow has been established in a positive direction, you can relax a little, cut down on your working hours, and add extra staff hours to replace your own.

Smaller caterers often have no full-time permanent staff. If they have enough business, they may be able to afford a permanent part-time chef or sales and marketing representative. They rely extensively on their list of on-call staff. This is exactly what you will need to build up.

Depending on the state of the economy and your location, you may have a relatively easy time finding staff. There are many young and even older people with solid food preparation or serving experience who want to earn a little extra money in restaurant kitchens or in dining facilities. For an on-call catering staff you will need people who want to earn extra income but cannot work full-time. These could be students, mothers with young children at home, or other people in small businesses who have flexible hours and some time available to work in catering. Avoid the unambitious, the ones who could but simply don't want to work more than a few hours a week. They are not suitable for your catering staff.

If you live in a community with a college or university, students are good sources for on-call staff. They often have some food experience. Your friends may refer people interested in working for you. You can even call other caterers and ask to share available staff for a particular time slot.

2. Presentable, hardworking, and reliable

Your staff selection must be extremely careful; they have to be almost as good as you and be exceedingly reliable. They must represent your catering business, arrive on time, work hard, and present themselves well. If you hire them for kitchen work, they must be experienced, good with food, able to follow instructions, efficient, and diligent. In a small catering business you often take the same kitchen personnel to the job site. They arrive in your kitchen in work clothes and must change into serving clothes before departure.

The staff's attitude and physical appearance should, if possible, be compatible with the style of catering you are running. If it is upscale or high-class, your people should be comfortable in a wealthy home or a plush corporate boardroom. Industrial catering requires a different style of staff. A subservient waiter in a tuxedo would look out of place in a "roach coach" and would intimidate the customers. An outdoor, south-of-the-border barbecue demands still a different character. Your selection of staff needs to conform to these aspects.

Catering an event is physically draining. Carrying equipment, food, and supplies in and out of the job site, setting up and serving, standing for several hours, cleaning up, packing up, loading, unloading, put-

ting the food away, and stacking dirty pots and pans — that is a total of several hours of fairly hard physical labor without much rest and certainly without sitting down. Often this is on top of several previous hours of food preparation.

Not many can or will undertake such "hard labor," so you must select people with strong backs and legs and explain in detail what they can expect. Unless you know the person, make sure you check his or her references. Your staff is crucial to the success of an event. You cannot afford no-shows, poor workers, or incompetents.

Until you know your staff well and can rely on them, overstaff your events in case someone fails to arrive. It will cost you an extra $40 to $60, which is a reasonable insurance policy against an unsuccessful or difficult party due to a missing staff member.

3. Your relationship with your staff

How you treat your staff is very personal, an art that has nothing to do with catering, just simple knowledge of how to deal with people. Some of your on-call staff will also be on-call for other caterers, which is fine as long as they don't give your secrets and your cherished recipes away. When one staff member talks a great deal about their work with other caterers and how they do things in their kitchen, you should be suspicious that he or she is doing the same about your business. Talk to your employee and explain how poor a policy it is to openly discuss his or her work in the competition's kitchen. If that fails, find another employee.

Since you will have a small number of employees, your relationship with them is particularly important. Let your staff try new techniques and be open to seeing their ways of presentation and preparation, provided it does not clash with your style of catering. You may learn a lot from your staff.

Give your staff feedback on their performance. Food preparation can be monotonous — for example, when you need to have 600 phyllo triangles filled with spanakopita. Have them take turns on the phyllo preparation and let everyone have a chance to do something more interesting, like preparing a platter that requires patience and creativity.

One thing in your favor when searching for catering help is that in many people's minds preparing and serving elegant food to classy guests is considered glamorous work. It can be and often is. Even though a lot of the work is routine and tiresome, your workers rarely do a monotonous type of preparation more than an hour before they move on to something else. It is not like restaurant food prep work with mountains of the same vegetables to peel day after day for hours, serving the same routine menu. Working with food in itself is an added incentive for many. In general, finding help for your catering operation is rarely a problem.

4. You make the rules

Set up the house rules early and enforce them. Don't allow food sampling, but be generous with any extra food after the event. For long days you may want to set aside some extra or leftover food for your staff. Or assign someone to prepare a pot of wonderful soup from all the vegetable and chicken trimmings, and your satiated staff will leave the client's food alone. It doesn't matter how you do it, but make sure everyone understands and respects your house rules. For more information about how to motivate your staff, see *Motivating Today's Workforce*, another title in the Self-Counsel Series.

If you have employees who work for you regularly, you need to have a written manual of company policies. The manual should cover a broad range of personnel matters. Hire a professional to make sure everything is covered to avoid lawsuits. Both new and old employees, as well as

you, the employer, should be familiar with this employee manual. You must adhere to it as closely as possible, regarding your employees' rights and other matters. As business consultants say, the only thing more damaging to a business than not having a consistent employee manual is to have one and ignore it.

b. Paying your staff

Most food preparation staff get very little money, with wages hovering at or slightly above minimum wage. The work they do often reflects the money they earn. Give your staff all you can afford. You will have more satisfied employees and a better chance of getting them on short notice when a last minute event comes up.

If your catering business is low or medium-class, your staffing requirement is much larger and you can pay less to produce food on a production line. For high-end catering, you need staff with better qualifications and the only way to get them is with better pay. A good policy to follow when you're a small business is to pay a little more than the average pay in that particular industry. You get less staff turnover and it's added incentive for them to work for you instead of the competition.

Give your staff plenty of advance notice when you want them to work a particular event. Reserve them at least 10 days ahead of the event. They will appreciate it and you can relax about staffing needs. The only problem is that the number of guests expected at an event is often

over-estimated. These numbers tend to go down during the last week before the event and a drastic reduction may force you to cut your staff. Cancelling reserved staff is a poor philosophy because you're jeopardizing their trust in you. It may be better to reserve less staff than needed and add an extra person the week before the event. Or if you must cancel, compensate them with a small cancellation fee of $10 to $20.

Now, what about your sales and marketing person? How does he or she get paid? Compensation of sales staff is more complicated than food prep people. It follows general guidelines of sales staff in other industries. Basically, a salesperson can be on monthly, weekly, or hourly pay, purely on commission, or any combination of the above. This issue is outside the scope of this book, but here is a brief summary of how this is handled by caterers.

Catering is a highly seasonal business and many catering sales personnel prefer to be on salary so their paycheck doesn't fluctuate with the seasonal highs and lows. Salary is the easiest to deal with for your business, too. As long as your sales person produces results without being on commission and he or she prefers a salary, agree readily to that means of compensation.

Commissions reinforce productivity. If the sales person sells more, he or she receives more money, and with higher catering volumes you can afford to pay more. There is little doubt that a person will work harder for you if the compensation depends directly on the work produced. The problem is that the commission is only paid after you receive payments for the events. That means a delay in paying the sales person.

Many caterers choose a combination of salary and commission. For a part-time sales person this is a good method of compensation. A modest hourly wage combined with a modest commission may be a good way to start someone off in your business. How much those "modest" figures should be is difficult since they vary from area to area, from small communities to large cities. Commissions fall broadly within the 2% to 10% range in catering. Large caterers with large volumes can pay less commission as the sales person makes enough by the sheer volume of business. Smaller businesses pay closer to 7% to 8% with little or no additional salary. Then there is the draw account, a somewhat complicated method of compensation not suitable for any but the largest companies. It is guaranteed advance pay for future sales in some businesses. In others, it is not guaranteed, so the sales person has to pay back anything drawn against the account from future sales.

Commissions are based on any item in your invoice that you make money on. You exclude delivery and rental charges, gratuities, or service charges, etc. Generally, it boils down to paying a commission on gross food and beverage charges. When discussing potential earnings with a new sales person, show him or her the amount of monthly total food and beverage charges you have been billing and calculate the potential earnings from that using the agreed-upon commission.

Bonuses also encourage further sales. In most sale situations, bonuses for most sales situations are given if certain predetermined levels of sales are reached or surpassed, but a lower bonus may be given if the goal is nearly reached by your sales person, say at 90% of the goal.

Make sure commissions and bonuses won't eat up a significant part of your profits. Offering commissions and bonuses requires a profitable operation. Make sure you have a written contract with your sales person. Make this up yourself or use the help of a lawyer. See Sample #2 for an example of a sales contract.

LETTER OF AGREEMENT

This letter of agreement is between John Dough, Dough Catering, and Jane Pastry, 415 Piecrust Canyon Drive, Sourdough, an independent sales and marketing representative. It is agreed that Jane Pastry will be employed as a freelance, independent agent to sell and market Dough Catering services. Compensation shall be $7.00/hour for approximately 15 to 20 hours a week. Working hours shall be determined by Jane Pastry, who will be working predominantly from her own office. Pay for her services shall be twice a month, on the 15th and last day of the month.

In addition to hourly wages stated in the previous paragraph, a commission of five percent of the net sales of all events catered by Dough Catering and directly attributable to Jane Pastry's efforts will be paid by Dough Catering to her after receipt of payment from the client. The net sales will be the total of all billed items that include Dough Catering's principal services, i.e., food and directly related services. It will exclude rental charges, catering service charges, delivery charges, and any charges that are included for subcontracting part of the event. However, if Dough Catering provides services, even though it is not directly food-related, such as bartending and flower arrangements, such services will be included as items for commission.

Frequent telephone or personal contact will be maintained between John Dough and Jane Pastry regarding progress. A brief weekly summary of Pastry's sales and marketing progress, including hours worked, will be submitted in writing to Dough Catering.

Day-to-day expenses directly related to work will be compensated by Dough Catering. Expenses greater than $50 must be preapproved by John Dough.

This agreement will be in effect for 60 days, but either party may request any change that seems necessary or desirable. Such changes will be in effect as soon as both parties agree to them.

This agreement may be renewed for another term, or the parties may decide on a new long-term agreement as they both see fit.

Jane Pastry shall start work on _____ and this agreement shall begin on the same day.

Dated:_____   Dated:_____

_____   _____

John Dough,   Jane Pastry

Dough Catering

c. How many staff?

You will need food preparation personnel who work directly under a chef, a kitchen manager, or you, serving staff that may be the same people, and a cleanup crew. For smaller events the initial cleanup can be done by the serving staff. For larger events, it is cheaper to pay someone a lower hourly rate just to clean up after the event. That person (or persons) could come to the job site near the end of the event and take care of the cleanup, stacking and loading equipment, china, glass, and cleaning the china and glassware in your kitchen either the same day or the next morning. If the china, glass, and silver are rented, they need to be rinsed and stacked into crates ready for pickup at the job site. Your higher-paid staff can go home an hour earlier, satisfied to earn one hour less to avoid cleanup duties, especially after a full day of tiring work.

You'll also need some bartenders on-call. You often need more than one and if so, someone should be in charge of all the bar duties, supplies, cleanup, and related work. Then you have one less thing to worry about, and you can concentrate fully on food catering. Bartenders demand a little more hourly pay than serving staff, but that depends on supply and demand in your area.

How large a staff do you need for a specific event? For a self-service hot meal, as a rule of thumb, you need one person for every 50 guests to be around the serving table to set up, replenish food, help when needed, clean up, gather plates, glasses, and silverware, change courses on the table, and be polite to the guests. Another person should be working with the food in the kitchen, keeping things hot, and making up new platters. For a reasonably simple menu, a team of two experienced staff can serve up to 70 to 80 guests. As the menu is more complicated or the length of the event is shorter, you should increase the number accordingly.

You also need one person in the kitchen for every 100 guests. For full-service meals, you need about one in the kitchen for every 30 to 40 guests and one server for every 20 to 25 guests, depending on how complex the menu is, what the facilities are like, and how far the servers have to walk from the kitchen to the dining area. Staffing requirements change somewhat with the menu; go down with simple meals and go up with more complex ones. For example, for a dinner party of 150 guests, served buffet-style, you reserve your chef and a helper in the kitchen and three more staff members outside. For a full-service dinner, schedule five helpers in the kitchen and six servers in the dining area. For simpler, lower-budget meals, reduce the kitchen staff. When each plate must be garnished and presented beautifully, increase the kitchen staff.

For reception food, one person can take care of 50 guests, with a very simple lower-budget menu, 70 to 80 guests or, in lowest-end catering, 100 guests.

For bartending, the requirement depends on the bar service requested. For simple bars of wine, beer, and non-alcoholic drinks, one bartender can serve 70 to 80 guests. For a full bar you reduce the guest number to 50 per bartender. If the bar is for a reception or open house over a relatively short period of time, you should figure fewer guests per bartender as all guests want to down at least a couple of drinks over the short period and the bartenders will be inundated. For an open house of three to four hours, the pace will be more leisurely, so a bartender can take care of more guests without being overworked.

d. Dress code

Dress code for you and your staff is something you have to decide on and stick to. Whenever you hire someone, explain the dress code and make sure the new person has the necessary clothing to look like a presentable member of your crew.

The more formal your catering business is, the more dressed up your staff should be. A uniform is a good idea for several reasons. The client appreciates having uniformed staff serve. It looks professional and businesslike to have everyone in the same uniform. Many businesses recognize this fact. That is why so many restaurants, bakeries, garages, and gas stations dress their staff in uniforms. It is also good for the staff. They don't have to worry about how to dress for the occasion and they have a sense of belonging to an identifiable team.

At the very least you should have aprons printed with your company's name, logo, or even a motto. The most classy outfit for catering staff, of course, is a white tuxedo shirt, black pants or skirt, and a bow tie. The bow tie could be black or your company's chosen color. Most companies that require a uniform ask employees to pay for it. Your catering company should use the same policy. Either have your new staff buy the needed garments if they don't have them, or buy a supply yourself, give a set to each new employee, and deduct it from their paychecks. You will find that many who have worked in the catering business already have the black and white.

Anytime your staff is serving, no matter what type of catering the event is, uniforms are worn. What about events when all you do is deliver, set up, and leave? Or when you just deliver the food? In general, it is always a good idea to wear the uniform. It represents classy service, and even though none of the guests will see you, the receptionist or the head secretary who is in charge of the event will be impressed. It pays to keep up your company image. This is the way to get the contact person to remember you and your company for events in the future.

As the owner and manager, you have the choice of wearing the same uniform as your staff or something that indicates you are the big boss at a larger event. If you are part of the working staff, it may be a good idea to wear the same uniform. If you are acting as the chief supervisor, you may want to wear a somewhat different outfit, a fancier tuxedo or a different colored one, a red cummerbund or a different-colored bow tie.

Make sure everyone's uniform and appearance is acceptable before you take off for an event. Have a few extra tuxedo shirts and pants available for emergencies. When a staff member forgets to bring his or her black and white and there is no time to go back for it or there is a last minute spill, you will be grateful for your foresightedness.

Make up a short list of your company's dress code requirements and hang it in plain view to remind your staff. Insist on their compliance. Here is a sample dress code to use as is or modify to your needs:

Dough Catering Dress Code

● Black slacks or skirt

● White tux shirt

● Black or dark shoes, clean and shiny

● Hair pulled back (neat and clean)

● No large or dangly earrings

● No earrings for men

● Natural-colored hose with skirt

● Black socks for men

● Conservative makeup

● Well-kept hands (nails short and clean)

8
Selling The Sizzle

a. Selling your product and services

1. Know your client

Selling services is much more difficult than selling a tangible item. Catering services are especially tough because it is such a significant monetary output for the buyer and because it is often a significant event in the buyer's life, something that can never be rectified if it is not perfect. The possibility of a bad choice in a once-in-a-lifetime event, like a bar mitzvah for an only male child, causes enormous stress. Even if it is a small brunch for 15 guests, a poorly chosen caterer can turn the event into a disaster or, at the least, an acute embarrassment to both guests and host.

In other services, like shoe repair, the biggest consequence is annoyance for poor service and the fault is usually easy to remedy. At stake is a relatively small amount of money. For catering even the smallest event, hundreds of dollars are on the line, and for larger events thousands are at stake. To add to the pressure, the merchandise is not returnable for exchange.

Whether you decide to do your own selling or hire a part-time sales representative, the average scenario for a typical sales transaction in catering is the same:

(a) At your first contact with the potential buyer, you determine qualifications (a quick personal assessment of the person and a few questions will tell you if you are in the same ballpark).

(b) At the first or a subsequent meeting early on, you discuss the proposed event in detail, the type of menu, service, and available dates.

(c) There is often further discussion with the chef, kitchen manager, or you about specific menu selection, service required, and the particulars.

(d) At this point, you prepare a written proposal for the client. (You may have to adjust this proposal after the client's initial approval.)

(e) The client confirms the event and hands you the deposit.

You or your salesperson should determine a number of selling points for your specific business. Chances are, you have a niche, some kind of unusual or even unique angle which makes your business different. You may have a number of unique "signature" food or beverage items, or perhaps an outstanding way of presenting food, or you may be known for serving the healthiest food in town, or using the freshest ingredients. Any of these can be a selling point to help convince the buyer that you will be the best caterer for his or her event. Stress that their guests will be impressed by having you as a caterer because no one else in town can do it as well as you can. Any host or hostess, business or social, will want to impress the guests. After all, that is one reason to hire a caterer. (The ones who don't care to impress buy a large deli tray at the supermarket at a fraction of the cost of catering.)

Sell your catering service in your own office. You are on home territory. You can give the potential client a good impression with your office, sample food, photos, and a clean and neat kitchen. You feel at ease and you can concentrate on selling. The client should see your working facility. Whenever possible, set appointments in your office to save you travel time. For a larger or more complex event, you will want to visit the client's facilities however. When making an appointment, point out the advantage of the client's seeing your operation.

2. Create a photo portfolio to show clients

Assemble an impressive collection of your photographs in a neat, professional-looking portfolio. Large, high-end caterers tend to produce the glossy, four-color, Madison Avenue-style brochures and professionally produced commercial photos of their events. Smaller caterers want to give a less expensive look, something that does not scare prospective clients away by giving a "too expensive" look to your business. But the other extreme, printing menus very inexpensively on cheap paper and with an unimpressive layout, is equally unacceptable. Your client may think your food matches the quality and care you put into producing the brochure. It is best to aim somewhere in between. Your decision should be based on the type of catering you want to develop, the type of client you want to please, and current trends at the time you open your business.

Recently, marketing experts have favored good quality snapshots for caterers as the best selling tools. The photos should show your staff in uniform at work, some of your food displays, and guests munching away. The better dressed the guests, the more suitable the photo. Limit the number of photos in your portfolio so anyone can page through within half a minute. Letters of recommendation are also good addi-

tions, as well as anything else you feel you should include. Don't crowd it and don't make it overwhelming. The photos could be of different sizes, neatly mounted, with or without labels, with your own personal touch. The clients should feel that the portfolio was not produced by a commercial enterprise. It is a simple collection of snapshots of your typical events.

It is best to produce two or more copies of your portfolio — one for your office, and one for each salesperson. You may not need more than one copy, but a spare may come in handy from time to time.

3. Business cards and menus

There are two other essential items: business cards and catering menus. The choices in each are very personal and it is not easy to give suggestions on styles and how much you want to spend on them. For caterers they range from simple to lavish. Naturally, the more high-end your business is the more elaborate your printed material becomes. In times of economic hardship, clients may not be impressed by three-colored glossy menus: they suggest high-cost catering.

Recent trends favor simple yet tasteful business cards and menus. The best approach is to collect your competitors' business cards and menus and see what they produce. Have a friend call around if you don't want your name be known to the competition and ask for all information from them. That may help you decide what sort of literature you want for your business. Besides business cards and menus, you need some general information that very briefly tells the prospective client what sort of food and services can be expected from your catering company. The help of a marketing expert would be useful in this task.

4. Choose your clients well

I have to caution you about one pitfall many beginning entrepreneurs won't escape —

taking all the business that comes your way. Be discriminating, even if things are extremely slow. There is nothing less rewarding than working with an impossible client. Start qualifying your clients immediately. At first, many clients can be tense and too demanding, knowing more about cooking, food, and catering than you do. But slowly they ease up when they see that they can trust you and that you are sincere. Some, however, will never soften up. They still keep telling you how to do your business, that your prices are unreasonable, and insist on your providing such and such a menu in spite of your explanation that fresh sautéed fillet of catfish is not only impractical for 95 guests, but virtually impossible. Do not waste your time with these types of clients. It may be best to refer them to your competitor.

Other potential clients you don't want to spend a lot of your time on are the ones without sufficient funds to pay for your services. Try to qualify these right away, even though it can be tricky. If you are a good salesperson, you can do it in no time. As soon as the budget looks questionable, send them politely on their way to a budget caterer. If you are already a budget caterer, send them to the supermarket.

As you work more and more with potential clients, you will develop your gut feelings about which clients you want and which ones you don't. Be suspicious when a client drastically changes a previously agreed upon arrangement, or when the promised deposits are not sent to you in spite of several phone calls or letters, or when the client appears to be unhappy with you. These are the occasions when it is best not to accept the event and even refund the deposit.

If you already have a heavy commitment during the time of the proposed event, refuse, no matter how good a client it is. Don't ever overcommit yourself and your staff, no matter how lucrative it appears.

Even though catering is difficult to sell, one powerful advantage you have over other businesses, as well as a good tool, is the food you can offer to visiting potential clients. If you are visiting the client, take a little plateful of samples. It is a very convincing selling argument.

Of course, there are numerous sales gimmicks, techniques that apply to any business and those which apply to catering only. This is an area where you or your salesperson can benefit from books or seminars on selling techniques.

b. Responding to requests

Most of your first contacts with a potential buyer will probably be telephone requests for information. If you have a display ad in the Yellow Pages, you will get many calls. Most of the callers from this source are price shoppers who call every business with a display ad. Some of them are blunt enough to say that all they want to know is how much a meal costs. These calls are generally a complete waste of time and money for a caterer, who won't even bother to send out the requested literature to the callers. Of course, before you disregard such a buyer, you are going to question him or her a little further. You can quickly get enough information to decide what to do with the call.

If you have a salesperson, pass the information on and delegate him or her to take care of it. If you are your own salesperson, send out a menu, which may be fixed or a sample, either with a cover letter addressed personally to the buyer, or a prepared information sheet about your business.

Certainly a personal letter gives a far better impression. It should explain everything about the company, the type of business you do, the kind of food you serve, the serving staff, and whatever else may help to convince the buyer to become a client. It is best to have at least two standard letters, one for corporate, and one for social clients, since each type of buyer may be convinced by a somewhat different approach. Right now, testimonials are in vogue in selling and marketing, so you may want to include the kind and complimentary words of a client who wrote a letter of appreciation to you.

Cover letters are very individual and I advise you to make up your own. However, the examples shown in Sample #3 may help you start the process of writing yours. Selling and marketing trends do change with time, so stay alert and change your letters when necessary. You receive a lot of unsolicited mail, like everyone else, and this is a good indicator of the latest promotional approaches.

Form letters on your computer don't have to be sent out unaltered. In fact, it is a good idea to include something in them that refers specifically to your telephone conversation with the buyer. That way the letter does not look quite so cold and impersonal, even though everyone knows that it is reproduced by the touch of a few buttons.

How should you handle price requests? Most experienced salespeople say you never, ever give out prices on the telephone. Anyone who is calling for prices is simply a price comparison shopper. You don't want their business unless your focus is on large, low-budget catering. These callers have little potential in using your services. You can answer a request for prices by offering to spend a complimentary half hour with the buyer in your office to discuss the upcoming event. Explain that once you gather more information, you will be glad to give him or her a proposal or a price. Tell the caller that you feel the telephone is not a satisfactory medium for discussing the event. If the buyer is willing to meet with you, it is worth a half hour of your time to pursue the matter further.

c. *Marketing your business*

1. Identify your market

Marketing runs parallel to selling, and both are essential to continued success. If you are fortunate, your salesperson is good at both selling and marketing. But some salespeople don't like to market and some marketers are not much interested in selling.

Many, but by no means all, standard marketing techniques apply to catering. Some unique marketing approaches are needed to increase the chance for success in selling your services. For example, it is generally agreed by most caterers and their sales/marketing personnel that media advertising is of little value except when targeting very specific markets. To verify this, scan your local newspapers or magazines. Rarely, if ever, do you see a caterer advertising in these publications. The only exception is a restaurant or deli whose sideline business is catering. Banquet halls and hotels often advertise their facilities with a word about their superb catering. Pure off-premise caterers put their marketing dollars into more productive areas.

There are innumerable marketing ideas in catering. Some ideas apply only to specific kinds of catering. Clients who want catering fall into these five areas:

(a) Corporate

(b) Social

(c) Contract

(d) Wholesale

(e) Budget

Focus your marketing dollars on the particular area(s) you want to target. No matter what type of catering you do, you will likely market to more than one of these basic categories. Most caterers will do both social and corporate catering. A few will do contract only and a few will focus on budget only. Both contract and budget catering are usually done by very large caterers whose food is produced in mass. An example of

August 3, 199-

Ms. Ginger Prosciutto
Spiced Ham Distributing Company
100 Clove Street
Tarttown

Dear Ms. Prosciutto:

Thank you very much for your interest in Dough Catering's services. We are proud of our reputation for quality food and service since 1983 and our prices make us indisputably the area's finest catering value! As Joe Clam from the Barrister Club put it:

"The participants were quite complimentary and you and your staff prepared great food and handled the occasion in a very professional manner."

In catering you get what you pay for. At Dough Catering our prices insure many things such as fresh, high-quality foods, sanitary preparation, on-time delivery, generous portions, and many small extras. And Dough Catering is the only caterer in town approved by the Great Plains Heart Institute's Dine Right program.

Our client list includes both large and small corporations with one thing in common: demand for fine food and good service.

Please call us at 555-7777.

Sincerely,

John Dough

John Dough, Manager
Dough Catering Company
35 Batter Road
Crepeville

August 3, 199-

Mr. Chuck Roast
100 Beefy Way
Lone Loin

Dear Mr. Roast,

Thank you very much for your interest in Dough Catering's services. We are proud of our reputation for quality food and service since 1983 and our prices make us indisputably the area's finest catering value! Joe and Nancy Smith put it best when they wrote us after their wedding:

"Thank you and your crew for a job well done. You made our day very special indeed."

Our very talented chefs have a wide range of creativity and skills. The food we prepare represents many years of recipe testing. We are quite conscious of the current need for lower cholesterol, fats, less sugar, and salt. That's why we are proud that we are the only caterer in town approved by the Great Plains Heart Institute's Dine Right program.

In catering you get what you pay for. At Dough Catering our prices insure many things such as fresh, high-quality foods, sanitary preparation, on-time delivery, generous portions, and many small extras. We are aware of the current recession worries and if your catering budget is not what you would like to have, we can suggest more economical ways without cutting corners in quality.

I will do everything I can to make sure you are absolutely satisfied with our services. Call me at 555-7777.

Sincerely,

John Dough, Manager

contract catering is doing the food service for an industrial cafeteria, where the contract is of several years' duration. In budget catering, food is prepared at the lowest possible cost, packaged inexpensively, and distributed. Large volume is necessary to realize profits since the profit margin is small. Making hundreds or thousands of sandwiches for the lunch trade is an example. It can be profitable, perhaps even very profitable. There are a number of books which specifically address this segment of the food industry.

As a small caterer, you can market to the corporate, social, and wholesale segments. Corporate and social catering are the best mix. It is a good idea to do some wholesale catering (i.e., sell to a retailer). This business, though not very profitable, is steady and fills in the voids between events. However, it does sometimes interfere with more profitable business if you overcommit on wholesale catering. Keep it to a reasonable level or at least have a fair degree of flexibility with the client on delivery schedules and amounts you supply.

In addition to these major marketing areas, there are certain catering niches that are suitable for a small caterer. These are discussed in chapter 1. Any of these niches can be targeted for your business, but don't attempt to target too many of them. Each needs a specific body of expertise.

2. Be sensitive to your client's needs

When marketing your business, you should keep in mind why your clients buy catering services from you. Let's look at the two major types of clients. Corporate clients buy mainly out of necessity and for convenience. Food is needed for a working luncheon, for instance. If the budget is really tight, they send out a secretary for deli trays, bread, packaged cookies, chips, and cold drinks. Unless you can compete with supermarket prices, you don't want to target this type of business. Some companies call in caterers to impress clients — for open houses, grand openings, ground breaking ceremonies, and other festive occasions when the budget is generous enough to provide high quality catering.

Finally, corporations use catering services to reward their employees. This is usually only once a year, during the holiday season. Some also provide company picnics in the summer. These tend to be fairly traditional events and the budget varies a great deal, depending on how the company is doing in its profits and how generous the boss feels toward his or her employees. Picnics are relatively low-priced, very casual affairs where standard picnic fare is expected. When caterers are called in for this service, it is for convenience and to save time and work, not for prestige. Holiday season events are much more festive and caterers are relied on because a festive meal is not easy to prepare.

Social catering clients have a variety of needs, too. Caterers save time and work and guests are impressed with the presence of uniformed servers, perhaps a chef in the kitchen, and the presentation and quality of the food. Many of the clients who demand elaborate and lavish cuisine want to compete with their friends and relatives, to show who can afford to provide this luxury and who can afford a more elegant service. This is especially true for bar mitzvahs, bat mitzvahs, and weddings. But some social clients are only looking for convenience and necessity in hiring a caterer.

Your targeted clients' needs should be the focal point of your marketing strategy. Your marketing person or you should spell out and emphasize that these are among the needs that your company will satisfy when you are hired to do a client's event.

3. Letters of recommendation and testimonials

If you provide excellent service and exceptional food, you will occasionally receive unsolicited letters of recommendation. These are wonderful to have, both for your ego and for promoting your business. Occasionally, you can mention to an especially pleased client that letters of recommendation are very welcome. It provides you with excellent fuel for your marketing efforts. Use quotes from these letters as testimonials.

Advertising testimonials are in vogue. You see them in newspaper and magazine ads, on billboards, and television commercials. Marketing personnel say that testimonials sell products. Notice that the name of the person being quoted is always mentioned. Use this marketing tool to promote your catering service. You may or may not need to ask for permission to quote from a letter in your promotional material. Use your best judgment in each particular situation, but err on the side of caution. These letters should definitely be a part of your sales portfolio.

d. Pros and cons of Yellow Pages advertising

What about advertising in the Yellow Pages? This is a controversial issue among caterers. Opinions differ and that shows you that this type of advertising is not a sure success for developing new business. You cannot imagine a locksmith, a plumber, or a restaurant without a prominent Yellow Pages ad. When someone is looking for a locksmith or a plumber, chances are the first place he or she will look is in the Yellow Pages. Not so for caterers. Someone

interested in purchasing catering services tries to remember a catered event he or she attended or the name of someone who deals with caterers who can recommend one. The Yellow Pages are a last resort.

People shopping for prices will go to the Yellow Pages and call up every caterer listed for the type of event they have in mind. Those are nuisance calls for all the caterers who don't get the job, a waste of time and money to send the menu off to the caller. Many callers will use up more than five minutes of your time on the phone. They want a free consultation, with numerous questions about how you would do the event, what is included, and the cost of each part. You have to decide how much time you can take educating the general public in the proper use of a caterer. Because of the numerous shopping-for-price calls, many caterers choose to be listed inconspicuously in the Yellow Pages.

However, some sales and marketing people claim they can get business out of Yellow Page callers. If you employ one of these people, maybe you should run a larger ad. But remember, a smallish display ad in the Yellow Pages will cost you at least $250 to $300 a month, which translates to $3,000 to $3,600 annually (1993 prices). Can you get that much business out of the Yellow Pages, just to break even? Or can you find a better marketing tool in which to invest, one that gives you a better return? This is your decision.

Reprinted with special permission of King Features Syndicate.

Since you must have a business telephone, you will get a listing in the Yellow Pages with the price of the phone. The general feeling among caterers in my community is that the more high-end they are, the smaller the Yellow Pages ad should be. A caterer's reputation travels best by word-of-mouth. As well, very few of the callers who saw the ad will have a budget or interest in high-end catering.

Low-end and medium-quality caterers will benefit more from the large display ads. They need volume. They are also the type of caterer most callers are looking for. This is my opinion. Check other sources to help you determine what is most appropriate for your business.

The National Yellow Pages Association conducted a survey in 1985-86 about the 62 most frequently called classifications in their part of the phone book. Caterers were not among them. If you do decide on a display ad, it is important to know which style will result in more sales with fewer calls. An advertising specialist can help you with this decision.

e. Client feedback

A good idea to help you get feedback from your clients is an annual survey. It is a strategy many businesses use, no matter how large or small. It is especially good when you really don't know why your business takes a sudden downturn. You'll find out if clients don't like your product, or if your prices are too high, or if the competition is cutting your market share. You may find it is simply that the economy has turned to vinegar and the first things your clients cut from their budgets are non-essentials like catering.

The cost of a survey is relatively low. Make up an intelligent questionnaire and send it to a small number of your clients along with a self-addressed, stamped return envelope. Expect a return rate of 15% to 20% from the survey. The number you

send out could be a dozen or hundreds, depending on your client base. The answers are very useful in finding the problem, especially if you allow clients to return them anonymously. If the results point to your service or product, correct the problem quickly.

Surveys must be brief. Most clients will not take them as intrusions; on the contrary, they feel that you care about their needs and requirements, that you want to serve them better. To add emphasis to this concept, you may want to start with the phrase, "in our continuing effort to serve you better..."

Sample #4 shows a cover letter that accompanies the questionnaire and Sample #5 shows a client questionnaire.

f. Competition

Caterers are as thick as flies in most communities, particularly larger cities. There is plenty of competition. Catering is a business that a lot of people think they want to get into. Then they discover how tough it is.

Your competition is going to be intense. If you have your niche, then you eliminate a great number of those listed in the Yellow Pages who don't have that same niche. But your competitors will still number in the dozens. To learn more about your competition, look at their brochures and menus. Pretend you are a client and have an event coming up and ask for their literature, even a price list or proposal, if that is the only way you can get it. Having that information for comparison is invaluable. Or offer to give your clients a small added service in exchange for proposals they garnered from your competitors.

Friendly cooperation among caterers is very desirable but difficult to achieve. It is particularly ideal when two or three caterers complement each other's services; for example, one can only do smaller events, the other is set up for larger ones. These two caterers can refer business to each

Dear Client:

In reviewing our accounts, we noticed that we have not received an order from your company for some time. We hate to lose a good client.

We feel it's important to keep informed of our customers' responses to our food and service so we can continue to serve them well. It is particularly important that we learn why old clients no longer order from us.

Won't you please help us by completing the following questionnaire and returning it to us in the enclosed stamped envelope? It will only take a minute and your answers are invaluable to us.

Thank you and we hope you'll be placing an order with us soon.

Sincerely,

John Dough

John Dough, Owner

DOUGH CATERING

Questionnaire

Why did you stop ordering from us? (Check all that apply).

- ❑ Dissatisfied with quality of product
- ❑ Prices are too high
- ❑ Dissatisfied with service
- ❑ No longer using catering services
- ❑ Other (Please explain) _____

_____

_____

_____

What will it take to get your business back?

_____

_____

_____

_____

_____

_____

_____

_____

_____

_____

_____

_____

other without hurting their own, and at the same time solve a caller's problem, which is the goal if you're tuned into marketing techniques.

Call up the owners of a few catering companies and suggest a mutual visit to each other's facilities with a friendly coffee and chat. Something like this can be beneficial to everyone, not only for referral business, but also for shared equipment, expertise on a specialized subjects (e.g., How do you make black pasta?), exchanged operational information (e.g., Where do you get your specialty produce in town?), and kitchen, bar tending, or serving help in an emergency.

Friendly cooperation may or may not be possible, but try it. You may find one or two caterers in your neighborhood who agree that cooperation can be mutually beneficial. Most, of course, will consider you a competitor and refuse to talk.

Any catering association in town may be worthwhile to join if the meetings provide you with useful information. It is a good way to meet other caterers, get a feel for what is going on in catering in the area, and monitor trends and problems in the field. However, catering associations are generally geared to help and serve the large caterers — those in huge hotel chains, institutions, banquet halls, and caterers running a large-volume business. Most caterers will learn little, if anything, from their meetings and large caterers tend to disregard you anyway.

9
Pricing

Perhaps the single most difficult problem for a beginning caterer is figuring out how much to charge the client. You are perfectly capable of producing the meal, delivering it safely, presenting it beautifully, and serving it with style, but what to charge for it is a mystery. This is natural since nearly everyone who considers starting a catering business has already been doing it for free — everyday dinners, festive occasions, and receptions for guests and family. But money rarely changed hands except maybe reimbursement for ingredients.

As a professional, if you've thought about this in advance, you'll tell your potential clients that the meal has to be priced out and you'll get back to them. That gives you some time to research pricing. If you give an answer on the spot, your price is usually too low, barely enough to cover your costs. This is a typical scenario and if you are in the process of converting from a cook with a reputation to a caterer, the time will come when you are confronted with this situation. Start doing your research now so you won't be at a total loss later. And remember, never give a price right away unless it is a standard item you are familiar with, and you know a reasonable charge that will include an acceptable profit.

a. Deciding how much to charge

There are several ways to arrive at the price you want to charge your client for your products and services. As a small caterer in

a small business, use the simplest calculation, which considers two factors:

(a) How much your competitors charge for the same or similar products and services

(b) What your cost is to produce the food items

1. What does the competition charge?

Start collecting your competitors' menus and proposals, at least competitors who are selling a similar quality menu to yours. That will give you an idea of what your prices could be. If your quality of catering is about the same, you cannot charge more. If you want to underbid those caterers to carve out your market share, charge less. But beware — if you charge significantly less, the client gets suspicious.

2. What are your costs?

The second factor, your cost, is not difficult to calculate either. If you paid attention to the advice given in chapter 6, you are already carrying around and filling in your little book the prices of everything you use in your kitchen. Using these prices, you can calculate the cost of the ingredients for a dish. Sample #6 is a typical chicken recipe with prices.

A few notes of explanation: unless they are major ingredients, prices of spices, herbs, salt, sugar, and flour can be disregarded. Just add a few cents based on your guess to the total, since these amounts are insignificant compared to the total. It is not

SAMPLE #6
PRICING A RECIPE

HUNGARIAN CHICKEN PAPRIKA 20 portions		
	Unit price	**Cost**
20 8-oz boneless chicken breasts	$3.00/lb	$30.00
24 oz chopped onion	$0.25/lb	$0.38
5 T Hungarian paprika	$3.65/lb	$0.28
4 t salt	$0.05	
24 oz chopped pepper	$0.75/lb	$1.13
1 lb chopped tomato or c paste	$0.30/6-oz can	$0.20
½ c sour cream	$0.60/c	$0.30
¼ c flour	$0.02	
Total cost	$32.36	
Cost per serving	$1.62	

worth your time to figure out their exact cost. In Sample #6, paprika is used in a relatively large portion and its cost was calculated as 28¢ cents. Usually spices, herbs, thickeners, and salt amount to a few cents per serving, of no significance compared to the meat or chicken or cheese in that dish.

For the chopped pepper, the price will vary depending on the season but also on the quality of the dish you want to present. You can use lower-priced green peppers, but if you want it to look prettier, a mixture of green and red peppers will cost more. The flavor remains the same. When you calculate your cost, calculate the presentation considerations, too.

It is a good practice to add this cost calculation to all your recipes. Note the year you figured the price to give an indication of how valid they are. Decide if it is still valid or if prices have gone up (they rarely go down). Having this information on most of your recipes will make pricing a good deal easier.

b. Calculate your overhead

Now that you know the total cost of all your raw material for a particular recipe, it is time to calculate your overhead and labor costs. Don't let this intimidate you. A simple way to figure these costs is by adding up a year's total cost (not including food and related expenses): fixed and variable expenses like rent, insurance, business taxes, utilities, depreciation, and so on. From this total you can derive your daily overhead expense. Do the same for labor costs. One advantage of being a small caterer is that you don't need to be exact on your figuring.

Another method that sidesteps these calculations, and which is commonly used in catering is to multiply the material cost by three.

c. Preparation time

This final figure still needs to be modified. If the preparation is very simple, like chicken wings that you brown in an oven with a barbecue sauce, you can charge less than three times your material cost and still make a good profit. If the item being served is bite-sized spanakopita with a labor-intensive preparation of small phyllo dough squares individually filled with the mixture, the multiplier is closer to four times the cost of raw material, partly because of the amount of labor and partly because ingredients for spanakopita aren't very cheap.

To return to our example of Hungarian Chicken Paprika, let's say we serve it with a side dish of poppy seed noodles and sautéed mixed vegetables. The cost of these two items is about 65¢ per serving. Add a bread roll and butter and another 35¢. The chicken dish is $1.62 per person, which makes the total material cost $2.62 per person. The preparation of all these items is simple, so if we multiply the figure by three, the price you charge will be $7.86 per person, a fairly reasonaly price for a main meal. Add a salad for $2.00 each and dessert for $2.50 each, and the total for this meal is $12.36 per person. Now think about this individual client's expectations, what

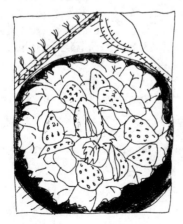

quality is expected. If it is a fancy meal, you inflate the price because you need garnishes for the plates or the table, fancier salads, breads, and vegetables.

d. Number of guests

Another consideration is the number of guests. If it is a small party, your price per person should be higher. If it is for a large event, with 100 or more guests, you can easily afford to reduce the price and still make a good profit on volume. Consider also the state of the economy and your booking calendar, and how much you need the business. That influences prices, too. If your catering business is running close to capacity, losing a job because it is too expensive for the client is not as crucial as when you're facing a near-empty month.

Take another look at the price you arrived at. Can the client get a similar dinner in a better-quality restaurant for that price? If so, your prices are too low. The price of a delivered catered dinner should be more than a comparable restaurant meal. Then look at similar items in your competitors' menus. If their prices are comparable, your price is about correct.

e. Perceived value to the client

The price also varies according to its perceived value by the client. A whole poached salmon on the buffet table is very impressive with an elegant presentation. The total cost of materials is not very high and the labor cost for preparing this item is moderate. Because of its high perceived value, you can charge a higher price for it. Another example is a chilled sour cherry soup laced with cabernet sauvignon. It is easy to prepare and the ingredients are not expensive, yet you can charge extra because it is unique and elegant. That is why restaurants come up with fancy names for otherwise simple dishes, so the perceived value is higher. You cannot charge the same price for spaghetti with meatballs that you could for the identical angel hair pasta with ground round smothered with fresh herbed Italian tomato sauce.

As you can see, pricing is very subjective. The factor of three is something to remember as a useful tool, but only to give you a starting point for pricing. Lately, caterers have been using a higher factor than three, because of their rapidly rising insurance, labor, utility, and rental costs.

This discussion has considered only a basic price for the meal. The total price might include chairs, glasses, tables, china, etc. Caterers differ a great deal in how they quote these extras. Many include the price of china, glass, and silver in the basic meal, and quote separate prices for tables, chairs, and linen as needed. Sometimes a separate price is quoted for the serving staff. Another way to give a total price is to list each item separately — food, beverage, rental, flowers, serving staff, and taxes.

The cost of serving staff can be by the hour or as a percentage of the food charge. Caterers commonly use both methods. Some caterers charge by the hour and add a percentage as well for gratuities. Some use gratuities only to pay for serving staff. A 15% charge is commonly added to the food and service as a gratuity. To avoid the sometimes unpleasant sound of a compulsory gratuity (North Americans, unlike Europeans, have never felt comfortable with

this), you can label it a catering service charge.

f. Receptions and buffets

What about reception food or self-service buffet items? Basically, you derive their price by a similar method but the final price can simply be the total of the prices of individual items. For instance, if the client chooses six items from your hors d'oeuvre selection for 35 guests, you simply add up the prices of the individual six items and use that as the price per guest for food.

Let's suppose that another client has a similar reception for 35 guests but wants to make it really lavish, so she orders 12 different items. Will your charge still be the sum of the individual items? That would be too expensive. Guests can eat only a finite amount. If there are six items, they will eat the equivalent of 3.5 ounces of cheese and meat combined (a realistic figure). If there are 12 items, they will still only eat 3.5 ounces of meat and cheese, so will eat less of each item. Even though it is much more work to prepare 12 items than six, you have to prepare a smaller quantity of each of the 12 items, so you can afford to discount. How big a discount is really up to you. There is no good guide or formula for it. Have a guide for yourself, a figure of 10% or 15%, and see how it works out for you profit-wise, then adjust if needed.

10
Getting The Contract

a. Safeguard against cancellations

It takes clever marketing and artful selling to win catering contracts. Many potential clients talk with half a dozen caterers and, when they've chosen your business (or *you* personally, in most cases) over your competition, you know you've offered something that the others didn't and you've impressed the client more.

It is time to have a mini celebration. But wait, maybe not quite yet. Although cancellations after receiving a deposit are rare, they do happen. In one instance we had a meeting scheduled with a potential wedding client, a young woman, at her home. When I arrived to discuss the particulars, she was still not home from work yet. Her fiancé said that she was delayed, but he would be happy to discuss our suggestions for the wedding.

The discussion took an hour. He was impressed with our food and service, we selected the menu that fit their needs and budget, and he wrote me a check for 50% of the estimated bill for a wedding scheduled in two months. I marked our event calendar in ink, but it turned out to be too soon. When the bride arrived home, she was furious that the discussion and selection of food took place without her. The next morning she called and demanded her money back. She cancelled the contract, no reason given.

1. Always ask for a deposit

Once the buyer decides that you are his or her caterer and becomes a client, the haggling over details is over. You have joined each other on the same side, and you are both fighting for the same cause, a successful event. There is no more mistrust. Once the client has decided to hire you, quickly assure him or her by saying something like, "Mrs. Paté, you made the right decision. We will make your daughter's wedding a most memorable event!" And now, if Mrs. Paté hasn't offered it yet, it is time to ask for the deposit.

Deposit policies vary among caterers. Some want to have one-third when booking, one-third one month in advance, and the final balance on the day of the event. Others want a nominal amount on booking (about 10%), half of the expected total (less the earlier deposit) a month in advance, and the balance on the day of the event. These are the most commonly used schedules. If the event is within five or six weeks from the day of the decision, ask for half of the expected total. If the event is scheduled far in advance (which is commonly the case for weddings and larger events), ask for about 10% or at least $100 to hold the date. Mention that you will require the rest of the 50% deposit a month in advance. Be sure to figure rental, taxes, gratuities, and all subcontractors' fees and charges into your estimate.

Some caterers are willing to refund the full deposit if the client cancels at least a month before the scheduled event. This is a good policy, especially if you use it as a selling point when the client is trying to decide. They know the door is still open to switch to another caterer. But that virtually never happens. In my business, with a full refund policy, it may happen once in two or three years.

A deposit is something that you must have, no exceptions unless you are dealing with regular corporate clients. Any time you do not receive a deposit, you are in danger of cancellation even at the last minute. We booked an event early in our business for a graduation party for a small gathering of about 40 guests. We didn't insist on a deposit. Sure enough, they called a week before the party and said they would have to postpone the event because of illness in the family. If we had insisted on a deposit, the party would have been held, illness or not. That taught us a lesson — never reserve a date without money down.

There are so many unforeseen circumstances that may result in cancellation. There are many more questionable reasons, and a deposit at risk can influence the final decision. If the computer crashes and everyone must stay to rectify the crisis, or important guests at the wedding party are delayed because of tornadoes in Texas, or

the family cat dies, the party will still be held if there is a deposit. If nothing is at risk for the client, the attitude is, let's postpone, to heck with the caterer. The deposit is necessary to cover any expenses you have already incurred.

Soon after you receive the deposit, you may want to get the competition's proposals from the client. This is information is of no value to the client anymore and probably will end up in the trash. For you it is invaluable. You want to know what you were up against and how your prices and menu look in contrast to the others. Offer the client something in return for the other proposals, perhaps a free coffee service or upgrading the disposable hors d'oeuvre plates to china at no cost. Offer something that will not cost you very much but will add an extra touch to the client's party. It is a win-win situation.

A few clients may consider your request for competitors' proposals unethical. In that case, drop the subject. Others are delighted with your cleverness in learning about your competition and will readily agree.

2. Always confirm the engagement

As soon as you receive the deposit, reconfirm the party with a letter, stating all details, the price of everything, what you will supply, and what the host or hostess will supply, unless you have already done so in a formal proposal. State clearly that you need to know

Reprinted with special permission of King Features Syndicate.

the guest count, or a guaranteed minimum number of guests, at least five days before the event. A small change after that date may be acceptable up to two or three days before the event, but a significant change (more than 5%) should incur extra charges, depending on the specific situation. Caterers customarily add a 15% surcharge over the regular per person charge for additional last minute guests. Explain to your clients that this is to cover the extra cost of having to buy small amounts at retail to provide for the added guests.

A written record of what you agreed upon — menu, prices, type of service — is essential for most events. For regular corporate events, like routinely scheduled luncheons, dinners, or breakfasts, this is not necessary. Even for a small social catered event, a telephone confirmation is often sufficient. Putting it in writing can be handled in two ways:

(a) A simple letter of confirmation you write and send to the client in duplicate. The client signs and returns one copy to you.

(b) A contract that spells out the legal aspects and is signed by both you and the client, with original signature copies to each. In addition to the contract, a letter or a standard form spells out the details of the party. A typical event contract and standard order forms are shown in Sample #7.

During the main discussion with your client, you must resolve the following details:

(a) Menu. Agree on the menu in as much detail as possible, but leave some options open so you have enough flexibility. If the event is a reception, the food items should be decided exactly since you will be calculating the price per person or total price according to the agreed-upon menu. If the event is a main meal, decide on the entrée and a side dish, the first course, and the dessert. Where seasonal items are to be considered — salads, vegetables, fruits — you and your client can decide tentatively, but keep the freedom to change according to what is available on the market and what looks best (and for your own benefit, what is priced the lowest). Most clients will understand this and let your chef do the final selection. Some are very particular and insist on specific items: "I want cauliflower because my husband loves it, but I also want green beans because that is Aunt Mabel's favorite and she will be the guest of honor." Agree to those requests, particularly if they are easy to satisfy. If it is creamed and pureed spinach the client insists on, don't agree. Explain that the honored guest will simply love your chef's creamed spinach but it is a questionable choice for the rest of the guests. Suggest a vegetable acceptable to more palates.

(b) The date of the event.

(c) The place it will be held at.

(d) Timing for the event. You need to know when the guests will arrive, when food and beverages should be served, and when the event will end.

(e) Approximate number of guests. Let the client know the final date on which you need a guaranteed minimum guest number. Also inform the client of your policy about last minute guest number changes.

(f) Style of service. Will it be self-service, full-service, or a combination? Let the client know the price of each style.

(g) Rental items. Decide on whether china, glass and silver, or disposable ware is to be used. Also, discuss linen and anything else that will

CONTRACT AND ORDER FORMS

EVENT CONTRACT
DOUGH CATERING CO.

CLIENT:_____**EVENT DATE:**_____

GUEST COUNT CONFIRMATION:

Dough Catering is reserving for _____guests. This estimate will be used as a basis for purchasing, scheduling, and preparation with a final guarantee to be given to Dough Catering five days prior to the event. Thereafter, the number may be increased at the quoted rate per person, but not decreased. An increase in excess of 10% may incur additional cost.

DEPOSIT AND PAYMENTS:

If the proposal meets your approval, please sign this agreement and return the original copy with your deposit by _____to reserve the date and confirm the event. Deposit of 50% of the expected total bill is required, including rental and other charges.

A final invoice detailing all actual charges will be mailed to you shortly after the event. Payment is due upon receipt. Unpaid invoices will be charged at the rate of 1.5% (18% APR) per month after 15 days.

CANCELLATION:

If you cancel the event before _____your deposit will be refunded. If you cancel the event after the above date, 75% of your deposit will be refunded or the difference between actual costs incurred and the amount of your deposit if in excess of 25%.

EQUIPMENT:

A count of silver, china, linen, glassware, and other equipment will be taken after the event and you will be charged for any missing items.

TAXES:

Local laws require that sales tax be charged on all food and beverage order items. If you are tax exempt, your tax registration number and a certificate of exemption must be returned with this agreement.

THE ATTACHED PROPOSAL AND THESE TERMS AND CONDITIONS ARE ACCEPTABLE.

By_____   By_____
        Dough Catering

_____   _____
                    Date   Date

EVENT ORDER FORM
DOUGH CATERING

Date of order:_____

CLIENT

Name:

Address:

Phone:

EVENT

Date:

No. of guests:

Place:

Time :

Occasion:

What service:

MENU/PRICE

Total price/person

Total price:

CSC (15%):

Tax:

Delivery:

Rental:

Flowers:

Bartending:

Other:

OTHER SERVICES

Beverage:

Tablecloth:

Napkins:

China, glass, silver:

Disposable:

Flowers:

Other:

STAFF

SPECIAL NOTES

EQUIPMENT REQUIRED

[ ] Deposit received

Date:_____Amount:_____

[ ] Bill out

Date:_____

[ ] Paid

Date:_____

need to be rented, like tables, chairs, and so on. Let the client know the exact price of each of these rental items. Even if you get a discount from the rental agency, make sure you charge enough to cover your costs and extra time you spend on getting the rental items. Also, they may charge a delivery and pickup fee and you may have to pay for broken or missing pieces that are very difficult to charge to the client when the damage is only a small amount, like for a few broken glasses. In addition, when dealing with china, glass, and silver, you will need extra help to rinse and stack them back into the crates at the end of the event. With disposable ware you can save several staff hours on the event. Include the extra staff cost in your rental charges, either by stating a certain number of hours for a cleanup charge or simply charging a little more for rental per person. If your client cannot decide right away, give him or her a deadline so that you can reserve the necessary rental items.

(h) Beverage service. Decide who will provide the beverage and who will provide the beverage service, the glasses, ice, fruit, mixes, and all other bar paraphernalia. Your client's needs may fall under any one of the following situations:

   (i) Full bar service, where the caterer provides everything and charges the client. You may or may not need a liquor license.

   (ii) The client supplies all beverages and the caterer supplies the bartending service at either a fixed price per bartender or an hourly rate.

   (iii) The client supplies the alcoholic beverages and the caterer supplies the non-alcoholic beverages. Include these details in your letter of confirmation. Spell out who is supplying what, including glassware, ice, table, or a more formal bar for the service.

(i) Miscellaneous. Discuss any other options like flowers, a special cake, music, favors, table decorations both for the guest tables and serving tables.

(j) Contact person/liaison. For some events, particularly weddings and other large events, you have to ask the client for a contact person at the event. The client, whether it is the bride, groom, a parent, or simply a host, will be far too busy to be able to answer questions during the event. A contact person should be agreed upon, usually a close friend or relative, who knows what is going on and who is available for quick questions or decisions. These questions could be little details like where the garbage can is, should we cut the cake or wait another half hour, should we cut off alcoholic beverages since there are some serious drunks among the guests, or what should be done with the extra food.

b. *Establish a refund policy*

What about a cancellation policy for when the party could not be held for a valid reason? There are no definite guidelines here. Use your best business instinct or wing it. If the event is far in advance and you have not refused other events on the same date, the best policy is to refund the deposit in full. If the event is scheduled within a month of cancellation, it is best to discuss it with the client personally. When the client calls to cancel on less than a month's notice and you are not sure how to handle the cancellation, postpone your decision. Tell the client that you have to check first with the kitchen manager (whether you have one or not) about what was already ordered for the event, how much money and time has already been put into it, what commitments you have made to subcontractors and your staff. That gives you time to calculate a reasonable amount to pay for costs you've already shelled out. Then refund the rest. It pays to be fair. There is a possibility of future business from this client.

If you made the mistake of not asking for a deposit, chances are excellent that you will not be reimbursed by your client for any charges you already incurred on behalf of the event. That is a business loss, an expensive lesson that will encourage your insisting on a deposit in future, no exceptions.

Another type of refund that some caterers recognize is called the embarrassment refund. This is initiated by the caterer. If you run out of a food item early on at an event or perhaps a server drops a whole tray of food that can't be reassembled, you must apologize to the client. Offer to adjust the final invoice to compensate for your error. This occasionally happens and it can be costly. Your invoice adjustment should be sufficiently high to console the client, so you want to avoid it when you can.

Sometimes an embarrassment refund is not voluntary and not a "refund" at all. If the client finds something unsatisfactory at the event, he or she may not want to pay all or part of your full invoice. In this case, there is not much you can do. If the amount involved is a large sum and you feel that the unpaid balance is not fully justified, you can argue your case with the client or even go through legal procedures if all else fails.

11
It Takes More Than A Hot Oven

a. Planning and organizing an event

The entire infrastructure of a catering business, including marketing and selling, exists for the sole purpose of executing a successful event. Nothing else really matters as long as both the caterer and the client are satisfied.

One of the issues when planning an event with a client is determining who will provide all the food for the same event. Inevitably, some clients will suggest that you bring some of the food and the rest will be supplied by various other people. This happens mostly in low- and medium-budget affairs, particularly weddings, and is always a headache for the caterer. There are two reasons a client may want to do this:

(a) your price will be lower because you are supplying only part of the meal, and

(b) because Aunt Mabel makes the most wonderful dips and providing them will be her gift to the bride and groom.

Your answer should always be a gentle but firm no. Explain why such mixing of the food cannot be done. One of them is legal liability. You are fully responsible for the food being served, but when all the food is not brought by you, your responsibility isn't under your control. Besides, your insurance policy will not allow it. Another equally good reason is quality and presentation. Aunt Mabel's dip could be one made with packaged powders and sour cream. As far as the guests know, everything on the table was catered. You cannot afford to have second- or third-rate tasting food mixed with your own high quality food. Your reputation is on the line. Never accept such compromises.

Once the client has reserved a date with a deposit, the caterer's job is to successfully execute the event. There still may be changes in the menu or in the number of guests or rental requirements, but these are usually minor and easily handled details. From now on success depends on the caterer's ability to plan and organize the event.

Neither of the three phases — planning, organizing, and executing — is difficult for an experienced caterer. The prerequisite for successful execution is planning and organizing in advance. Without this step, an event is unlikely to be fully successful. However, no matter how much time was spent on careful planning and organizing, if the execution is not done exactly right, the client is not likely to be pleased. All three phases are equally important.

There are additional complications when several events are being planned and organized simultaneously, especially if they are large, complex, and difficult affairs. Smaller events are less of a problem. As a matter of fact, several smaller events can be planned and organized with less total time than it takes to plan and organize each one individually.

b. Thinking ahead

How far in advance you should plan an event depends on you, on the type of event, and the type of catering you do. Determine this by experience and eventually you will come up with a reasonably comfortable schedule for when to start planning an event. Until you get comfortable and secure, start very early so that you aren't frantic the day of the event.

If you need hard-to-find ingredients or items you must order in advance, schedule the search and ordering at least two weeks before the event. There's always the problem of the exact number of guests changing significantly even a week before the event, but that is a chance you have to take. Compensate by over-ordering a little. It's low-priced insurance and the extra food is comfortable to have even though it bites into your net profit. Give the extra food to the client at the end of the event, if possible. The payback in good relations justifies the extra cost. (Regarding extra food, see the discussion in chapter 12, section d., about storing food, and chapter 14, section h., about contaminated food.)

When planning several events with dates close together, it pays to have similar menus for them, or at least some duplicate items. If you or your salesperson played the cards right, the menus will be identical.

Plan the menu using ingredients that are freshest and lowest priced at that particular time of year, or something you over-ordered the week before because you could get a case at a lower unit price. Use it for the next corporate luncheon. That should not mean that you sacrifice quality, of course. All it means is that you are using up the available ingredients or that you are taking advantage of seasonally low-priced products.

For a second, or even a third event spaced closely in time, the same menu means much less work. Some things can be prepared or partially prepared at the same time — for instance, spanakopita fill for cream puffs. For others items that must be prepared fresh, time can still be saved. For example, if at Thursday's luncheon you serve pasta salad, you can serve the same salad at a Friday luncheon if you mix the salad fresh on Friday from ingredients premade the day before. On Thursday morning you cook your pasta, cut up and blanch vegetables for both salads, then divide it into the Thursday and Friday portions. Friday's salad ingredients go into the refrigerator for storage. (Toss the pasta first with a little oil). Friday morning you combine the salad ingredients with the dressing and it's ready to go.

Again, the decision about how much you can make ahead is yours.

c. Checking the site beforehand

Should you plan to visit a new client's facilities before the event? Some caterers feel that you definitely should at all times, no matter what the event is. Others feel it is an unnecessary waste of time. My own policy is determined by the event. For a larger party with several food stations, bars, and a complex menu, a preview visit is advisable. This is the time to scout out the following:

- Nearest door you can park at to unload; where you can leave your truck so it won't be blocked by the guests (they love to do that)

- Shortest, easiest transportation route from the truck to the party site

- Kitchen facilities — if there are none, a staging and storage area (sometimes an empty office is fine)

- Availability of tables for preparation

- Refrigerator, freezer, and oven facilities (don't count on space in refrigerator or freezer unless you arrange it ahead of time)

- Where to set up food and bar tables

- What the logical traffic flow is

- Availability of electrical outlets

- Water and cleanup areas if there is no kitchen

- Trash disposal

Check the electrical outlets both in the kitchen and serving areas whenever you have several appliances you are planning to use. Most heating appliances use high wattage and older circuits are not wired to deliver the amount of electric current needed to run them. You blow the circuit when you overload the wiring, a real nuisance when you can least afford the time. You have to find the host or someone to reset the circuit and that can cost you 10 to 15 minutes in an office building. It could be even worse on a Saturday evening when no maintenance person is around. An alternative is to carry your own multi-plug strip with an overload reset button between the appliances and the wall outlet. If the wiring is too weak, your circuit breaker will be tripped. Before resetting, you can take one of the appliances to a different part of the house or use the equipment one at a time. Carry a multi-plug strip with you to all events.

We learned our lesson on a Saturday morning workshop for judges and lawyers in an old courthouse. The building was nicely remodeled and modernized except for the wiring. We only had two coffeemakers and an electric tea kettle, and when it was hard to find an electric outlet, we should have thought about the fact that the original wiring in the building was not meant for 20th-century appliances. We had to run an extension cord from a bathroom socket, the only one we could find near the buffet table, an outlet that was designed for the power of an electric razor. As soon as we plugged in one of the coffeemakers and an electric kettle, the circuit blew.

We moved our equipment downstairs and cautiously plugged in both appliances on two widely separated sites, praying that they were on different circuits. It worked and soon after that, the maintenance person reset our triggered circuit upstairs. Since that event, we have always carried our own multiple plug cord with built-in circuit breaker.

Coincidentally, there was a second lesson that was to be learned at that courthouse breakfast. To get into the building, we had to go through a metal detector that immediately got all excited by our metal equipment. The guard would not, under any condition, let our knives through. We needed those knives to cut the freshly baked walnut-date bread, one of the items on the buffet table. In the end we had to send someone back to the truck with the knife, a cutting board, and the breads to finish the job.

For a smaller, simpler event, an advance visit is usually unnecessary. If you feel better about looking the place over, by all means go. With experience, however, you will learn how to quickly evaluate every new situation and in no time work out all the particulars of the event within minutes after arrival. If you have not visited the site previously, you should allow an extra 20 or

30 minutes to work out the details on the day of the event.

Sometimes the client asks you to visit the facilities. If you feel that it is an unnecessary trip, say so. If it makes him or her feel better, visit the place anyway.

d. The supply list

The first stage of planning is to prepare your shopping list. If you personally use your kitchen a lot, you know how much you have of most items and if you always replenish items as they run low, your list will only include fresh and special products for that particular event. If you don't do the cooking in your business, work out a schedule with the chef so that you have the list far enough in advance to complete the shopping comfortably.

A good, efficient shopping list is not at all what most people carry into the supermarket. A professional list is well organized to save you shopping time. Divide your list into at least four parts: meats, dairy, produce, and other items. Then, with color coding or by some other visible means, mark items according to where you expect to purchase them. Or if you prefer, have separate lists for different shops you expect to get your supplies from. Cross each item out as you get it and before you reach the checkout

counter, take another close look to make sure nothing has been forgotten. The goal is to cut your shopping time to a bare minimum. Occasional forgotten items are inevitable, but the better organized you and your kitchen are, the less likely a second trip will be needed. A forgotten but essential bunch of parsley can cost you a half hour, provided there is a store nearby! It's important to work at making those forgotten items a rare occurrence.

For smaller events, one shopping trip can take care of all necessary supplies. For large events you often need at least two trips — one several days in advance to purchase ingredients for items that hold well, things like dressings, stocks, marinades, pastry crusts, concentrates for punch, fillings for quiche, and so on. Items that must be defrosted have to be bought early too: chicken, shrimp, some vegetables, and juices.

The second trip should take place either the day before or on the day of the event. Shop for the fresh items that don't hold well: vegetables, fruits, pastries, bread, and dairy products.

If your business is large enough that suppliers will deliver to you, your shopping is reduced but not eliminated. The planning is about the same. Your lists will consist of items that you can order from different suppliers and your job is to coordinate the deliveries so they arrive when you need them.

e. The work schedule

1. Minimize preparation time

Now that you have your supplies, you can make up a schedule of what to prepare and when. The idea is to have as little left to prepare at the last minute as possible but still have everything as fresh as possible. This isn't always easy but it can be worked out. If you were a good planner with your client, the menu won't include too many items that either must be prepared at the last minute or on location. Many things can be partially or fully finished days ahead. Some items are better prepared in advance.

Eventually you will devise your own system of mapping out a schedule. In the meantime, here is one efficient way to do it. Start at the day of the event. List all items that absolutely must be prepared that last day. Then list jobs that can be done the day before and continue listing backwards a day at a time until all jobs and items are taken into account for that specific event. Your motto should be to prepare as much in advance as possible. Check your refrigerator, freezer, and storage to make sure you are not preparing some things unnecessarily.

When your schedule of food and beverage preparation is completed, checked, and rechecked, assign an approximate preparation time for each item. The daily total will give you the food preparation time required for that day and will tell you how much labor is needed. Add extra time for cleanup, breaks, telephone calls, and miscellaneous contingencies.

The actual preparation of the food is just one of the many things that takes up the total preparation time, though it is by far the most time-consuming. Another important part is the presentation. You will have to think about how the food is going to be presented, how the table will look, and what you will need to acquire and purchase to follow through on your presentation plan.

If you have a simple catered event with a modest budget, the presentation should match it. It is always nice to have a few items to adorn or garnish your tables or trays. They don't have to cost a lot: a few radishes trimmed into flowers, the tender inner leaves of celery, sliced scallion greens, even lemon slices and a few flowers can add a great deal. Whatever you choose, you have to plan and add these items to your shopping list.

Be sure to schedule time to collect all the required equipment for the kitchen. For this you need a checklist (see the event checklist in Sample #8). Without a checklist, the chance of forgetting something essential is much greater.

2. Organize your equipment

It is a good idea to have a separate list of items that should come out of the freezer and refrigerator for loading at the last minute. Since in most kitchens both freezer and refrigerator are quite full (often more than full), cold and frozen items needed for a particular event cannot be isolated easily. It is best to list them separately and check them off as they are loaded on the truck just before leaving.

It is also good to have a catering box permanently loaded with items and equipment that may be needed at any event. This box is always carried to all events, like a life vest on a motor boat. Here is what I carry in mine:

- extra menus, business cards

- business card holder for the buffet table

- disposable plates, containers for food left for the client

- oven mitts

- extension cord

- multiple outlet strip with circuit interrupt on it (so you don't blow the line that supplies all the electricity to kitchen outlets on-site)

- cutting board

- chef's knife, paring knife, serrated knife

- salt/pepper shaker

- dish towel

- wiping cloths

- roll of plastic wrap or aluminum foil

SMITHS' LUNCHEON

☐ tablecloths, napkins

☐ plates, cups, glasses

☐ flatware

☐ serving platters, chafers

☐ serving utensils

☐ trays

☐ electric kettle (quickly heats water for chafers, tea, etc.)

☐ hot plates (keeps extra food hot in kitchen or on buffet table)

☐ extension cord

☐ circuit breaker (always use it when plugging more than one electric appliance into a socket)

☐ water pitcher

☐ coffee server, carafe

☐ ice, ice bucket, and scoop

☐ oven mitts

☐ chef's coat and hat

☐ aprons, serving jackets

☐ extra bow ties

☐ can opener

☐ corkscrew, bar equipment

☐ cutting board, carver, serrated knife

☐ colander, strainer, bowls

☐ vegetable peeler

☐ measuring cups, spoons

☐ wooden spoons, whisk

☐ candles, matches, sterno

☐ salt, pepper

☐ sugar, cream, their containers

☐ disposable containers and wraps for extra food and drinks

☐ trash bags

☐ dishwashing detergent, dishcloth, sponge, wash-up bowl

☐ dish towels

☐ food umbrellas (small umbrella-like food covers made of gauze-like material to cover food outdoors; comes in different sizes — can be found in Asian variety stores)

☐ beverage tub

☐ water bucket

☐ bus tub

☐ disposable wine glasses (to exchange wine glasses of reluctant-to-leave guests at the end of the party so you can go home)

☐ invoice

☐ business cards, menus

☐ catering box

- rubber spatula to scrape used plates

- matches

- corkscrew

- champagne bottle opener (hard to open dozens of bottles by hand quickly)

- champagne bottle stopper

- oven thermometer

- rubber bands, wire twists

- tape, thumb tacks, string

- pocket timer

- cake cutting chart

Note: A cake cutting chart is a useful thing to have if one of the servers must cut a cake. Cakes have to be cut by different methods to produce nice, even-sized pieces and to keep the cake from collapsing when the support is removed. You will find a sample cake cutting chart in Appendix 1. Ask ahead what shape cake has been ordered and decide how it should be cut.

3. Coordinate your staff

Next you will need to schedule your staff. You may be able to do smaller events, for instance, a buffet business luncheon for 20 guests, by yourself or you can assign the whole event to one staff person. For larger events you have to calculate the number of staff needed and reserve them sometimes weeks ahead of the event, especially in a traditionally busy season. Reserve the food preparation and cooking staff, serving and cleanup crew, and bartenders and their helpers.

For larger events or several simultaneous small events, you may also need a kitchen manager, someone who is experienced and knowledgeable enough to direct the kitchen operation in addition to being part of it. During the busy holiday season it is often essential to have a kitchen man-

ager. You may also need a cleanup crew to come in right after the event or the next day.

4. Other details

Reserve rental items as far in advance as possible. Also book florists, musicians, ice sculptors, limousine services, and any other subcontractors whose services you are responsible for well in advance.

Another thing you should remember is to check the client's address if you or your event manager don't know exactly where it is. You cannot afford to search for a location when you're on a deadline. Write down the exact directions for everyone who has to get there, including staff members driving on their own.

Finally, prepare an invoice to take with you to the event. Have a folder or briefcase ready for your paperwork: invoice, notes for the event, staff schedules, staff work assignments and telephone numbers of your staff, rental agencies, subcontractors, and anyone else who is scheduled to deliver anything to the job site. And one more important item: take some cash with you for any emergency shopping. It is embarrassing to send someone out for another bottle of vodka and no one has enough money to pay for it.

f. Transportation

Your carefully prepared food, gleaming glass and china, shiny silver, and brass have to arrive at the event site in the same condition as they left your kitchen. That also takes some careful planning, a good transportation system, and plenty of experience. Many catering disasters occur in transportation. That is where the vulnerable food and equipment are in the most danger of damage.

Use boxes or crates to transport equipment efficiently. Organize the packing systematically — serving equipment is separated from plates and flatware, kitchen and cooking equipment are separated, and garnish, greens, and table decorations are all together, and so on. Assemble as much of this as possible the day before the event.

When you are transporting raw or partially cooked food to be prepared on site, the danger is much less. For many events, especially receptions where kitchen facilities are not available, food is transported ready to be served. A sudden stop or an unexpected bend in the road can send the food skating across the truck.

There are some types of food that transport easily, provided they are well secured on the truck and well wrapped on their serving dish: fruits, vegetables, breads, pastries, and anything in chafing pans, etc. Others are harder to transport, like stuffed eggs or other stuffed items without a flat base, any food on an unstable pedestal server, and large arrangements of fruits or vegetables. To transport these items, you have two alternatives: start preparing them in your kitchen and finish them on the event site, or prepare them fully and devise ingenious accident-proof ways to carry them in your truck.

Often the first alternative is better, provided you have some time and space to finish them at the party site. If it takes 20 minutes to finish the food, that means arriving 20 minutes earlier, which also means that other menu items need to be held an extra 20 minutes outside your own safe holding facilities. Keep in mind things like the refrigeration or warming facilities at the party site, how much labor you have available, and how difficult it is to transport your food item safely when fully prepared.

For example, stuffed cherry tomatoes are really hard to keep from sliding around in transit. One way to prevent them from moving around is to set them in a bed of chopped parsley. Even if they slide around a little, they will remain undamaged. Or, have the cherry tomatoes hollowed out and transport them in a carrying container. The filling is in a pastry bag, also easy to transport. On arrival the tomatoes are put on their designated serving platter, the filling is squeezed into them from the pastry bag, and the platter is ready in minutes. You won't need to do them all, just a first batch as a starter. A little later, when the pressure of setting up is off, you or one of your helpers can fill the rest in your spare time.

Liquids are easy to transport. Just make certain they are in tightly closed containers. Sauces, juices, or liquids that are part of cooked food are more of a problem. They spill easily if they are in chafers since these cannot be closed airtight. Covering them with aluminum foil seals them reasonably well, though they can still spill a little. Another possibility is to pour most of the liquid off (or drain it off with a baster) into a tight container for transportation and add it back when you arrive. This is for cooked or baked dishes. If you plan to prepare the food on site, then don't add the liquid until you arrive.

12
Executing The Event — It's Show Time!

Now we are down to the most important part of your catering business: conducting, directing, and executing the event. This is the culmination of all your planning, preparation, and work. This is when your client finds out if all the promises you made were just empty promises or you're as good as you said you were.

a. Arrive well ahead of the guests

How long before the event should you arrive at the party site? That really varies. For a simple, small breakfast, a half hour should be sufficient, provided everything is all ready to serve and you've been there before. For a larger or more complicated event, schedule at least 45 minutes to an hour. For a very large, complex party even more time is needed.

If you have to set up tables, chairs, china, silver, glasses, etc., an advance crew can be sent to handle that part. The food and the rest of the equipment can arrive later but still at least 45 minutes before the first guests arrive. This assumes that there is little or no food preparation being done on site. If food is being prepared on site, schedule the arrival so everything can be comfortably prepared and cooked by serving time.

How the event is executed differs with the various types of functions. The three most common varieties are reception catering, self-service, and full-service meal catering.

b. Receptions

Reception catering is generally of three different styles:

(a) Full-service meal with staff in attendance

(b) Meal delivered and set up but no staff in attendance, pick-up later

(c) Delivered on disposable ware, no staff in attendance, no pick-up

Full-service is most commonly used for better quality receptions. Many middle or high-end caterers will not do anything but full-service receptions. The logic is that reception food cannot be left unattended and still look presentable.

For smaller events where food can be delivered, set up on quality, non-disposable platters. Since the equipment is picked up later, no serving staff is needed; however, menu items are limited to food that holds up well or needs a minimum of preparation and no replenishment. This type of service is limited to events with simple food and no more than about 25 to 30 guests.

Reception food delivered on disposable platters along with an invoice is not common in better-class catering. It is akin to pizza order and delivery with advanced reservation. This type of food cannot be presented quite as well as the same items on china, glass, silver, baskets, or wood. However, very good quality disposable ware is available and is perfectly acceptable for certain types of events, like a picnic. High-quality disposable ware is fairly costly and you have to consider that when pricing the event. Ordinary, inexpensive disposable ware can also be used if it is completely covered with layers of greens, chopped parsley, paper, or even cloth napkins. For low-budget catering, you don't even need to do the covering. The client gets what he or she pays for.

1. Setting up

Let us presume that you, your staff, the food, and the equipment have arrived at the job site safe and sound, on time as promised. First, take a quick look inside the truck to make sure there is no problem that may have occurred as a result of transportation. Survey the facilities if you haven't done so previously. Take ten minutes, if necessary, and plan where everything goes. Where will the serving and bar tables go? How well can you manage in the existing kitchen facilities? If there is no kitchen or dining room, set up your staging area in an empty office or another room. In a private home you often need a small storage area as well, like a laundry room, office, or even a garage where you can stack up the extra equipment, food, and transportation crates. Watch out for cats. They adore your jumbo shrimp or poached whole salmon and can wreak havoc in a very short time.

There are clients, mostly in social catering, who hover around you and your staff during the entire setup period, making you feel uneasy. Or they sit down near the reception table and just quietly watch you working. Try to ignore the client's presence. The worst, of course, are the clients who not only sit down next to your work, but also chatter nonstop, asking you questions when you are trying to concentrate on making their event a success. Or they criticize and disapprove of arrangements, color, the order of platters, and so on.

2. Unloading

However, let's assume that all went well with your planning, and you and your staff are left alone. Now comes the time to do the most unpleasant task — unloading. Unloading is a thankless job. It is also physically taxing, particularly when cases of liquor, china, glass, tables, and other heavy equipment are involved.

Office settings are easier to set up. There are no stairs involved so you can use your cart and dolly. There are almost always stairs or steps in a private home, so you often have to carry everything in by hand. You can sometimes park your vehicle close to the kitchen and reduce unloading time.

Planning and organization are still critical, but you can slow down on your worrying. If your planning and organizational skill got you this far without any obvious problems, you can execute the event as well.

When unloading, try to arrange things right away in an orderly fashion. Food items go into the kitchen or staging area, anything that belongs to or near the buffet table is carried to that area, and so on. The idea is to lift each piece only once and put it down where it will be used. China, glass, and silver for a buffet dinner can stay near the table in their boxes and be unloaded later directly onto the table. At a full-service dinner, plates are taken to the kitchen; glasses and silverware are deposited in the eating area ready for table setting.

For a self-service event, the next step is to set up the food table as much as you can to eliminate some of the clutter of food and equipment. Plates, silverware, glasses, napkins, and some of the food items can go on the table. Anything that needs to stay cold should wait in the refrigerator or on ice until the last minute. Food to be freshly prepared should also wait. If the event includes hot food and it is ready, it can go in the chafing dish. Bring the water to a boil in your electric kettle or in a pot on the stove and pour it into the bottom half of the chafer, light the sterno, then put the pan of food over it, cover and forget it. Many caterers use hot water from the tap for the chafers. It will not keep the food as hot as if the water is brought to a boil first. When you see steam escaping from the bottom half of the chafer, turn the flame down a little to save fuel, especially if you have a long reception and your fuel must last several hours.

3. Staff pep-talk

For a larger event, once the entire staff has arrived, it's useful to have a brief organizational meeting. Explain the event in a few quick phrases, especially timing. Mention the name of the host and hostess and any other important guests, and where they will be seated.

Go through your event plan briefly, outlining the various phases. Then assign each person specifically to his or her role and tasks during the event. If you have new or fairly new crew members, mention again the various rules you want them to follow.

Mention the continuous cleanup mode during the event. Anyone who has any free time can collect dirty plates, glasses, and ash trays to keep the site clean. Also make sure that equipment is not mixed up. There could be your equipment, the rental agency's, and the client's. They all must be in separate piles at the end of the event. It is time-consuming to return someone's china and flatware, and costly to lose yours.

Make sure everyone knows the name of every food item. The little spheres of meat in the chafing dish are *not* meatballs but Latin albondiguitas. And the other chafer holds not chicken wings but chicken drumettes.

Scrutinize the crew to make sure everyone looks up to your standard. Always be pleasant to your staff. They will pass your pleasant attitude on, and ultimately, your business will benefit.

A meeting of this sort should not take more than ten minutes, possibly much less, and it is a very useful exercise. The crew will appreciate knowing their exact roles and having the event clarified. You may also get some very useful feedback and questions from your crew, often about things you have not considered or may have overlooked.

4. Keep everybody busy

While you or one of your staff is working on the food table, someone else should be busy in the kitchen finishing the food that still needs preparation.

Next, bring all food in the kitchen as close to finished as possible, but never sacrifice quality by preparing too early. It is better if the guests have to wait a little longer. A little waiting is acceptable, especially at leisurely evening or weekend social occasions. At corporate lunch functions or any other function with a tight schedule having speakers or similar programs, waiting should be kept to the absolute minimum. Some sacrifice in quality is even acceptable over keeping the guests waiting in these situations.

Reception food is ideally small, bite-sized finger food. For lower-budget and simpler events it could be only two to three items, such as the popular (because they are cheap to prepare) fruit and vegetable platters, cheeses, and cold cuts. More extravagant

events will include at least six to eight different items, some hot, some cold. Cold items are the easiest for the caterer, not only to transport but to serve and maintain on the serving table. If hot items are served, the easiest are those served in chafing dishes kept hot over steam. The most difficult are those that are to be served fresh out of the oven.

5. Hot and cold foods

Let's assume that we have a better event with mixed hot and cold food. After unloading from your vehicle, the cold food can be placed directly on the serving table. The hot food served over steam can be transferred and kept warm on the table. If an oven is available, hot food should be held in the oven to save the sterno fuel for later.

The buffet table should be the most visible part as soon as guests arrive, so set it up as fully as possible. Many guests arrive quite early. The table should look good by the time these early people arrive, even though it is not quite finished.

There is a nightmare story a caterer told us about an elegant, high-priced, lavish reception. The table was set up, looked gorgeous, and had a huge crystal chandelier over the center. The first

guests were just arriving. The bartender walked over to admire the table while opening a bottle of champagne. The exploding champagne cork hit the chandelier in the center, broke many of the crystals, and the shattered glass pieces dusted most of the table and freshly uncovered food. I don't know the ending to the story, but it could not have been a happy one.

Anything to be baked or broiled is kept aside, ready to go into the oven at the proper time. These foods are best brought to the event site fully prepared for the oven so there is no extra work with them. It is up to you to decide when to serve these hot items.

6. Keep small batches circulating

Food should not be served too early or the later guests may not get any. Few people eat right after arrival. Most will start at the beverage table, then socialize and finally drift over to the food table.

The best way to deal with hot food is to prepare it in small batches throughout the reception. Don't attempt to bake everything at once and keep it hot. Have enough servings to serve half of the guests present; when you run out, announce to the guests that fresh ones will be ready in a few minutes. They'll anticipate your food. Plan the baking so that items come out of the oven every 10 to 15 minutes in small batches. Assign one of the servers to pass it out at once. When everyone has been served once, wait a while with the new batches, perhaps 30 to 40 minutes. If this hot food item is one of the main foods on the menu, it should be served more continuously than if it is one of many items.

Someone should be in charge of ready-to-bake items, equipped with a small timer in his or her pocket. It is easy to forget that something is burning until the smell reaches you. People, especially the client, start sniffing and wonder what the caterer just ruined. Don't let that happen; carry a timer.

7. Replenish some items, ration others

Traditionally, in mediocre catering (often hotels and banquet halls), what the first guests see are huge platters of food set up on large tables. The later guests see the same but the platters are less than half full. The food is disarrayed and much less appetizing than the original setup. Guests arriving late see even worse conditions. The food is beginning to look like leftovers and has definitely lost its appeal.

Better caterers serve on smaller tables on small serving platters and replenish the food continually, carrying full platters to the table and taking the half-empty ones off. This type of service takes more staff time, but the last guests will find the serving table virtually in the same condition as the first guests. Plan to serve in this style if at all possible.

Certain food items may not need to be on the serving table all the time like hot, freshly prepared food that you carry around or items that need to be rationed. Steamed jumbo shrimp, for example, are devoured in huge quantities. Unless the budget is unlimited, these are best rationed. Serve them by carrying them around every 15 to 20 minutes or have them on the table so that half the time there is shrimp and the other half there isn't. Guests will ask you about the shrimp when it is not there. Politely inform them that a new plate is just being readied — they must be prepared absolutely fresh, you may add. Make sure that the host or hostess is offered the first choice from each freshly carried full platter of these rationed items. That way he or she will have the impression that someone is carrying a full platter around all the time, having an unlimited supply in the back.

No matter how you ration these very popular items, some guests will "pig out" on them. It is horrifying to see a guest take a dozen large shrimp and add nothing else to his or her plate; there goes your estimate for two-and-a-half shrimp per person. There is nothing you can do except to stare that guest into shame, and even that won't work. Guests with a full plate of shrimp are very thick-skinned. Usually there are also a number of guests, however, who are either allergic to shrimp or dislike it and that makes up for the greedy ones.

For the caterer, the pressure will be at its most intense during the first third of the event. This is when you are setting up and attempting to get everything on the table. Once the table is ready, you have a respite until the first few guests drift over to the serving table. Soon after more come, the ones who are starving but did not want to be the first ones at the food. Then come the hordes. Constantly replenish platters, adjust garnishes, wipe up spills, add plates, napkins, and answer questions and requests. About halfway through, the pressure eases. This is the time to carry platters around the room, offering items to individuals. This shows off your good service and extra attention. Always start with, or near, the host or hostess and any honored guests.

Guests will take anything you carry around, so offer items that you have plenty of. Food that you're running short of should remain on the table. Push the guests to eat items that will not keep. Hold back food that can be used in the future. If you have anything that did not turn out as well as expected, don't pass it around. Leave it on the table.

The last third of the reception is the winding down period. An important part of your staff's job is to keep everything in beautiful order on the table until it is removed. If you calculated your food correctly, there should be enough left in the last third of the reception to keep the platters reasonably full and attractive. Near the end you may be running low on some items, so you cannot fill a platter completely. In this case combine two or even three items, or switch over to even smaller serving plates. If you're combining items, they should complement each other. Don't combine the raspberry tarts with the pickled herring or the fruit sticks with the pesto tortellini, just because both are on skewers.

8. Clean as you go

This is the time to start your continuous cleanup, too.

Pick up used plates, napkins, glasses, bottles, and ashtrays, and clean up spills.

Finally the hour approaches when the party is scheduled to end. Your instinct tells you that it is time to clear the food, clean up, present the bill, and head home. Don't listen to your instinct. Keep the table looking nice and leave the food there. Don't ever appear anxious to leave. Start the cleanup process in the back. If it isn't obvious to the guests, start carrying a few unneeded items to the truck. China and glasses can be rinsed and put back into their carrying cases or bus tubs.

Once the scheduled end of the reception is reached, assess the situation. If it looks as if your food is no longer needed, ask your client if you can start clearing the table and cleaning up. If there are still guests around (there almost always are), suggest that you will consolidate the food on a few disposable plates for anyone who may want to nibble some more. Or ask if he or she wants the food left in the refrigerator (or wrapped to take home if this is a reception hall). Most clients will agree that you can go ahead and clean up. Some may ask if you can stay for an extra half hour because they are still expecting a few late arrivals. Generally you should agree; there isn't much of a choice unless you can make a nice arrangement of your food on disposable platters. Some caterers simply charge an extra half hour for the staff time. Consider specifying this in your contract.

Once the client agrees that it is time for you to clean up, gather your equipment and leave. Some guests, particularly close friends or relatives and people who won't depart unless they are shown to the door, are still standing around with your wine glasses in hand. How do you collect them? A good plan is to carry disposable wine glasses with you and ask those guests to exchange their glass for the disposable. No one will object.

9. Leftovers

Finally comes the tricky question of the leftover food. This has always been a dilemma for caterers. There is no clear solution. The client may claim that it belongs to him or her, particularly when far fewer guests showed up than expected. You may claim that you prepared extra food not paid for by the client and for safety and legal reasons nothing can be left behind. The caterer is legally liable for what he or she serves and leaves behind. While the food is under your control, there will be no problem. Once you leave it with the client, you don't know how it is going to be stored and taken care of. It may have already been sitting out on the serving table for an hour or two and if it is not eaten soon, its safety could be in question. If someone gets sick, you can still be blamed.

Here is a partial solution. Discuss extra food with the client while planning the event. Have the client understand that anything you deem safe will be left behind; other items will be removed.

But the food may still be perfectly safe though no longer very attractive. You hate to leave a bad impression. To avoid such a complication, leave extra food either on your truck or covered in the staging area. Remove everything extra from the staging area before the end of the event and the question of extra food may not come up at all.

If you donate leftover food to a nonprofit organization, remember that legal liability lies with the delivery person. If he or she pick it up from your kitchen, you are no longer responsible for it.

c. Self-service meals

A full meal buffet is the easiest on the caterer. However, this takes the least number of staff members, so whoever sets it up has the extra burden of loading and unloading alone or with a small staff. Arriving early is essential. Count on 45 minutes to a full hour to unload, carry everything into the work and serving area, and organize and set up a smaller luncheon or dinner, depending on how much last minute on-site preparation is needed. If the meal is at a previously unvisited place, allow a little extra time.

It is important to have corporate meals ready on time when the schedule is tight and they expect to eat at the appointed time. When meetings are scheduled with out-of-town visitors, this may not happen. There are often travel delays for guests. Plan ahead by having extra fuel for the chafing dishes and plan the menu with this eventuality in mind.

Like reception catering, the self-service meal is also of three different styles:

(a) Self-service with server in attendance to assist

(b) Delivered and set up, no server in attendance, pick-up later

(c) Delivered on disposable ware, no attendant, no pick-up

If an attendant is present to assist, the caterer has two choices: food that is brought in fully or partially prepared, or food that is prepared on the premises. Planning is somewhat different for each as was discussed above, but the execution of the event is basically the same for both types. When food preparation is required on the premises, you change your planned arrival time.

Most corporate functions are the first type, when food is delivered almost fully prepared. This is because cooking and food preparation facilities are not commonly available in a corporate office. However, there are corporations with small, fully equipped kitchens (not cafeteria kitchens) next to the executive offices. These are meant for meal preparations for executive meetings, but they are often available for use at other corporate meal functions. If you are a permanent caterer with such a corporation, you can set up, stock, and equip the kitchen for your convenience and cook meals there regularly for your client.

Self-service on disposable ware is not common in middle- and high-end catering. But from time to time, clients want to have a full meal delivered ready to go into the oven. The client can take care of all food preparation after drop-off. For brunches and picnics this is acceptable, especially when all the food is served cold or at room temperature and no preparation is needed by the client except uncovering the disposable serving dishes. (Some clients will need instructions on how to do this.)

d. Full-service meals

Full-service meals commonly have the highest per-person costs of any event. Clients ordering full-service meals have adequate or even unlimited budgets. Full-service meal clients are your favorite ones. Cherish them, treasure them, nourish them.

The difference in price between self- and full-service is mainly in the labor costs. It takes one server for every 10 to 15 guests for full-service, but one server can handle about 50 guests in a self-service event. You also need additional kitchen staff to prepare the plates individually for a full-service event.

Food costs remain the same, or even less. When you pre-plate food for full-service meals, you don't need to prepare much extra food, just enough to serve the number of guests for the order and a little extra. For the pre-plated dinner you end up with virtually no food in the pots and pans when the last plate is served if you have learned to calculate accurately, so waste is nearly eliminated.

On the other hand, each plate is individually garnished for full-service meals. Preparation time and the cost of the garnish offset the reduced food cost.

There are five common styles of food service:

(a) American (or plate) — food is portioned out, garnished in the kitchen, and served.

(b) French — the food is partially prepared in the kitchen but the final preparation is done at the table as well as adding sauces, garnishing, and plating.

(c) Wagon — similar to French in that finishing is done at the guests' table, but requiring no cooking skill, such as carving or tossing salads; only the illusion of French service remains.

(d) Russian (or platter) — the finished food is served on platters and transferred to the guests' plates; it requires skill and practice to transfer the food properly.

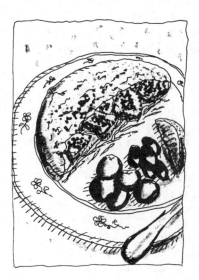

(e) Family — large bowls and platters of finished food are placed on the table for guests to serve themselves.

In full-service catering American-style food service is used almost exclusively. Very high-end catering may use other styles. Whatever you use, remember: food is served from the left, taken away from the right. All liquids like water, wine, coffee, and soup are served from the right and also taken away from the right.

1. Full staff

Unlike reception and self-service catering, full-service can only be done with a full staff, so there is only one type — full staff in attendance serving guests individually. The only exception is a type of catering with a blend of full- and self-service, something that is used fairly commonly. In this case there is a partial aura of serving staff but not the cost of a full-service meal. An example is when the entrée is served buffet style but the salad or soup is pre-plated and placed at each place setting. Dessert can also be pre-plated and served or passed by a server from a tray to each guest. You do need extra staff which you will have to calculate and add to your price for this type of service, but not a full staff as for individual serving.

2. Kitchen facilities

The food for the full-service event is also prepared as much as possible in the catering kitchen but by its nature, final preparation, cooking, and baking is done on-site if feasible. This is usually not a problem for smaller, more intimate meals but it may be tricky for a large group, depending on what sort of kitchen facilities are available at the site for the caterer.

Make sure you know what the kitchen facilities include. We had a holiday, full-service dinner party for 35 guests in a house with small kitchen facilities. I met the client at the house and inspected the site carefully. I told her that it would be tight for that many people but we could do it. She said she had two ovens. I went in the kitchen and, sure enough, there were two ovens. This was somewhat of a surprise because the house was older, from a time when putting in two ovens would have been very unusual.

I told the client that with two ovens there would be no problem. We could do the entire meal on location. When we arrived several months later, our fancy marinated chicken breasts were in pans ready to be baked. We were in no hurry to turn the ovens on; there were hors d'oeuvres ready to be served; the evening was going to be slow and leisurely. Finally the time arrived to heat the ovens up. This was when we discovered that even though the hostess had two ovens, only one worked. For the next hour we had a terrible time using one oven to bake two ovens' worth of food. By rotating pans every 15 minutes in and out of the oven, we finally cooked all the chicken breasts, though not to perfection. We were only a little behind schedule in serving. Our servers kept serving wine, hors d'oeuvres, and bread diligently to divert the guests' attention. No one noticed the difference, although the host did complain that his chicken was not quite hot.

With good planning, many things can be done ahead of time. For instance, all garnishes can be ready for the plates, salad ingredients cut up, blanched, or prepared ready for plating, vegetables partially cooked or blanched, meat cut up and perhaps browned or half-baked, hors d'oeuvres ready for the oven or ready to be passed, desserts half or fully prepared, and coffee measured out. All this early preparation will free valuable time at the event site.

The very busy, high pressure period is somewhat different, too. In the self-service meal most of the pressure is at the very beginning — before and during setup and the first part of serving. With the full-service meal the pressure comes later, mainly around the serving of the entrée. This is the most time-consuming part of the meal, the preparation of a garnished plate with piping hot food served to the guests with a minimum of time from stove top to table. Once the entrée has been served, the pressure eases somewhat. It will take a while before guests are ready for the next course, and since the main part of the meal is in front of everyone, the guests will have more tolerance to wait. In fact, they should be allowed to have ample time to finish the entrée, socialize, cleanse their palate, and digest.

3. When to take the plate away

Don't start collecting plates until most guests are finished at a table. Often there is the problem of an overly talkative guest who forgets to eat. Or someone who has to leave for some reason and comes back to start the meal when almost everyone is finished. This is a problem with no obvious solution. The servers just have to wait as long as possible, but if it is obvious that there will be too much delay, it is best to clear the table and leave the last guest talking with the food getting cold. Eventually he or she will get the message. Often such a person ends up sending the barely touched plate back. Don't be offended. For some people, talking has priority over food.

Before dessert and coffee are served, the table must be cleared of everything that was used for the previous courses, including china, glass (except what may be used still, like wine and water glasses), and silver. The servers should clean off any serious spillage as well as they can or cover it with a napkin.

It is best to serve the hot beverages before the dessert. That gives the kitchen staff a little extra time for the dessert preparation and plating, but also, most people like to have the coffee or tea right after the meal and with the dessert.

If this is the last course, then the only service left is refilling the hot beverage cups and eventually removing the dessert plates. The pressure is off, but the enormous drudgery of collecting all the equipment and cleaning up is still ahead. It is very helpful to have one or two inexpensive cleanup staff who come in relatively late to relieve the tired serving and kitchen staff.

When all is finally complete, the client's kitchen looks better than it has for years, the truck is loaded up to its rim (for some unexplained reason there is always more to haul back than what you brought), and the exhausted staff can hardly drag themselves to do the loading.

Now it is time to present the invoice. You always hope that you will get a check for the balance of the invoice right away, but if not, cheerfully tell the clients that there is no problem with dropping it in the mail tomorrow.

It is up to you how you divide any gratuities that you might receive. You can do it in equal portions among the staff and yourself or in unequal portions as you see fit. Or keep it all to yourself if you want to, especially if your staff did a lousy job.

Last, if your event was not a regular business meal, a thank you note to the client is a thoughtful gesture. To make it sound personal, add a sentence on something about the particular event.

e. After the event

Once the event is over, and the equipment and leftover food is transported back to the kitchen, the final step is cleaning up and putting everything back in its place, ready for the next time. Make sure that whoever is putting equipment away knows what goes where. You can't afford to waste time looking for items a half hour before departure time on the next event. If the cleanup person doesn't know what goes where, have him or her leave the clean equipment out for sorting instead of putting it away on the wrong shelf. Perfect order in your kitchen is another prerequisite for an efficient operation.

Carefully store any leftover food that can be used again and discard the rest. For instance, cheeses can be grated and frozen

Reprinted with special permission of King Features Syndicate.

to be used in cooking. Vegetables may be used for stocks or soups or some can even be used in salads if they are in good condition. Pickled items are reusable, breads can be frozen, and leftover pasta is fine for salad. Only keep leftover and extra food if you feel it is absolutely safe and its quality on reuse fits your established standards.

To know what is absolutely safe and what is doubtful, you must be familiar with spoilage and deterioration rates of various foodstuffs. You must also know how that particular food was stored and handled since it left your kitchen. If something was sitting out on the kitchen counter or buffet table for several hours, be suspicious. If it is cheese, not much can go wrong with it except drying out. It will be perfectly fine for cooking, grating, and baking. Serve the leftover potato salad with mayonnaise

dressing to your own staff only if you think it is really safe. Either you or a trusted staff person should sort the food as it is unloaded and judge its usability. Naturally you want to reduce waste to a minimum without risking your reputation. If you provide linen for an event, time must be scheduled for laundering as well.

The goal is to get your kitchen and storage room back to normal as soon as possible after an event. If you have other events planned soon after, then you want to clean and sort even faster so you can get on with the scheduling of the next event.

If you and your staff are especially busy with events during high demand season, it may be a good idea to hire extra help just to keep the kitchen, work areas, and storage space clean and ready at all times.

13
Diary Of A Caterer

In a small catering operation there is no such thing as a "typical" catered event; each one is unique. When you are fortunate enough to get a steady corporate client with fairly routine orders, usually luncheons, this is as typical as your events ever get to be. Catering never gets boring, that is the reason tension is always high. You never know what to expect next.

Let's walk through two events from beginning to end so you get a feel for what to expect. Since there is no typical event in small catering, let's call them "average" events: a reception and a full-service dinner.

a. Event #1: A reception

1. The beginning phase: client-caterer contact

You receive a call from a Ms. Ginger Prosciutto from the Spiced Ham Distributing Company. She tells you that they are new in town, they are opening a branch office, and they are looking for a caterer for their grand opening reception six weeks from now on August 1. Your catering business was highly recommended to them by a client of yours in the building they just moved into. She wants to know prices, what is included, what you recommend for beverages, what types of food you serve, etc.

You tell Ms. Prosciutto that you would be delighted and honored to cater the reception and you need to check your calendar to make sure August 1 is still open before further discussion. You put her on hold and look at your calendar. There is nothing scheduled for August 1. You tell Ms. Prosciutto that fortunately that date is not yet booked and the next step is to meet personally to talk about details, budgets, and menus. You also tell her that generally you recommend that new clients meet you in your office, so they can inspect your facilities and get an impression of how your operation works. She can even taste some fresh tidbits from your repertoire. Ms. Prosciutto agrees and you give a secret sigh of relief. It saves you a trip, and also it is an advantage to meet clients on your home ground.

Two days later Ms. Prosciutto shows up in your office on time, giving you a good impression of the kind of client you like to work with — professional, business-like, and pleasant. She accepts and compliments you on a glass of your fresh peppermint iced tea. You give her your photo portfolio and menu to look at while you ready a tiny plateful of goodies that you carry in on a little silver tray. Now you are ready for business.

You may want to go through some of the photos in the portfolio and talk about the kind of event they represent, perhaps pointing out a few things like your professional-looking uniformed staff, etc. Then you find out all about her reception — time of day, length, number of guests invited and expected, facilities available, type of food wanted, beverage service, and the budget allocated. This is what she tells you:

They are inviting about 130 guests and requesting an RSVP. They will invite the staff, some retailers, and other companies that are potential clients. They want to distribute their own spiced ham. They have scheduled an open house reception from 2:00 p.m. to 6:00 p.m. Their facilities are minimal — just a small lunch room, with a tiny refrigerator and a microwave oven, that doubles as the office storage room.

However, the office is in a prestigious, high-end, high-rent office building in a new development downtown. Ms. Prosciutto tells you that budget is no problem and they want a very classy affair. They want to impress their potential new clients as well as the old ones who are already distributing their ham. They want a full bar service. The only condition, she says, is that the food must feature their ginger-spiced prosciutto ham as one of the buffet items.

No problem, you say, since you know that their ham is excellent. So you discuss the menu in detail for the next 40 minutes. Ms. Prosciutto would like to have two of the items she has just sampled on the reception menu because she liked them so much. (This is one way to steer clients into choosing certain items.)

You tell her that a four-hour reception is hard on the host, staff, and the guests and could result in very thin attendance. You recommend no longer than two-and-a-half hours. She agrees, provided her boss approves. The event is now tentatively scheduled from 3:00 p.m. to 5:30 p.m.

You also tell Ms. Prosciutto that to reserve the date, you will need about half of the expected total as a deposit as soon as possible, the balance being due at the time of the event. You offer to send a proposal letter with all the details and a copy of the contract the next day.

The total consultation time takes one hour and 15 minutes and almost all the details for the reception are worked out. This is a fairly typical amount of time for a

first consultation. You should generally expect to spend an hour to an hour and a half, including coffee and chitchat.

After Ginger Prosciutto leaves, you think about the meeting briefly, look at your notes and jot down anything you may have forgotten. The meeting went well. Ginger was impressed with you and your kitchen and she liked your food. You liked her, too. This will be a good client to work with. But the job is not yours until you receive the deposit.

The next day you send the client a letter of proposal (see Sample #9). This sets out the arrangements you have discussed and the cost.

Three days later Ms. Prosciutto calls to tell you that she received your letter, all looks fine, and she has requested a check for you from their head office. Mark your calendar in pencil for August 1. If you don't receive the deposit within the next week and someone else calls you about another function for August 1, consider whether you can do both. If not, call Ginger Prosciutto and explain the situation. If the check is already coming, tell her that you will refuse the other event but you cannot hold the date open for more than three days without the deposit.

The check and the signed contract arrive as promised. Now the event date is marked firmly in ink on your calendar and you can forget it until July 20.

So far this event has been very easy and has cost you only a couple of hours work. This is not typical, though; you must expend a lot more energy to obtain many events.

For other clients it may take much more haggling, letter writing, and telephone followup. Business clients are more businesslike than social clients and they don't want to waste any more time than you do. Social catering clients, especially for weddings, are often much harder to pin down. Some take three, even four meetings, none

Dough Catering Company
35 Batter Road
Crepeville

June 17, 1993

Ms. Ginger Prosciutto
Spiced Ham Distributing Co.
100 Clove Circle
Tarttown

Dear Ms. Prosciutto:

It was a pleasure to meet with you yesterday. We are honored to present you with this proposal for your grand opening reception on August 1. The menu we agreed to is as follows:

- Ginger-spiced prosciutto wrapped around honeydew melon wedges
- Poached whole Atlantic salmon
- Baked brie en croûte with fresh-baked french bread and cracker squares
- Sour cherry sweet potato tarts
- Italian pesto torta made with fresh basil
- Tortilla roulade with a spicy Tex-Mex flavor
- Cherry tomatoes with a southwestern corn salad filing
- Our own fresh-baked dessert display

This lavish meal will be presented elegantly and beautifully on buffet-style service with uniformed staff in attendance. We know that you, your staff, and your guests will be impressed with both our food and our service. The price will be $14.50 per person, assuming approximately 130 guests and including china and paper napkins.

One bartender should be able to provide full bar service with some help from our food staff at times of greatest demand. Should the number of guests go up, we may need two bartenders, though due to limited space, only one bar will be set up. Bartending service is $75 per bartender, including ice, fruit, and miscellaneous bar items. Glasses are $2 per person and I understand that you will supply all beverages, including mixes.

A 15% catering service charge and 7.75% tax will be added to the final bill. We would like to have a final guest count five days before the event.

We sincerely hope that you will choose Dough Catering for this important function. We would be very pleased to serve you and will do everything we can to make this event memorable for you and your guests. We will reserve August 1 for your event as soon as we receive a deposit of $1,300 or about half of the expected total.

Sincerely,

John Dough

John Dough
Manager

shorter than an hour. These clients do not use caterers on a regular basis, they are uncertain and afraid of being "ripped off." Your first job is to convince them they can trust you.

2. The middle phase:
planning and organization

July 22 arrives, ten days before the event. It is time to reserve your staff. You haven't heard from Spiced Ham yet about the exact number of guests, but you don't expect that for a few more days. You assume there will be about 130 guests, and chances are that the number will go down as RSVPs slowly arrive. This is based on my experience with previous events.

The menu is not difficult. No food needs to be freshly prepared on site. The staff will replenish trays and cut up the full pans of food into portions. Excluding bartenders, you can handle it with one helper, but it will be tight. One bartender for that many guests is really cutting it close. As a compromise, have one bartender and two helpers, and one of your helpers can also assist the bartender from time to time. That way you have a total of four staff, including yourself.

Wait before reserving the second helper until you hear from the client about the final count, just in case the number goes down drastically. You know that it could easily drop 20% to 30%. Ginger appears to know what she is doing, but be ready for anything.

Look at your menu again with a critical eye. Any out-of-the-ordinary ingredients should be ordered ahead of time, as well as anything that needs special attention.

A week before the Spiced Ham event, on July 25, it is time to look at the menu and start planning. First, write down the staff schedule; don't leave it to memory. The bartender, Curry, should be on location an hour and fifteen minutes prior to the event, at 1:45 p.m. She is reliable and she should be able to set up well before 3:00 p.m. Your

helper, Clove, will be in the kitchen at 8:00 a.m. on July 31. Put these notes in the Spiced Ham file.

Of the various menu items, you pick ones that can be done ahead of time to keep last-minute preparation to a minimum. Here are things you can do in advance: puff pastry wrap for brie, pie pastry for sour cherry tarts, pesto, and possibly some desserts. You note that none of the items needs too much preparation. You can't begin any of them until the final guest count is given.

Fortunately the next day Ginger Prosciutto calls you and keeps the count at 125. Now you sit down and prepare a supply list and a detailed schedule. But first you should call the second helper and reserve his or her time. After calling several, you find that Pepper is available that day. He is reasonably reliable as a server but not very good in the kitchen. So you reserve him for August 1 to arrive in the kitchen at 1:00 p.m., dressed in your standard serving uniform.

Sample #10 is the menu showing reference page numbers in your recipe collection and the number of times the recipe should be scaled up. Sample #11 is the supply list and the detailed schedule (giving approximate preparation time in hours) for the event.

This schedule is a fairly complete list of jobs to be done for the event. The times given to accomplish each task are approximate, but with experience you can get rather close in your guess. It is best to allow a generous time allowance.

Here is a brief description of the preparation involved in some of the menu items:

- The prosciutto is thinly sliced and will be wrapped around bite-sized melon wedges, secured with a toothpick, and stuck into half a red cabbage. Once the red cabbage is full, the remainder is prepared and kept in a storage container for replenishment.

Item	Recipe File	Scale of Original Recipe
Ham/melon	(no recipe) 250 skewers	
Salmon	p. 36	
Brie	p. 12	pastry 3X
Tart	p. 52	2.25X
Pesto	p. 54	3X
Roulade	p. 21	10X
Corn salad	p. 40	3X
Dessert:		
plum tartlets	p. 12	4X
lemon-walnut	p. 43	4X
biscotti (already prepared)		

This can be replenished very quickly so half a cabbage is enough.

- The salmon is garnished and ready to be put on the table. If you can get one large enough so only one is needed, then that goes on the table and kept looking neat during the reception. If you have two pieces, the first one is replaced when most of it is gone. The brie is also ready but there are four to six of them. Only two are garnished and ready to go and one is placed on the table; the other one is backup. The rest will be garnished and used as needed.

- The sour cherry tarts are cut up into small pieces, trayed, and garnished on the job site. There is always one plate prepared ahead ready to go on the table.

- The pesto torta is cut into several pieces, two are plated and garnished, one of which goes on the table. The rest is backup. The roulades are on two plates, ready to go. The remainder is cut up and can refill plates quickly. The dessert display is on two platters, the rest is on reserve. They are also quick to replenish.

The schedule shows that, if you have the time Saturday, you can do the work by yourself. You could also work on Sunday, too, if there is no other business and you want to save on labor costs. Monday, you and Clove have four hours each, so starting at no later than 8:00 a.m. is advisable, especially for you as you may be interrupted by telephone calls and so on. But both of you should be able to finish and have a quick bite by noon. There should even be time for a fast cleanup. With Pepper's help you should be able to load the truck and be ready to roll by 1:30. The client's office is only 20 minutes away.

SAMPLE #11
SUPPLY LIST AND DETAILED SCHEDULE

MEAT	DAIRY	PRODUCE	OTHER
12½–13 lb. salmon	6 lb. brie	1 red cabbage	toothpicks
4 lb. spiced prosciutto	7 lb. butter	4 lge. honeydews	crackers
	10 lb. cream cheese	12 lemons	7 baguettes
	24 eggs	8 limes	9 oz. black olives
	3 c. milk	3 lb. yams	2 lb. corn
		3 bu. basil	hot chili oil
		3 lb. carrots	stuffed olives
		9 oz. pimento	maras. cherries
		120 cherry	1 bt. wh. wine
		tomatoes	10 burritos
		6 scallions	70 lb. ice
		2 bu. parsley	
		garnish: table	
		salmon	
		trays	
		greens for trays	
		flowers	

Schedule

SAT		SUN		MON	
roulade mix	1.25	pesto torta	1.0	prep prosc/melon	1.5
puff pastry	1.5	poach salmon	1.5	cut up roulade	0.5
cookie dough	0.75	bake brie	1.5	cherry tomatoes	1.5
tart pastry	0.5	corn salad	0.5	bake dessert	1.5
pesto	0.5	prep invoice	0.5	cut up tart	0.5
order bread		prep equip	1.5	tray dessert	0.5
		tray salmon	0.5	load	0.5
		wash truck	0.5	pick up bread	0.5
				contingencies	1.0
Totals	4.5 hrs		7.5 hrs		8.0 hrs

Depart 1:30 p.m.

Work to be done on site: Tray cherry tarts, tray and fill tomatoes

3. The final phase: day of the event

Before you all leave, you go through the menu and your notes one more time, perhaps the third time, to make very sure everything is on the truck. Take your time to check off each item and think about every component of it that needs to be taken. Some of the food items are in more than one piece, like the cherry tomatoes. Remember the garnishes, flower, ice, and fruit for the bartender. These should all be on your checklist. Then look into the refrigerators and freezer for a last minute visual check in case some prepared plate is still hiding in there. The equipment was already carefully checked and loaded earlier. Your final check complete, the team is ready to take off.

A few minutes before two o'clock, you arrive in front of the office building. Curry, the bartender, is already there waiting.

Your two helpers, Pepper and Clove, with Curry's help can load up the rolling cart, while you go upstairs to check in with Ginger in Spiced Ham's office. Decide with Ginger where the bar table and food table are going to be. Your staging area will be very small but will have to do. The dining area you were told was small is really tiny, not much counter space, just a small table.

By 2:40 p.m., everything is upstairs and the empty truck is parked. One helper sets up the table, one takes care of the bar and

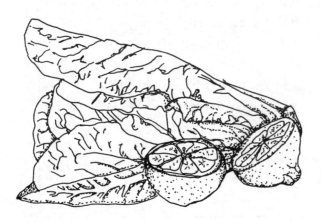

two of you prepare the trays that were left to be done on the job site. The loaded trays are checked for any necessary adjustment. By the time they are finished, the table is ready. A few minutes before three o'clock, both the bar and buffet table are ready. The food looks gorgeous. Ginger, her boss, and the office staff ooh and ah in front of the buffet. The guests start arriving shortly after.

You and your helpers can relax for a while. Only Curry will be busy at the bar. The guests attack the bar first and only a few will nibble.

By four o'clock the place is jammed and everyone is busy. You can keep up without difficulty but Curry needs help. You assign Pepper to help Curry as needed. The food is going well but there is plenty of extra left by 5:15. The reception is obviously a success for the Spiced Ham Company as well as for you.

Although the reception was supposed to be over at 5:30 p.m., many guests are still hanging around both the bar and food tables at 5:45 p.m.. There is no choice but to put a smile on your face and pretend you are thoroughly enjoying the extra half hour with these exciting people.

So the time is not completely wasted, you can all start collecting equipment without making it too obvious to the guests. Leave the buffet table and the bar alone. There are plenty of other things to clean up and pack into boxes or crates. Any extra food that you would rather not leave behind is now discreetly taken down to the truck to avoid discussion with the client later.

By 6:00 p.m., it is time for the bartender to go around with disposable wine glasses and ask everyone with a real glass for an exchange so we can pack up our glasses. Ask Ginger if you can break down the table. Ginger readily agrees, thinking that this may be a further hint to the last unobliging guests. It will take half an hour to break everything down, pack items away, take them down to the truck, and reload. In the meantime, all the guests have disappeared. Only Ginger, her boss, and a few office people remain, ready to lock up. You offer some food items that are safe for them to take home. From your catering box you take out a couple of paper plates, fill them up with food, wrap them tightly with plastic wrap, and give them to Ginger, along with the final invoice.

By 6:25 p.m., the truck is loaded, Curry is gone and you, Clove, and Pepper leave. The truck needs to be unloaded, which takes another 20 minutes. Things must be sorted and any perishables put away in the freezer or refrigerator. Let Pepper and Clove help themselves to whatever they want from the extra food. You take care of a few last minute things in the office and by 7:30 p.m. you can lock up the kitchen.

Cleanup has to wait until tomorrow. You make a mental note to send a thank you card to Ginger, mentioning what a pleasure it was to serve the Spiced Ham Distributing Company and adding some specific sentence about the party.

b. Event #2:
A full-service dinner

For our second example, let's walk through an elegant full-service dinner party.

1. The beginning phase: client-caterer contact

Mr. Chuck Roast is a partner in a law firm for whom you have catered everything from full receptions to holiday dinner parties. He calls to ask about catering for a surprise birthday dinner party for his wife, Tender Roast, in six weeks. You ask him for the exact date to make sure that your calendar is clear. It is scheduled for Friday, September 16. You inform Mr. Roast that the date is his. You set up an appointment in your office for Thursday.

He arrives at your office as scheduled, and since it is a warm day, you offer fresh iced tea, a piece of cranberry sweet potato tart, and some fresh lemon-walnut cookies. He accepts them with delight. Since he has attended several of your parties, he knows that he can trust your food and service. That eliminates a lot of sales talk, show-and-tell, and negotiating. You get down to business at once.

He is planning to invite 36 guests for his wife's 40th birthday celebration. It will be a surprise party. He wants a full-service, elegant dinner party and, though his budget is not unlimited, he will pay whatever it takes within reason.

Here is what he wants: tables, chairs, and linen set up in his backyard, along with an ice sculpture, flaming torches all around the yard, flowers on the tables, and live musicians. He also wants a limousine service to take his wife on a hoax trip supposedly to meet him for dinner and keep her out of the way while things are being set up. Can you arrange it all? Of course, you assure Chuck, no problem at all.

As for the dinner, he wants your suggestion for an appropriate menu that is elegant, unique, and pleasing to every palate. He also needs a bartender for a full bar, along with china, glass, and silver. You say that your proposal will be in the mail within the next two days. Since you have

no event scheduled for the rest of the day, you settle down to write it up. Easy, you think. The greatest prospect for a caterer is when the client trusts you to choose the menu. Menu items that are relatively easy on the caterer, hold well, and will be appreciated by the guests can be selected.

Occasionally a client comes to a caterer with a full, preconceived menu in mind. The menu is often completely inappropriate for several reasons. The food will not hold and must be served absolutely fresh, (e.g., sautéed fish), or it is a dish like a stew that cannot be presented well, especially on a buffet table. The ingredients are too costly for the meager budget (the classic champagne taste on a beer budget), or the ingredients are out of season (asparagus in mid-summer). The items could be out of the caterer's style or range of food. Sometimes a client requests food that few guests would be willing to eat or appreciate, such as seviche or herring.

In mid-afternoon Mr. Roast calls to tell you that he also wants a birthday cake, something beautiful, not too sweet, and with a great flavor. In your files, you should have a cake cutting chart so you know how to cut the cake so there are enough pieces for each guest. (A cake cutting chart is included in Appendix 1.) Also, he reminds you that all correspondence and telephone calls should be directed to his office, not his home.

It takes about an hour to prepare a proposal. You have all the subcontractors' prices in your files. Sample #12 is the proposal letter you type up for Mr. Roast.

You send this proposal the next day. Chuck Roast calls you two days later. He basically likes the menu and the proposal, but would like to change a few items. He doesn't care for The Squealing Pig Quartet. He would rather have a country western band, his wife's favorite. You agree that it is no problem to arrange this, but most country western bands are just too loud to accompany a dinner where guests would like to socialize. You promise to find one that is willing to turn the sound down (though you know this will cost you extra).

He is also uncertain about the iced sour cherry soup. You assure him that the sour cherry soup will be well received, though not everyone will be willing to taste it because it is so different in appearance and flavor. The older generation will love it. Younger guests will be suspicious. You remind him that it will be a very elegant beginning. Chuck finally agrees and says that you can make the reservation firm since he is putting a check in the mail today.

You mark your calendar from pencil to ink, complete your notes on the Roast affair and put the file away for four weeks. Call all the subcontractors and reserve September 16. Wait to do this until you have the deposit in your hand. You will have to send a deposit to the ice sculptor and the musicians. Others you pay at the end of the event.

2. The middle phase: planning and organization

Two weeks before the Roast party, on September 2, you retrieve the file and take a look at the menu to refresh your memory. Is there anything you need to order ahead of time? No, there are no unusual or exotic ingredients that you cannot get from your usual sources. However, it is time to reserve the subcontractors. All of them are people you have worked with before; they all give you a 10% discount. The only exception is the country western band with whom you have already made arrangements after talking with Chuck Roast. It will cost more than The Squealing Pig Quartet, so you need his approval. This is a four-piece band, including a female vocalist, the Bellowing Bisons. They agreed very reluctantly to turn the volume way down.

Now it is time to reserve all the other subcontractors: the cake, the flowers, rental equipment, limousine, and ice sculpture,

Dough Catering Company
35 Batter Rd
Crepeville, CA 94066

August 3, 1993

Mr. Chuck Roast
The Law Firm of Partridge, Squid, and Roast
1 Meat Avenue
Butcherville, CA 94067

Dear Mr. Roast:

It was my pleasure to meet with you yesterday regarding your plans for a surprise birthday party for your wife on September 16th. I can assure you that we will do our best to help you give Mrs. Roast and the invited guests a great meal with a beautiful presentation. Here is my tentative suggestion for the menu:

- Hors d'oeuvres: fresh baked artichoke kisses, steamed marinated jumbo shrimp in snow peas and our own pesto torta with cracker squares (these will be passed around by the servers)
- Iced sour cherry soup served in melon halves
- Boneless fresh Atlantic salmon fillet with chopped eggs and dill in individual paper packets
- Pork tenderloin medallions with peppers in paprika sauce
- Seasonal vegetables
- Rosemary linguini
- Fresh-baked Italian bread, rolls, and butter
- Light chocolate cake with raspberry and Bavarian custard filling, decorated with fresh flowers (no inscription)
- Bite-sized fruit tartlets and lemon-walnut cookies
- Choice of fresh coffee and teas

The prices for 36 guests are as follows:

Food	@$31.50	$1,134.00
Dinner china, glass, silver	@$3.25	117.00
Ice sculpture		200.00

Flowers	180.00
5 tables @ $7.00, 36 chairs @ $1.00	71.00
Linen	53.00
Bartending service, including ice, fruit, bar glassware	121.00
Chocolate cake	120.00
Yard decoration and bar rental	285.00
Music, The Squealing Pig Quartet	320.00
Limousine	225.00
Subtotal	$2826.00
15% catering service charge on food/beverage	188.10
7.75% tax on subtotal	219.02
Estimated total	$3233.12

All set-up will be completed before guests arrive at 6:00 p.m. We will start serving hors d'oeuvres by 6:30 p.m., giving early guests time to order drinks first. Champagne will be ready for toasting by 6:45 p.m., when Mrs. Roast is expected to arrive by limousine. Dinner will be served at about 7:30 p.m. We will have one bartender who will also help pour wine at the tables during dinner, a chef, and a helper in the kitchen, and three servers. At the end of the meal, the kitchen will be cleaned up and refuse removed. Rental items will be stacked by the back door, ready to be picked up the next morning. The Squealing Pig Quartet will play from 7:00 p.m. to 10:00 p.m. with two short breaks. We will supply everything for the party except beverages, which will be supplied by you.

We have tentatively reserved September 16 for you. As soon as we receive half of the estimated total as a deposit, the reservation will be firm. We would like to know the final number of guests by September 11, though variations of up to three are acceptable until September 13. The price for the food is based on 36 guests. Since we have to reserve several subcontractors, we would appreciate hearing from you as soon as possible.

The weather should be pleasant on the date of the event, but if the forecast is for rain, we will arrange for tents to be brought in and set up.

Thank you for asking Dough Catering to serve you. We will do everything possible to make Mrs. Roast's 40th birthday a memorable event.

Sincerely,

John Dough

John Dough
Owner

giving the subcontractors an exact guest count (subject to change), the address, and any special instructions. The limousine will pick Mrs. Roast up at a friend's house. She thinks they will then pick up Chuck Roast and take both of them to an unspecified restaurant for dinner. The surprise is that she will be dropped off at her home with 34 guests and her loving husband waiting.

Reserve your staff. Curry will be your bartender again, and Cinnamon will be your chef. You'll help her plate the food in the kitchen, and Clove, Pepper, and a new helper, Chili, will be the servers. You reserve them tentatively, but since no firm schedule is set yet, you postpone telling them the exact hours of work until a few days later.

It is time to put the schedule on paper so the staff can plan their time. Sample #13 shows your planned schedule.

The numbers on the Friday schedule are estimated hours needed for each job. A total of 6.25 hours should finish the preparation. The Thursday hours are not specified since nothing is very time-consuming. Two-and-a-half to three hours should complete the job; you will be doing this yourself. Departure time on Friday, considering rush-hour traffic and the

SAMPLE #13
PREPARATION SCHEDULE FOR THE FULL-SERVICE DINNER

Prior	**Wednesday**	
Prep marinade for shrimp	Defrost shrimp	
Order cake	Boil 4 eggs for salmon	
	Pastry for tartlets	
	Cookie dough	
Thursday	**Friday, 9/16**	
Steam and marinate shrimp	Finish shrimp	0.5
	Artichoke kiss	1.0
Pesto torta	Tray pesto torta	0.25
Cherry soup	Melon for soup	0.5
Peel, chop eggs	Prepare salmon	0.75
Bake tartlets	Prepare, cook pork	1.0
Invoice	Pick up bread	0.5
Collect equipment	Bake cookies	0.5
	Tray dessert	0.25
	Load contingencies	1.0
	Fruit for bar	
	Total time	6.25

fairly distant location, should be 4:20 p.m. Even if traffic is heavy, 30 minutes should be sufficient to get there and by 5:30 everything should be unloaded and organized in the kitchen.

Ask Chili and Pepper to meet you at the Roast residence at 5:00 p.m. on the 16th. Chili, who has not worked for you yet, needs to be reminded to wear a tuxedo shirt with black slacks. You tell him that you will bring the bow ties and aprons. Even though Chili appears to be very reliable and was highly recommended to you, you have no experience with him, a slight cause for worry.

Clove, the third server, will take care of the torches and decorations, so she is instructed to arrive at 4:00 p.m. Rental equipment, including a portable bar and torches, will be delivered earlier the same day. (Mr. Roast has arranged for Tender to be away from the house for the full day).

You schedule Curry to be at the residence at 5:00 p.m. to set up the bar. It will take close to an hour to complete the job, including glassware. The fruits for drink garnishes will be prepared before you leave your kitchen. Cinnamon will be putting in about six hours in the kitchen doing the bulk of the dinner preparation. You will assist her as needed.

Flowers, the ice sculpture, and cake will be delivered by 5:00. Musicians will arrive at 5:45, and start playing at 6:30.

The next step is to prepare your supply list. Ordering on Monday, September 12 is adequate as this is a fairly easy, small dinner party. Sample #14 shows the order list.

This list does not include every ingredient you will need to prepare the menu. Spices and herbs are on the shelf. Before purchasing the supplies, you check the shelves for anything already available to eliminate duplication.

You'll need several shopping trips. Some supplies will be needed early in the week. The fresh produce and dairy products should be purchased on Thursday. Another buying trip is needed on Friday for the fresh bread, and the individually wrapped butter patties need to be taken out of the freezer. You always have a supply of these on hand.

3. The final phase: day of the event

Your chef, Cinnamon, arrives at 10:00 a.m. on Friday. You give her a rundown of the menu and let her work at her own speed to have everything complete by 3:45. You take care of the bread pickup, loading the truck with equipment and other basics, including the halved melons. She can do the rest comfortably.

The shrimp is marinated. One snow pea split in two will be wrapped around each, secured with a toothpick and stuck into half a red cabbage. Extras are transported in a covered pan. The artichoke kisses are prepared and half baked. The pesto torta is trayed, garnished, ready to be passed around, and accompanied by crackers in a tiny basket.

The salmon fillet is cut into small serving pieces, allowing two ounces per person. Most guests will take a pork tenderloin as well, also in two-ounce pieces. If a guest doesn't eat pork, he or she can take two or more pieces of salmon. There are 40 servings of the salmon. Each piece is put on a square of parchment, sprinkled with chopped boiled egg and fresh dill, and closed to form a cute little packet. They will be baked just before serving. It only takes 12 to 14 minutes in a hot oven.

The pork is half finished. It will take about 20 minutes of cooking on site to finish it. Pasta can also be cooked at the host's kitchen. Freshly chopped rosemary is taken in a plastic wrap to be added to the pasta right after cooking. Vegetables are blanched and ready to be sautéed on site with garlic and fresh tarragon. They only take ten minutes to heat through and finish cooking.

SAMPLE #14
ORDER LIST

Item	Recipe file	Scale of Original Recipe
Artichoke kisses	p. 45	0.2X
Shrimp	p. 40	
Pesto torta	p. 50	0.5X
Crackers		
Cherry soup	p. 20	3.0X
Melon		
Salmon	p. 61	3.0X
Pork	p. 12	3.0X
Vegetables		
Linguini		
Bread/butter to pick up		
Cake ordered		
Fruit tartlet	p. 27	1.0X
Lemon cookies	p. 21	1.0X
Coffee, tea, cream		

Produce

2½ lb. onion
1 bu scallion
50 large snow peas
1 bu basil
1 bu dill
1 bu tarragon
1 red cabbage
4 lemons
2 limes
18 melons
1½ lb. red pepper
1½ lb. green pepper
7½ lb. mixed vegetable with entre
Garnish for hors d'oeuvres
    plates
    dessert

Meat

4 lb. shrimp(21-25 count black tiger)
5 lb. salmon fillet
5 lb. pork tenderloin

Dairy

4 oz. parmesan
1 c. heavy cream
Cream for coffee
8 eggs
1 lb. cream cheese
1 lb. unsalted butter

Other

1 lb. phyllo dough
25 oz. marinated artichoke hearts
Crackers for pesto torta
3 lb. canned sour cherries
1 bot. red wine for soup
24 oz. tomato paste
4 ½ lb. linguini
50 lb. ice

The cherry soup is finished, resting calmly in the refrigerator. Heavy cream and the red wine need to be swirled into it as a final touch just before serving. Dessert will be trayed on-site and passed to guests. This is in addition to the cake, an extra touch, and most people will take one or the other. Some will take both. The cake will be cut in small portions.

You have scheduled enough helpers, so the bread can be sliced on-site, stacked in baskets for each table along with butter. The servers will replenish them as needed.

All is going according to plan. At the last minute it occurs to you that you neglected to provide some garnish for the soup. Is one needed? There is enough heavy cream, for example, to whip some up and add a tiny dab on top of each serving. Or a thin half slice of lemon could be hung on the edge of the scooped-out melon half in which the soup will be served. You confer with Cinnamon. She says no, it is overkill. The soup will be served in a fruit bowl, it is a dark-colored, unusual-looking soup. Anything extra will be too garish.

By 3:30 p.m., everything is just about complete. You and your crew have just enough time to give a quick cleanup to the kitchen.

By 4:00 p.m., the truck is loaded except for a few things in the refrigerator and freezer, for which you have a separate checklist. You know that Clove is very reliable, and she will take care of everything at the Roast residence. Nevertheless, you are anxious to leave. You and Cinnamon go through the checklist of the menu one more time, then take the frozen and refrigerated items out and place them in the cooler on the truck. According to health regulations, any potentially spoilable food should maintain a temperature of less than 45°F (4.5°C) in transit. In this case, the shrimp and the salmon are the only potential hazards during a 30-minute transit. But you want to serve the pesto torta and the soup

cold, too. They all fit in the cooler along with the 50 pounds of ice for Curry, the bartender.

You and Cinnamon have changed into your uniforms and are ready to leave shortly after 4:00 p.m. To your surprise, the Friday rush hour traffic is not too bad. Still, you drive at a respectably slow speed in consideration of your precious cargo. When you arrive at the party site at 4:40, the decorations are in place, the cake and ice sculpture have just arrived, and a few minutes later you see the rest of your staff driving up. Mr. Roast is not ready yet but comes out to greet the staff and tells you to do whatever you want, the house is now yours. He shows you where the trash is and the two refrigerators, one of which is half empty. The other is filled with champagne, wine, and a variety of other chilled drinks. Curry will soon take care of emptying that one, too.

By 5:15 the truck is unloaded, Cinnamon is busy in the kitchen, Curry is setting up the bar, and everyone else is working on the tables, chairs, linen, and silverware. The china remains in the kitchen. By five forty-five everything is done, including the ice sculpture, flowers and cake, and the place looks fabulous. The band is just setting up. They have brought their huge sound system. Will the lowest level still be too loud for a quiet conversation? It doesn't matter so much by the middle of the party when people had enough to drink and the level of conversation is no longer quiet, but at least during the early part of the dinner the music should be quiet.

A few minutes before 6:00 p.m. the bell rings; several guests have arrived already. You check progress in the kitchen and all seems fine. The shrimp and pesto torta are ready, the artichoke will not need to go into the oven until close to 6:30. Cinnamon does not need to do much with dinner until close to 7:00. Even though dinner is scheduled for 7:30, chances are it will not be served until later. These leisurely parties never stay on schedule.

By 6:30 the place is humming and so is the band. Surprisingly enough, the music is pleasant, relatively soft country ballads, very nice as background music. The female vocalist is excellent. The bar is busy, and you decide to wait with the food until more people arrive. You know that everything is ready in the kitchen. The oven was turned on 15 minutes ago, and the artichoke kisses will only take five minutes to bake.

Pepper reminds you that Tender should be arriving in ten minutes, and shouldn't we serve the hors d'oeuvres. You agree and the two servers appear with two trays, passing the food. All seems well so far. The hors d'oeuvres go fast, people seem to be hungry but there is a lot left in the kitchen. Only about half of the kisses have been baked. They are light, so they can be served even shortly before dinner without spoiling appetites.

The limousine arrives exactly on schedule at 6:45. Everyone is waiting at the front door and Curry has 36 champagne glasses ready inside on two trays. She will start with five bottles of champagne that are open and one bottle of non-alcoholic fizzy drink. That should be enough for the first round. The surprise for Tender is successful. Curry and the three servers pour and distribute the champagne for the toast. In just a few minutes everyone has a glass in hand. Curry returns to the bar and leaves several bottles of champagne with the servers for refills.

You check the kitchen. The water is ready to boil for the pasta, and the pork is being finished slowly. The melons are ready for the soup and the plates are stacked up, ready to be garnished once the soup is served. That will be your job. Everything else is last minute preparation.

Check with Chuck Roast about dinner plans. He says he would prefer to postpone it a little since no one seems to be ready to

break up the socializing. You and Chuck agree on 7:45. That means that the entrée won't be served until nearly 8:15, so you inform the chef of the new schedule. She agrees to put the salmon in the oven at 8:00, as well as the bread to warm up. The pasta can be cooked at 7:45, ready to be served by 8:00 (it holds well), and the vegetables can also be started at 7:45, too.

At 7:35 the soup is served in the melon half-shells and placed on the table at each place setting. Bread baskets and butter are put on each table, water glasses are filled with ice and water. Two servers distribute them; the third one is still passing the hors d'oeuvres, making sure that the host and Mrs. Roast are always served from a fresh plate.

The soup, like any unusual food, is a mixed success. Shortly after 8 o'clock the soup containers are collected and water glasses are refilled. Curry and one server are filling the wine glasses. Everyone else is in the kitchen helping to plate the entrée. The 36 plates are laid out on the counters and tables, and each one is garnished. The whole job takes four or five minutes. On every plate a packet of salmon, a portion of pork medallion, pasta, and vegetables are placed in a beautiful, colorful arrangement. As soon as half a dozen plates are finished (in less than a minute), they are taken out by the servers. Wine has been poured, so all three servers can work on the distribution of dinner. Another six plates are ready by the time the servers return for them.

Everyone has been instructed on what the food is. If a guest prefers no pork or no fish, then Cinnamon can make up a separate plate which is delivered with the next set. In less than ten minutes, the entire dinner is plated and served. It is time to replenish the water glasses, wine, bread and butter. The pressure is off. The remainder of the meal should be slow and leisurely.

It is close to 9:00 p.m. by the time plates can be collected. A few of the guests ask for seconds. The amount of food left on the plates tells you a lot. If it is too much, you either served too large portions or they didn't like the food.

It is time again to refresh the wine glasses, there is no hurry with dessert. The coffee pots are ready, both regular and decaffeinated, and the electric kettle is plugged in for tea water. In a few minutes the tables are rechecked to make sure nothing from dinner is left before the coffee is served.

By 9:15 the guests are ready for coffee. While Cinnamon is organizing the kitchen, you and the three servers distribute coffee with cream and sugar and tell guests that both black tea and a variety of herb teas are available. Several prefer tea, so you bring out tea bags neatly arranged on a plate for choice. When someone makes a choice, you take the tea bag back to the kitchen, pour freshly boiling water over it in a cup, and bring it back to the guest.

You tell Mr. Roast that it is time to cut the cake. After a brief ceremony and many good wishes, Tender cuts the first slice and Curry finishes cutting 36 servings. They are distributed quickly and the fruit tartlets and cookies are passed by two servers. As predicted, almost everyone takes one or the other, or even both, in addition to the piece of cake in front of them.

By ten, no one wants to eat or drink anything. The servers collect the plates and only leave the coffee cups on the tables. The kitchen is in good shape. All dinner china is rinsed and in bus tubs. With everyone helping, the rest of the china, silverware and glasses can be put into crates fairly quickly.

By 11:00 p.m. most guests are gone. The band is packing up, the tables are cleared, and the truck is half loaded. Pay the balance due to the band, complimenting them on the very good job they did. By 11:15 only

a few guests are left, probably close friends. Ask Mr. Roast if he would like to keep some extra food. He says yes, so Cinnamon wraps a generous portion of leftovers up and puts it in the refrigerator. The remainder of the cake is also wrapped and stored in the refrigerator. Other food is placed in the truck by the servers. In the meantime, you hand your invoice to Mr. Roast who compliments you for a very successful event and superb food.

He returns in a few minutes with a check for the balance due. After verifying that the kitchen is scrupulously clean and neat, checking the refrigerator, the freezer, and for any of the catering utensils or equipment that may have been forgotten, you take one more look to make sure all the rental equipment is in crates and stacked neatly in one pile, ready to be picked up. You say farewell to Mrs. Roast and depart with the staff. The time is now 11:40. Back at the kitchen the truck is unloaded, extra food is quickly put in the refrigerator to be sorted out tomorrow, and dirty dishes are put in the sink to soak. It is well past midnight. The facilities are ready to be locked up.

There is another two to three hours of work left to clean up equipment and the kitchen, put everything back in its proper place, and store or discard leftover food. There are also a few tasks in the office: mark the file, mentally check off the menu to see if any notations need to be added to the recipes regarding either portions or ingredients. Then add the gross earnings to your books, mark down staff time, pay the various subcontractor bills, and send a thank you note to Mr. Roast.

You made a very good profit on this event. Adding to your own profit is 10% of each subcontractor's invoice. You planned it well, organized it down to the finest detail, and executed it perfectly with a good team. You deserve your profit.

14
The Cookhouse: It's Not All A Picnic

a. Running a small catering kitchen

Before you can efficiently run your catering kitchen (whether it is in your home or in a properly approved commercial facility), you must have equipment and skill. However, it is unreasonable to expect that you will drop into a fully equipped kitchen with the skill of a seasoned professional at the beginning of your catering career. Both equipment and skill come slowly and gradually. In the meantime, accept some compromises. Your kitchen won't run as smoothly and efficiently as it could, at first. You'll pick up skills and purchase equipment gradually as needed when extra funds become available from your profits.

Let's presume that when you first start your business, you'll be in the process of acquiring many of the necessary physical skills for food preparation and cooking. Let's also presume that for quite some time now you have been busy testing recipes and accumulating a store of cooking and kitchen reference books. These activities are essential, no matter what sort of catering you have chosen.

b. Recipes

Learn to write recipes in an abbreviated, professional way. You'll soon have enough cooking experience to need a minimum of explanation to follow a recipe. Often, the recipe becomes a mere checklist of ingredients. Sample #15 shows a simple recipe written for a novice. Compare it to Sample #16, a recipe written for the professional.

As you can see, the second recipe is written in shorthand style, giving you ingredients and pointers on preparation. You know the rest. The preparation is slightly altered for quantity commercial cooking, but the results will be the same.

What measure you list quantities in on your recipes depends on you and your equipment. If you prefer to use scales, use weight measurements. For liquids, use cups. For quantity cooking, weight is the most convenient method because it is easy to check and it is easy to scale a basic recipe

Reprinted with special permission of King Features Syndicate.

HUNGARIAN CHICKEN PAPRIKA

1 cut-up chicken, about 3½ pounds

1 chopped medium onion

3 tbsp. vegetable oil

4 tsp. Hungarian paprika

1 tsp. salt

1 chopped medium green pepper

1 chopped medium tomato or
   1 tbsp. tomato paste

2 tbsp. sour cream

2 tbsp. flour

Brown onion and chicken pieces in the oil in a heavy pan over medium heat. Turn heat low, sprinkle with paprika and salt, and stir until chicken is thoroughly covered with paprika. Cover pan and sauté on low heat with steam from chicken for 30 minutes.

Add tomato and green pepper, cover pan and continue cooking for another 30 minutes on low heat, stirring occasionally. Add a little water, if necessary, if there is not enough liquid in the pan.

Meanwhile, stir flour into sour cream in a small bowl with a wire whip or spoon, slowly adding some hot liquid from chicken until it forms a thin, smooth paste. Remove chicken pieces from pot, gently stir sour cream/flour paste into sauce, and heat slowly until almost boiling, stirring continually. Turn heat very low, continue stirring until sauce thickens. Return chicken pieces to pot, heat once more slowly. Serve over hot poppy seed noodles or spaetzle, accompanied by traditional Hungarian sweet-sour marinated cucumber.

Serves 4-5.

HUNGARIAN CHICKEN PAPRIKA

20 8-oz. chicken breasts

24 oz. chopped onion

5 T Hungarian paprika

4 t salt

24 oz. chopped pepper

1 lb. chopped tomato or ¼ cup paste

½ c sour cream

¼ c flour

Brown chicken breasts in oven. Sauté onion. Add paprika, salt, cook for few minutes, add tomato, pepper, cook 30". Blend sour cream, flour, little sauce, combine with rest of sauce. Pour over chicken, cook 30" in 300° convect. oven or on range. Serves 20.

up or down from the amounts indicated. Most commercial kitchens deal with weights even for liquid ingredients. Never write "to taste" on any of your recipes; it is hard to scale up or down. It will add to your preparation time when you have to think about how much salt to add to a french vanilla cream written for eight portions and salt is shown as "to taste." Change it to a definite quantity, like one-eighth of a teaspoon; that way, 40 portions will be five-eighths of a teaspoon.

Once you begin collecting recipes in earnest, you'll soon realize that you need an excellent system of organizing and retrieving recipes. If you are a good organizer, develop your own system. Put recipes on a computer if you have easy access to one at all times, but you'll still need hard copies for kitchen use. Both professionals and non-professionals tend to organize recipes by class of food: meats, soups, desserts. That is how cookbooks are organized, too.

However, there are other systems. The one that I use is especially suitable for commercial operations:

- Collect recipes in random order in any form you wish — loose leaf binder, index card, bound book, whatever you have. Number each page or card. Compile a master file in which each recipe is listed under the standard headings acceptable to you, like soups, salads, chicken, fish, etc. You may want to divide each of these headings into subheadings. For desserts, for example, you can have subheadings for cookies, cakes, pies, miscellaneous pastries, and basic preparations.

- Only the name of the recipe and its page number appear in the master file. Of course, references can be made to cookbooks on your shelf, too. Just choose a brief name for each by title or author and the appropriate page number. To illustrate, say you are looking for a recipe for Bavarian Trifle. Open the master file to Desserts. Trifles are found under the Miscellaneous subcategory since they don't fit into any other standard dessert preparation. It takes you 15 seconds to discover that Bavarian Trifle is on page 52 of your collection. Open the collection book (or card box) to page 52. In less than a minute, you have found the recipe.

The advantage of this system is that your collection can be completely random as long as either the pages or the recipes are numbered. It is foolproof, except when you cannot recall the name of the recipe or what category you put it under. Cross indexing in your master file is advisable when something is ambiguous, for instance a lemon-herb salad dressing that can also be used as a dip should be listed both under salad dressings and under dips.

When you are collecting new recipes, which should be a continual process, keep in mind the broad areas they should fall into. Think twice before keeping a new recipe if it cannot fit in any of those categories.

Your personal catering recipe collection, tested, revised and modified over years, is an invaluable asset to your business. Losing your collection is something you cannot afford. It needs to be protected like any other valuable business asset. First of all, to protect the written recipe for everyday use, each page should be separate from the rest of the material so when you or your kitchen staff use a recipe in the kitchen, just that single page or index card leaves your office. If the page falls into the boiling minestrone soup, all you have to replace is that single page — no great tragedy. (The soup is fine, too). But if the whole collection falls in, you have a much more serious issue.

Second, each page should be protected individually from spillage in the kitchen. Ideally, it should be sealed in a transparent, washable cover. While permanent sealing is the best protection, it also prevents you from adding remarks on timing, baking temperatures, and serving sizes, etc. Recipes in a good kitchen evolve continuously. No recipe is permanent; it should change with time, following food trends as well as changes in your own taste. Various transparent protection covers that the page or card can be slipped into are available in all sizes. They're a must since you can't avoid all spills no matter how careful you are.

Third, you should have a backup copy of your recipe collection at your home or at a location other than the main collection in case of fire, theft, flooding, or whatever. Treat your collection as one of your most important documents. Update it regularly with the notations you make when using the originals.

c. Labelling

Run your kitchen as if it were a laboratory as far as labelling is concerned. Every item in the freezer and refrigerator should be labelled and dated. This is also true for your regular shelf items; nothing can be left unlabeled.

Make sure that when food is prepared for an event, everything is also labelled as to which event it was prepared for. This may sound like an unnecessary step when you only have one event. But it *looks* better when it is delivered to a client's home or office, suggesting a busy caterer's kitchen where several parties were prepared that day. So that little unnecessary step may be a good client relation strategy.

This procedure is an absolute necessity when two or more events are being prepared during the busy periods. It is important to read those labels with great care when loading the truck.

On one holiday party someone was not careful enough and our wonderful, freshly prepared cranberry sauce ended up on the wrong truck even though everything was meticulously labelled. It was meant to accompany a holiday turkey at a private, full-service dinner for about 30 guests. The meal was lavish, elegant, and beautiful. But there was no cranberry sauce anywhere. We didn't have much choice; someone quickly got in the truck (left on the street so no one could block it!) and ran off to the nearest supermarket for a few cans of horrible cranberry sauce. The guests were grazing on their salad and the next course was due in a few minutes. No one could see our horrible crime of opening cans of cranberry sauce for the high-priced dinner. Since opening cans is an unusual occurrence, a can opener is something that we don't carry with us. However, we discovered an electric one sitting on the counter in front of us. We thought our troubles were over until we tried to operate it. It gave out a horrible screech and whine that could be heard by the whole neighborhood. Conversation stopped for a moment in the dining room until the host stood up and announced that it was just the can opener. He came in the kitchen to assist us. We were thoroughly embarrassed but he neither noticed what we were opening or cared. The dinner was good enough that the third-rate cranberry sauce probably was not noticed very much. The nice home-made sauce was brought back from the other event and devoured by the staff. It was good!

d. Continuing your education

Continue collecting information from any source that suits you, whether it is magazines, new cookbooks, foreign cookbooks, or your own old books. On your shelf alone there are thousands of untried recipes. Your changing recipe collection is a major marketing tool in the fierce competition among caterers.

Think about the staggering number of new cookbooks appearing every year, with hundreds of recipes in each, plus scores of food magazines with their own hundreds

of recipes. But after you compare those many new recipes to the basics, you will quickly come to the conclusion that new recipes are not new at all.

Many recipes, especially desserts, are virtually the same in most cookbooks with nothing more than a change of name and possibly a few minor changes in ingredients. Many of the new recipes are adaptations of older, standard recipes with trendier titles. Spaghetti with tomato sauce and meatballs becomes angel hair pasta with ground eye of round smothered in Italian spring tomato sauce and herbs. Same thing, but the spaghetti was changed to a thinner cousin, angel hair pasta (previously know as vermicelli), with virtually no difference in flavor or appearance.

There are a few cookbooks with really new recipe collections, written by people who were able to successfully create their own new concoctions. Those are the books you're looking for, books that suit your taste and style. These will be the cornerstone of your research for new ideas. You can sometimes use the recipes as they are written, but more often you have to modify them to your taste and style. Don't blindly trust any cookbook. Your well-tested favorites are fine, but treat any new ones with caution. Some of them have obvious errors in them which is bad news when you are testing their recipes.

Even after you have tried out a recipe, the product may turn out quite differently than predicted. The more you know about food and cooking, the more likely you can predict the outcome of a new recipe and errors that you may make with a difficult preparation. Here is a simple example.

I was in charge of a church dinner once as a volunteer. The expected guests numbered 180. I planned the dessert to be fresh-baked lemon bars, a simple recipe with only a few ingredients producing very delicious, traditional lemon bars. Anyone with a minimum of baking skill can produce this recipe with minimal effort. I bought the ingredients for 180 servings, divided them into nine equal portions, and gave each portion to one of the nine volunteer bakers along with a photocopied recipe that gave instructions on how to prepare it in a standard 9" x 13" baking pan. Each person was to cut the dessert into 24 squares, plate them, dust them with icing sugar, then bring them to the dinner.

The results were totally astonishing. It was as if nine completely different recipes had been used. They looked vaguely similar, and with a few exceptions they all tasted good, although unexpectedly different. And the difference could have been due to only two factors: oven temperature and preparation. (Or did a few bakers keep the nice unsalted butter I bought and substitute margarine?).

Learning on the job is by far the best and most pleasant way to continue your education. But it is often by trial and error, a slow way of learning as well as somewhat risky to your client's food. Learning through formal training is another way. Advanced cooking classes can be useful and from time to time classes are given specifically for caterers. Unfortunately, these are mostly geared for the large caterers and institutional types like hotel catering services. Nevertheless useful information can be picked up at these workshops and seminars. Of course, they are costly.

e. Sharpening

As mentioned in chapter 5, sharp knives are the single most important tool for a chef or caterer. There is nothing you can do without them, unless your catering business is based on buying and reselling ready-made food products.

From your experience as a cook, you probably know the importance of having *very sharp* knives at all times. You may also know that the accidental cutting of fingers is more often the result of using a dull knife; sharp ones can be controlled fully; you know the result of each cut you make. Dull knives can slip and cut fingers.

You have probably attempted to use knives in other people's kitchens on occasion, and you may well wonder how they manage to cut butter with those knives. It is amazing how cooks can prepare anything with their dull instruments. As a matter of fact, dull and poor quality knives may be the single biggest reason why many people hate to be in the kitchen, unless they're eating.

Make sure that all your knives are razor sharp any time you use them. If you have watched professional chefs and butchers work, you know they sharpen their knives often, every 15 minutes or half hour when working with them continuously. They can work faster and safer with less effort, and they know it.

A good way to make certain your knife is sharp is to try dicing tomatoes. Tomato skin is tough and a not-quite-sharp knife has problems penetrating it. You have to exert pressure. A sharp knife cuts through a tomato as easily as through a ripe peach, with no effort and a minimum of pressure.

You can always send your knives out to have them sharpened, but it is much better to learn how to do it yourself. That way, they're always available when you need them. All you need is a sharpening stone and a sharpening steel (or ceramic). It is easy to resharpen knives provided they weren't misused and aren't nicked, or you didn't let them become very dull. For dull or nicked knives, power grinding is necessary to restore the original bevel (angle or slant) of the blade. You can achieve the same with a file and plenty of elbow grease. Remember, too, that eventually sharpening steels lose their fine steel ridges and won't effectively sharpen your knives. Don't use a steel that seems to have too little resistance when a knife is drawn against it. It may be too old to do much good.

Three different cutting edges or bevels are used on common kitchen knives. The heavy french knife, your very basic tool, has a V-shaped grind, the tip of the V coming to a sharp, very thin point in cross-sectional view of the blade. The edge that comes to a sharp point combined with a heavy blade will give you the sharpness and strength needed to do a lot of chopping. The carving knife has a thinner blade and the cross-sectional V-shape is narrower. This is called the hollow grind. This knife has even more of a sharpness thanks to the thin blade, but not as much strength as the french knife because it is only used for carving reasonably soft food items. There is also a concave grind for even thinner bladed knives that are not used much in catering kitchens.

The first two are the most useful for you. Don't worry about how to achieve a V-shape, hollow, or concave grind. Just sharpen the knife well and try to keep the original configuration of the blade.

The sharpening stone, or whetstone, can be used two ways: sharpen with a moist stone, dipping the stone into water often while sharpening, or keep an oil stone. If you use an oil stone, you don't need to add anything to it. To make the oil stone, soak a stone in light machine oil for several hours. Lift it out of the oil, wipe it clean, and you have an oil stone. Keep it in a plastic bag so dust won't settle on it, otherwise it may become clogged.

Most stones have a course and a fine surface. When your knife is quite dull, start sharpening on the coarse side, keeping the blade at the original angle against the stone. As soon as it appears sharper, switch over to the fine side and continue sharpening. For larger knives it is easier to hold the stone against the blade. For smaller knives, hold the knife against the stone. Keep up a good pressure on the blade, but gradually ease off the pressure until you just barely push the blade against the stone. For a

sharp knife that only needs keening of the edge, the process takes 30 seconds. For a duller knife, it takes a minute or two.

A sharp edge becomes dull from contact with the cutting surface. Try not to cut on hard surfaces like metal, pottery, or glass. Hard surfaces dull knives fast. Wood is the gentlest surface for knives; plastic cutting boards are in between.

As the blade touches the cutting surface, the very fine cutting edge bends slightly on a microscopic scale and eventually looses its razor edge. To restore it while working with the knife, you don't need the whetstone. Just stroke the blade against the chef's steel for 15 seconds. Start with good pressure, then ease the pressure off gradually. Try this when cutting several pounds of tomatoes. Start with a sharpened knife and resharpen with a steel after dicing about two pounds of the tomatoes. You can notice the difference immediately.

Whetstones are only used occasionally, when the edge of the knife is duller than a steel can remedy. You will be able to tell when it is time for the stone as you get used to working with well-sharpened knives.

A serrated knife rarely needs sharpening, but don't use it on other than fairly soft food material. It will keep its edge for a very long time. There is a special sharpening steel available for serrated knives, but

it isn't commonly available. A well-equipped hardware store may have one if you feel the need for it.

The blade of the food processor also needs sharpening just like your knives. When it is used often, sharpen it often with a whetstone. Food processor blades have one bevelled edge and one flat. When sharpening, keep these original angles. Sharpen the bevelled edge only, and when it is sharp, pass the whetstone gently over the other flat side of the blade a few times to get rid of the rough surface that the whetstone produces while sharpening the bevelled side. When cutting certain acidic foods (like a lot of parsley), the manufacturer recommends resharpening the blade frequently.

One more item that should be sharp is the vegetable peeler. Replace it soon as it does not peel with the lightest touch.

If you don't yet know how to sharpen knives, learn how, either by yourself or have someone else show you the technique. Get into the habit of using these sharpening devices continually while working with knives. The habit will make your kitchen work much easier.

f. Kitchen supplies — shelf life

Replenish all your supplies as soon as they get low. It is a sin, and a major dent in efficiency, to run out of a critical item in the middle of preparing a meal when every

minute counts. There is no choice but to run to the nearest store, wasting valuable time. Train your kitchen staff (and yourself) to write everything that needs replacing on a board or note pad and remember to add it to your shopping list.

For perishable items, use the refrigerator or freezer, but use good judgment and leave enough space for other things.

When buying and storing your supplies, remember two things:

(a) You don't want to buy too small a quantity of items you use often. But neither do you want to buy huge quantities that tie up your money and take up too much storage space. Find the balance that is correct for you. Consider cheaper unit prices when you buy in larger quantities. For example, capers are costly when bought in small jars. A four-ounce jar costs 68¢ an ounce. The unit price is much lower when you purchase a 32-ounce jar for 36¢ an ounce. Since capers keep perfectly well in your refrigerator for a very long time, if you have the space and use them frequently, the larger jar makes better sense.

(b) Most items have a finite shelf life. There is no sense buying large quantities if the shelf life is much shorter than the time it would take you to use all of it. This is a common fault in household purchases. You see huge spice containers in many kitchens simply because it is cheaper in large containers. Four, five, or even ten years later the same containers are still sitting in that kitchen, and the cook is still using the same spices that lost their flavor three years ago. You might as well add talcum powder to that chicken dish instead of the five-year-old garlic powder; the taste will be the same, and talcum powder at least helps thicken the sauce!

You should learn the shelf life of items you stock in your commercial kitchen. There is no overall guideline for shelf life, unfortunately. You can study cookbooks, food manuals and reference books, home economics texts, and government publications. A wide range of values on the shelf life of various foodstuffs can be found. And when you see that some of them are obviously wrong, how can you trust the rest? One reference book mentions that salt and sugar have a shelf life of one year. But I know that they both keep indefinitely as long as they remain dry. Another says honey is no good after two years. Yet perfectly good honey was found in the Egyptian pyramids, proving that its shelf life is indefinite, at least for our purposes. I just haven't found a reliable guide to food shelf life.

Legumes, dry goods, and canned items will keep for years. Items in your refrigerator and freezer vary, and the taste will tell you. The guides you find in food reference books are much too conservative.

Once you read a great deal about food (and that is what I'm advising you to do), you can reason out shelf life for most things. For instance, storing food in the freezer can produce freezer burns if oxygen comes in contact with your food. Properly wrapped food suffers a minimum of freezer burn, but it is difficult to completely eliminate oxygen without a vacuum seal. In frozen fruits and vegetables, the enzyme action eventually breaks down flavor. If the produce is blanched before freezing, the enzyme action stops. Storage life will be much longer but not indefinite as both the flavor and nutritional content will slowly drop with time.

There should be very little deterioration in dry legumes. With years of storage they become even drier, requiring a slightly longer cooking time, but you can challenge anyone to tell the difference in flavor be-

tween a kidney bean stored for six months and one stored for six years.

Spices and herbs are another matter. They do lose their flavoring oils, called essential oils, with storage. These are the items you should purchase in very restricted quantities, certainly not more than a year's supply if the spice is ground. If it is whole, it will keep longer.

Discard it when in doubt. Flavors are so important in your cooking that you can't afford to use old spices and herbs.

For your spice and dried herb supplies, look for a source where you can buy in bulk (not commercially packaged) but in small amounts. Make sure the resource has a good turnover of stock by smelling the spices and herbs. They should have a fresh, pungent, spicy smell, not a dried, grass-like odor.

You may want to keep certain spices that you have to buy in ground form (curry and chili powder, paprika, ground chili, etc.) in the freezer to keep them fresh if you have the space.

Find out what keeps well in the freezer, what can be reused after defrosting, and what can only be used in cooking and baking. You will always have leftover food, much of which can be reused or recycled, like cheeses, dairy products, meats, fish, breads, and pastries.

g. Waste reduction

Wasted food is probably the single most serious plague of the food industry, a business already operating at marginal profit levels. Many restaurants and caterers go out of business because they cannot make enough profit to justify their existence.

There are two categories of wasted food in catering:

(a) Beyond the caterer's control:

(i) Client overestimated the number of guests and ordered more than needed.

(ii) Guests consumed less food than expected

(iii) Cancellation of the event

(iv) Extra food prepared to insure sufficient amounts

(b) Within the caterer's control:

(i) Food waste during preparation

(ii) Overestimating ingredients needed

(iii) Spoilage

(iv) Theft

In the first category, food is actually wasted but is paid for by the client, so it doesn't cut into profits. Some of the extra food can be left with the client; it is not all wasted in the physical sense. How much extra food is prepared as insurance against running short of food is really within the caterer's control, but is necessary and included in the pricing. The number one complaint against caterers in general by the public is that "they ran out of food." With experience the amount of extra food prepared can be a minimum to reduce waste. Ten percent is a good rule of thumb if you figure your portions precisely. With lower budget catering it can be reduced even more, and for full-service pre-plated meals it is minimal. When pre-plating food, the chef or kitchen help carefully divide food on the prepared plates so there is just a little left in the pots when the last one is dished out.

The second category is the one you should worry about. In the first list, waste hurts for ethical reasons, simply because wasting food is a crime when much of the world's population is hungry. But at least you are not losing money on the food. In the second category, however, you waste not only the food but the money you paid for it.

Waste can be reduced significantly with good organizational skill and efficiency, but it can never be fully eliminated. Some waste is necessary to run your business efficiently. For example, you need to keep

milk and coffee cream in your refrigerator for events and sometimes they become outdated or spoiled. That is a small expense compared to someone's unnecessary trip to the store just to get cream for the next morning's breakfast event because you ran out two days ago. Some of the extra food is there as an insurance policy against such contingencies and a small waste is justified.

1. Supplies

To order supplies close to the right amount is an art that comes with experience. In some cases it is easy: if you need salmon steak for 34 guests, you order 34 pieces and a few extra for a possible increase in the number of guests. In the case of salads, you have to figure the amount a person consumes plus 10%. But no matter what, you have to over-order somewhat to avoid unexpected problems — unacceptable pieces of fruit, for instance, errors in the kitchen, spillage, and sampling by staff all go into this category.

Theft is a problem discussed in chapter 3. This is usually well within your control, though not always easy to do. Losses due to theft could be significant. The larger your operation, the more likely you are to have a problem here.

2. Staff

Another area of costly waste in catering is staff time. The more routine work your catering business does, the easier it is to plan staff time. If much of your business consists of corporate breakfasts and luncheons, they are all of similar menus and you can predict preparation, delivery, setup, and cleanup times fairly closely. Your staff time waste is minimal.

But with a high-end reception where menu, setup, and everything else is completely different from one to another, you have to plan extra staff time for contingencies. You can't afford to schedule your staff so closely that as soon as they are finished in the kitchen, it is time to leave. There are many things that can go wrong. You have to allow extra staff hours for such eventualities, and at times everyone is finished an hour before the scheduled departure time. This is expensive but necessary.

The second most frequent complaint against caterers is that they arrive late. This is an easy problem to eliminate; usually all it takes is careful planning and organization.

3. Space

There are other kinds of waste to consider, too. If you are running a small business and you don't have many events scheduled to keep your kitchen busy, your rented space may be wasted if it sits idle too often. If you can find another entrepreneur in food preparation who can use your health-approved kitchen, sublet your space for some extra income. Make sure you don't interfere with each other's activities, and that the other person is properly insured, licensed, and trustworthy, and that you have permission to sublet from your landlord if you are renting the space yourself. Don't sublet to someone who may be or could be your competition. Keep your files and recipe collection under lock and key when you are not in your kitchen.

h. Cleanliness and cleanup

1. Avoid contamination

It is vital to your business to be clean and hygienic at all times in the kitchen. One error and your business can be ruined. Your food must be perfectly and absolutely safe without the slightest doubt. There should be no possibility, no matter how remote, of someone getting sick from your kitchen's product. Strictly observing all sensible rules and regulations of food preparation will virtually eliminate this possibility. Many caterers and restaurateurs are wiped out overnight as a result of some careless error in spoiled or contaminated food.

It is not enough to keep everything hospital clean. As a caterer and chef you need to learn and understand what causes food poisonings and how it can be eliminated.

In a nutshell, there are five micro-organisms that are the most common causes of food-borne illnesses:

(a) botulism, incubation period 12 to 36 hours, very serious

(b) salmonellosis, incubation period 12 to 24 hours, moderately serious

(c) trichinosis, incubation period two days, serious

(d) staphylococcus poisoning, incubation period three hours, not very serious

(e) clostridium perfringens poisoning, incubation period 10 to 12 hours, mild

All five are easy to prevent if you know just a little bit about them. Poisonings by salmonellosis and botulism have been increasing, while trichinosis is decreasing over the years. The other two are rarely reported because they are rarely recognized as food-borne diseases and their symptoms are relatively mild. There are many books available on the subject. Take one out of your library and study food-borne illnesses.

In addition to knowing these food-borne problems, you should stay up to date with reports in the food industry regarding their occurrences. For instance, eggs have not been a serious cause of salmonella until recent years when a large batch of salmonella-infected eggs found their way to consumers. That means raw or barely cooked eggs are no longer considered safe for you and your guests.

There are many preparations that use slightly cooked and raw eggs, including various sauces, poached eggs, eggs Benedict, and Caesar salad. Even though salmonella-infected eggs are very rare, many, if not most, hotel and restaurant kitchens stopped preparing foods that call for raw or not-fully cooked eggs. You're the one who decides whether you will also follow that safety precaution, or take a chance, tiny as it may be. It is just a question of time before perfectly safe eggs (perhaps irradiated to kill any possible infection) are available again. But it is your responsibility to seek out current information on food safety on a regular basis.

2. Staff

If you feel that your food preparation techniques are absolutely safe, your only worry is your staff's personal hygiene and food preparation practices. Observe how each staff member works in the kitchen. You can guess at their personal hygiene, too, after observing them.

It is mandatory in the food industry that staff wash hands with soap after using bathroom facilities so there is no chance of transferring any disease-prone organisms into the food. How do you check that? There is no easy way short of staying with them in the bathroom, and that isn't an acceptable alternative to most of your staff. Your next choice is to hire people who are clean in appearance and seem to take good care of themselves. Chances are their personal hygiene is good, too.

3. Utensils and equipment

Continuous cleanup is highly beneficial to kitchen efficiency. Pots, pans, utensils, and whatever is being used in the kitchen should be washed on a continual basis. As soon as one project is finished, utensils and containers should be washed. No matter how busy the kitchen is, mountains of unwashed dishes are never present. It helps efficiency because whenever you need something, you know it is ready to use. It is psychologically beneficial, too. You don't have to contemplate an hour's washing up at the end of the cooking time. A few minutes here and there are far easier to swallow. Finally, it is much faster to wash

almost anything right after it was used rather than hours later when everything is congealed and caked on.

The cleaning of floors, work tables, and walls is also part of the continual cleanup mode of a catering kitchen.

The continual cleanup mode requires a quick, general cleaning. Your kitchen equipment is washed well and thoroughly, but your floors, walls, sinks, and tables are only cleaned superficially during food preparation. After the food preparation is completed, usually after the event, a more thorough cleaning is needed so no remnants of spilled food are present. It eliminates bacterial growth as well as insect infestation.

Surfaces should be washed with disinfecting cleaners. Work tables and cutting boards are constantly in contact with food and are vulnerable to bacterial infections. Soap and water will do a good job, but occasionally a spray bottle filled with chlorine should be used to spray them for a thorough disinfection. Chlorine will also take food stains off cutting boards and work tables. If you are using any wooden surface, rub some vegetable oil into it from time to time to prevent drying out, thus preserving it for the long term.

Always keeping your kitchen spotless pays off in the long run. There is less chance of bacteria and insects, as well as a better working environment for you and your staff. A person working in a clean kitchen tends to clean up more as he or she goes along.

4. Work space

A properly sealed kitchen should be virtually bug-free. Needless to say, all food must be in tightly sealed containers with nothing exposed even overnight. As long as there is nothing for them to eat, they will go to someone else's kitchen.

Spiders and flying insects are not so easy to keep out. The wonderful smells coming out of your kitchen will attract flies, and when you have to leave your door open for loading and unloading, they will be delighted to join those smells. That keeps the spiders happy, too. So try to have the door open as little as possible. Obviously, no insect spray of any sort can be used in the kitchen. A fly swatter is one of the only weapons allowed. To kill ants, crawling insects, and spiders without using insecticides, you can use a spray bottle of laundry stain remover such as Spray 'n Wash. Even though it is not poisonous, make sure it is wiped off of surfaces that will be in contact with food. When sprayed on insects, it kills them in seconds and is a perfect alternative to insecticides.

Beware of food in boxes brought into your kitchen. They are potential bug carriers. Empty the boxes right away and remove them from your inside area.

Another kitchen problem to deal with is hair and fur. Few things will turn a guest off faster than a stray hair in a tantalizing dish. Hair in the food is a disaster. No animal of any sort, unless it is completely bald, should ever enter your kitchen. It is much harder to maintain a crew of bald helpers! If you or one of your employees has a problem with flying hair, insist on a hair net for everyone. Never let anyone comb or brush their hair anywhere near the kitchen. Again, frequent cleaning of your facilities will reduce this problem.

Keeping your facility clean means you're always ready for an unexpected health department inspector's visit. You want the inspector as a friend and the less violation he or she finds, the less trouble you will have in the future. Once an inspector knows that your kitchen is always clean, he or she will not even look around much on visits and will just have you sign the papers. That "no violation at the time of inspection" notice gives you a wonderful feeling and can even be used as a marketing tool.

i. Health department code

Health department codes for your commercial facility are strict and vary depending on where you live. Generally, field inspectors visit twice a year, in some cases three or four times a year.

Larger, more heavily populated areas have stricter codes. Enforcement is probably more strict in large metropolitan areas with good reason, too, if you think of some of the sleazy-looking restaurants you may have passed in the seedier parts of town. Just looking at the restaurant's visible areas lets you imagine what the non-visible kitchen and storage areas must look like.

In the United States, the federal model health code was introduced to have all states adopt the same, uniform code throughout the country, but due to the many regional variations and politics, it was never adopted. It won't happen in the near future. Canadian and American regulations are quite similar, with variations ranging from province to province and state to state rather than across international borders. The differences are considerable within the same province or state between large municipalities and small communities. Investigate your local regulations.

To give you at least a vague idea of what regulations are like, here is a summary from the California code, which is probably the strictest on the continent. Only the part of the code that may apply to small catering facilities is included here. These codes are strictly enforced with inspectors visiting about once every six months. The visits are not announced so there is no chance to bring the kitchen up to par the day before. If your kitchen is well-maintained and if it generally conforms to the code, you should have no problem with the inspectors. In general, hygiene codes look at these problem areas:

(a) Doors and windows

    (i) Exterior door: rodent and insect-proof with no opening greater than one-half inch and equipped with heavy-duty self-closer

    (ii) Screen door: equipped with heavy duty self-closer

    (iii) Windows: equipped with screening

    (iv) Restroom doors: equipped with self-closers

    (iv) Other openings entering buildings (pipes, etc.) sealed

(b) Interior material and finishes

    (i) Floor smooth and washable in all rooms where food is prepared or stored, and in toilets

    (ii) Base of continuous four-inch cove sealed between floor and walls

    (iii) Walls and ceiling smooth, washable, light colored, sealed

    (iv) Exceptions allowed where food is stored in unopened cans, bottles, cartons, sacks, or other original shipping containers

(c) Toilets

    (i) Hand washing facilities within or adjacent to toilet room. Must provide soap dispenser, towel, paper dispenser, and hand wash sign

(d) Lighting

    (i) Minimum 20-foot candle intensity in food preparation area

    (ii) Minimum 10-foot candle in storage area, toilets, dressing room

    (iii) Protective cover over light bulbs or use of shatter-proof bulbs

(e) Ventilation

    (i) All areas must have sufficient ventilation to facilitate proper food storage and comfort to workers

    (ii) Toilet must have exhaust fan or openable screened window

(f) Kitchen

    (i) Canopy-type hood with six-inch overlap on ends and sides over stoves, grills, soup kettles, steam jacketed kettles and fryers — duct, fan size, air velocity must comply to specified code

    (ii) Thermometers in refrigerators and freezers, accurate within plus or minus 2°F (1°C)

    (iii) Tables, counters, shelves made of hardwood, formica, metal, or other approved easily cleanable material

    (iv) Food storage shelves six inches above floor

    (v) Utensil and equipment stored so as to be protected from contamination

(g) Washing facilities, four options:

    (i) Dishwashing machine with 180°F (82.2°C) rinse

    (ii) Dishwashing machine with 120°F to 140°F (48.9°C to 60°C) chemical rinse

    (iii) Undercounter dishwashing machine with 120ÉF to 140°F (48.9°C to 60°C) chemical rinse

    (iv) Three-compartment metal sink and hand washing according to code: dishwashers must have two metal drain boards or adjacent two-compartment sinks with two drain boards; sinks and drain boards must be stainless steel; vegetable sink indirect waste connection to floor sink; dishwashing sink direct waste connection; dishwashing machine direct waste connection.

(h) Refrigeration equipment

    (i) Indirect waste connection or self-contained evaporator unit

(i) Cleaning area, two options

    (i) One-compartment non-porous janitorial sink, hot and cold water

    (ii) Concrete slab, curbed and sloped to drain, connected to sewer, hot and cold water with anti-siphon device

(j) Grease interceptor

    (i) If required, must be readily accessible for cleaning

(k) Water supply

    (i) Hot water heater minimum 120°F (48.9°C)

    (iii) Hot and cold water to all sinks

    (iv) Water of required minimum temperature to dishwashing machines

(l) Refuse

    (i) Adequate facilities to store and dispose of all waste material

(m) Other requirements regarding catering food facilities:

    (i) All potentially hazardous food must be held below 45°F (7.2°C) or above 140°F (62.8°C) at all times

    (ii) No food prepared or stored in a private home can be served for sale or given away in a food facility

    (iii) All food preparation employees must wear clean, washable outer garments or uniforms and keep their hands clean. They must wash hands and arms with cleanser and warm water before commencing work and after using toilet facilities. They must wear hairnets or caps. They must use tongs to serve food

(iv) No smoking in food preparation, storage, and cleaning areas

(v) All poisonous substances, including cleaning material and insecticides must be labeled properly, kept in original container and stored in separate closet away from any food material

(vi) All waste is stored in leak- and rodent-proof containers and removed frequently. Food preparation facilities must be free of litter and rubbish

(vii) Manual sanitization according to code specified

(viii) All living and sleeping quarters must be separated from the food preparation area by a wall. No door or other opening may connect the two directly

(ix) Vehicle used in food transportation must have smooth, easily cleanable, easily accessible interior surfaces

15
The Office: No Picnic At All

a. Planning the office space

While your business is reasonably small and you do most of the work yourself, you can expect to spend equal amounts of time in your kitchen and your office. Once your business picks up, the amount of time in your office tends to increase and kitchen time decreases. However, you do have some choices here. If you really hate office work, have someone take care of that part-time so you can spend more hours with your food. Whatever the final outcome, you will need a well-equipped, comfortable, presentable, or even elegant office that will reflect the type of business you wish to impress upon your visiting clients.

For example, if you run a low-end, large-volume barbecue operation, your office should still convey to your client that the business is doing very well. There is no need for a lavish office with exotic, trendy flower arrangements. The client may get the wrong impression, thinking that you are too pricey for a barbecue. A small bouquet, arranged by yourself or even a few single stems are sufficient.

The higher the class of catering you run, the more presentable your office should be. Nevertheless, a personal touch in the office will help sell a client on you much faster than the cold plastic look of an interior-designed bank manager's office. You need to give the client a favorable first impression of you and of your establishment. Then you can impress him or her with your menu, pictures, and samples.

Your office should be comfortable for you and your guests, and it should definitely reflect the fact that a caterer occupies it. Many caterers, if they have the space, set up a little "tasting" table that will seat two to four guests. There your client can sip fresh iced coffee with little scones and plum jam, or taste tidbits of presentable items that you pulled out of your refrigerator. Whenever you expect a client's visit, plan to have something fresh, even if it is just chocolate chip cookies. The aroma of anything freshly baked is welcome at that time. Your client will want to order whatever you serve for his or her event, so don't offer something out of season, or an item you don't like to prepare, or something obviously out of the client's budget.

If your office is too small to have a separate table for clients to sit around, have a little coffee table where you can set a beautiful little tray of refreshments. Anticipate extra people showing up; prepare some extra food. Set four or five glasses in the freezer on a summer day to serve chilled beverages. Many clients find it fun to visit a caterer and sample the food, so extra people may join in at the last minute.

If your office is too small for that many visitors, set up some kind of a little reception area for guests elsewhere in your facility if it is at all possible. Even if it is not very fancy, the clients will understand that this is primarily your working kitchen, not a reception room. Make serious attempts though, to give your reception area a little zing.

b. Basic equipment for the office

Your office needs a desk, filing cabinets, and bookshelves to store cookbooks and various items, like your collection of antique tea kettles. These items, of course, should preferably be food-related. A collection of antique rat poison containers may be frowned upon by your clients, as well as by the health inspector.

You will need either a good electric typewriter, word processor, or computer for billing and letter writing. A poor quality letter written on an outdated typewriter reflects poorly on your business; the quality of your correspondence should conform to your business style. If you are planning to run a middle- to high-end business, you need a versatile computer and laser printer. However, if you are not into computers, you don't need one for a small catering business.

There are several companies who make software specifically for restaurateurs and caterers. By the time you read this there will likely be even more available. These are geared mainly for larger businesses, but a smaller caterer can benefit from them, too. Computer software can scale recipes up or down, give you quantities of ingredients needed, costs, prices, and profits at a given price, search for recipes, and so on. The catch is, of course, that all your recipes must be keyed in, as well as prices of every ingredient. Any change you want to make on the recipe and any time there is a change in the cost of ingredients (which is all the time), you must key it in, too. But that also has to be done with a manual system.

The software is most useful in a large business if your gross is over $100,000 annually. But it can be useful in any size business if that is your style of running the business. The cost of software is not high. To give you an example, a company called At-Your-Service Software in Bronxville, New York, markets a program named Recipe Writer Pro for $295 (1994 price).

However, before you use a computer for all these functions, you must be able to do it by hand and with your head comfortably, quickly, and competently.

Your standard office equipment should include a good calculator. If possible, you should have one in the kitchen as well. A telephone answering machine, voice mail, or answering service is a must for catering since someone cannot be at the telephone all the time and clients with last-minute changes in guest numbers or menu items should be able to leave messages for you. The fax machine is becoming a standard piece of any office's equipment; it does help to get a menu or proposal instantly to your clients, some of whom often request information be faxed to them even though their planned party is several months away. It is just the new office trend to have everything at your fingertips instantly.

A cellular phone is also optional. More and more larger caterers equip their delivery vehicles with a car phone. Although it is a drain on your budget, having one can be very convenient. Not only are you easily accessible, but you are not tied to your office quite so much. And when heading to an event, a car phone comes in very handy to keep in contact with your help, sometimes your kitchen, and even the client if you cannot find the address or you are slightly delayed. A car phone is another one of those choices that is left to you to make. The size of your equipment budget will help you make the decision, as well as the current price of these phones.

c. Bookkeeping and other records

There is constant office work of all sorts associated with any business that not only

132

must be done, but some of it is legally required. The secret to having all your books in order hinges on two basic tenets:

(a) Keep good written records of everything related to your business

(b) Keep your records and books fully up-to-date at all times

If those two principles are not observed, your office work will become a menacing black cloud over your head most of the time and a chore even if you generally don't mind the books. If, on the other hand, your records are good and orderly, keeping up the book work is not very difficult and literally a few minutes of your time daily will take care of the majority of the necessary office chores. Once a month there will be extra office work to keep up with monthly records, labor reports, payrolls, etc., and once a year your annual records, taxes, reporting of employee earnings, and similar tasks will keep you busy for hours, even if you have a bookkeeper who does the bulk of the reporting.

You must keep records all the time, no matter how busy you are, and you must keep your books up-to-date at all times. Even if you are working long hours and can barely keep up with your holiday events, keep up with the office work as well as you can. Schedule a little office work into your general plans or just do it routinely. If you prefer to have someone else do this work, be sure the business records necessary for the other person are orderly and also up to date. He or she can only accomplish record keeping as good as the raw data you are supplying. And if it is very poorly organized, it will cost you dearly to have your bookkeeper organize it for you.

As soon as you anticipate your first few business expenses, open a separate business checking account. Keep your business and personal checking accounts strictly separate — never mix the two. Choose the type of business checking account that fits your business needs best. Some small business people use the same simple system of a personal checking account, some prefer a more elaborate system, like "one-write" checks which gives a carbon copy of all checks and a spreadsheet.

Accountants say that if you are processing more than 30 or 40 invoices a month, a computer accounting system should benefit your bookkeeping.

1. Records

Keep records of all your expenditures, supported by receipts or at least canceled checks. Even if your business is very small, it is wise to keep these records in a regular accountant's book with ten, 12, or 14 vertical columns for different expense categories. The vertical columns will automatically give you the breakdown of expenses that is required for tax purposes once a year.

You can break the expenses down into categories any way you like but it is preferable to have them in groups that will eventually help calculate your taxes. If you have a tax accountant, he or she will give you the categories. Here is an example:

(a) Food and related supplies

(b) Office expenses

(c) Insurance

(d) Advertising

(e) Rent

(f) Utilities

(g) Repair

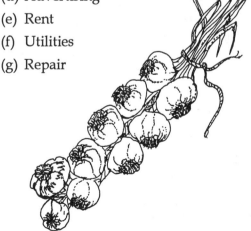

(h) Equipment purchase

(i) Vehicles

(j) Rental, flowers, subcontractors, miscellaneous

(k) Salaries

(l) Total

Have a separate set of records for each month. Each entry should include the date of purchase, where the purchase was made and, if it is out of the ordinary, what the item was. To keep up such a record is easy and best done by you even if you have a part-time bookkeeper. For occasional items, a missing receipt would probably be acceptable if you have to undergo a tax audit, provided a receipt is difficult to obtain, the item is not expensive, and it is infrequent in occurrence. An example is a purchase made at a local farmer's market. To make it even more acceptable, you can list on a piece of paper the date and approximate total purchase of produce and nuts and sign it. Include it in the collection of receipts.

2. Records of employee hours worked

You can keep the record of employee hours in a separate book on regular employee time cards. At pay time, multiply the hours by your employees' hourly wages and mark the amount paid on the card.

3. Events and appointments

Never leave any of these to memory. If you forget to mark down an item you purchased or your chef's hours for a day, you may end up with slightly misleading records or a dispute with your chef. If an event didn't get on your calendar, you have a disaster on your hands. Make sure that all events you are asked to cater are on the calendar at once! Also mark any deposit you have received from a client. An unmarked deposit can lead to unpleasant consequences, too.

4. Client and event records

As soon as you are contacted by a client, open a file for him or her. What system you use for each is immaterial as long as you are consistent and the records are easily retrievable. You can use a separate file folder or just a sheet of paper for each client where you record the date of first contact, name, address, telephone number (preferably both home and business), and two pieces of clearly visible information: the date of the prospective event and the number of guests expected. Add any details about the event that you have been told, including price or price range quoted. Any subsequent contact with this client should be recorded on the same paper or in the same file folder, including everything that is new in connection with the party.

Every item can be useful in planning the party so your notes should be detailed. File the information in some order so that you can retrieve it readily. Reserved events can be filed together by month. If you don't have too many, each event can be randomly placed within a folder for that month. If you have many events, you may want to separate them by weeks or alphabetically. However, keep in mind that since you cannot remember each client's name, alphabetical listing is only helpful if you have cross-referenced the name, maybe on your event calendar. If you remember that the event is in May, you can scan your calendar until the name in May comes up and find your event notes in the May folder. Whatever way you choose, make sure it works for you.

5. Invoicing events

The easiest, most straightforward way of invoicing is to take an invoice with you to present to your client at the end of the event. This is possible in many cases. Hand your client the invoice, and thank him or her for choosing your catering company for the event. Often you will get a check for the balance. This saves time and you have a check in hand ready to be deposited in your bank. This is a common way of billing in social catering.

For corporate catering, a check must often be requisitioned, which will take a few weeks, but carrying the final invoice with you will save some time in mailing. Chances are you will get your check a few days earlier. Some corporate clients carry a blank check with them, so having a ready invoice with you can pay off.

In some cases, however, you cannot make up an invoice until after the event. For such clients, you must send the invoice by mail. The sooner you send it, the sooner you get paid. For more frequent clients, you may bill monthly. This bill should be made up as soon as you know all the event totals for that month. It is best to schedule invoicing time as part of your event-planning time.

6. Accounts of events

As soon as an event is over, you should record it, giving a brief summary of the event on a single line or two with name of client, date of event, type of event, number of guests, gross receipts, amount of sales tax included in the gross, and a column to check off once you receive payment with the date of receipt. To double check the receipt of payment, it is a good idea to mark outstanding invoices in the client's file as well. Since many clients are potential repeats, mark down anything that may be useful for you to know for a future event for the same client — names of relatives or close friends, food likes and dislikes, and so on.

7. Notes on past events

Once you become a seasoned, well-established caterer, you will rarely need notes on an event you catered, but even then you might want to mark down anything new that happened from the caterer's point of view. When you are still learning (this goes on for a long time yet — my education is still in process), it is important to learn from mistakes you made. Write down anything unexpected and significant, especially with regard to food. Was the quantity enough or too much? Did you run out of some item too soon? Did everything arrive in top condition? Did the guests especially like or dislike a menu item? Make notes on staff, too. Did you plan for just the right number or were idle staff talking in the corners? All these observations should be filed in the appropriate pigeon holes — notes about the staff in one file, and food quantities with the recipe file, or wherever you keep your notes for such things.

8. Inquiries and requests

Many of the calls coming in are from potential clients not ready to make reservations. Respond to these appropriately, sending the information requested, making your notes with enough detail for the next call from the potential client, and file it separately from the reserved events. Again, the best plan is to set up monthly files. Some inquiries are general with no specific event in the client's mind. These cannot be filed by event date, so keep them in a separate folder called "General Inquiries." Check this folder from time to time and recontact the potential clients.

9. Paying your bills

Prompt payment of your bills is essential, particularly when starting up a new business, to establish your credibility and to gain the confidence of your suppliers. That will eliminate future problems and headaches. Of course, during the beginning period, virtually all suppliers demand to be paid on pickup or delivery of your order. No one trusts a brand new business until it has been financially established and proven itself to be viable.

Your orders will be rather small and suppliers don't need small business too much, so establishing the image of a trustworthy, upcoming new business is a good idea. There are times when you need their help in a sudden, last-minute emergency order, or when they have to drop off an order by your back door when no one is in your kitchen and trust you to send a check by return mail. You adore the client who carries a blank check with him or her to an event to pay you with. This will be just as much appreciated by your suppliers. While you are small, you depend on them more than they depend on you.

Utility bills, rent, and other payments should be paid promptly, too. To anyone supplying you with anything the only proof is your payment.

d. Monthly summary

It is a good habit to add up your books once a month and feel the pulse of your business. No doubt, you have some idea how you are doing anyway, but sometimes those numbers come back with a different answer than you expected. Sometimes it's a pleasant surprise, other times not so pleasant. You want to know if your cash flow is a trickle, or if it is flowing out instead of in. You need to remedy that situation fast. The books will give you an answer and if you don't add them up at least once a month, you won't know what's going on. Also, if the business is doing better than you suspected, you can afford to adjust your pricing a little for new requests and you can refuse marginally profitable events that you don't want to waste time on. This is important!

At the end of each month add up your total expenses by categories, check if there are some unjustified expense leaks, and add

up your receipts as well. Subtracting the sales tax and any other expenses that either you collected on someone else's behalf or were not related to your business, compare the total receipts to your total expenses to get the approximate bottom line figure of how your business did that month. This figure will not be quite accurate as it does not take into account any change in inventory, but in a small catering business that is not significant enough to be worth the bother. Provided you kept your records up-to-date at all times, adding up your books monthly should take minimal effort.

e. Payroll

Organizing your payroll can be done in several different ways. People working for you on an occasional basis generally want to be paid frequently, often right after each event. For a really occasional worker, there is no problem with that. For someone working more frequently, weekly, bi-weekly, or monthly payment is preferable. You want to keep your staff happy and working for you in the future.

Even if you are not a pleasant boss to work for, the bottom line for them is your prompt payment. Your helper will swallow a lot if he or she knows that the check is forthcoming regularly and promptly, as expected. Make sure that they are not disappointed in you. Establish your credibility with them as carefully as you do with your suppliers. When they know that they can count on your punctual payments, they will be more likely to work for you in an emergency situation.

In addition to your regular record keeping and payroll chores, there are also periodic legal requirements that you must observe. These are discussed in full in chapter 16. They include filing business records, renewal of licenses, and completing tax returns. Again, the answer is to do these things promptly. If there is payment involved, the forms are often sent to you months in advance, in which case prompt payment is not a good idea. Put the deadline date on your calendar if a missed deadline will result in a fine. Establish a system to help you remember these dates if you have a habit of ignoring the calendar.

f. Annual summary

Once a year, add up the total of each of your monthly summaries to feel the average annual pulse of your business. Again, if you did your homework every month, this is not a big job and will tell you a great deal about the progress of your business. The procedure is no different than your monthly summaries, but you will have to deal with 12 sets of figures, one for each month.

g. Income taxes

Your annual tax returns will be more complicated by having your own business. Most small business owners find it best to have a professional accountant familiar with small business taxes do the chore. Business tax laws change from year to year, and you may have difficulty keeping up with the changes on your own. In addition, a good tax accountant will be able to advise you with the right combination of various allowable deductions and options on equipment depreciation so you pay the minimum of income taxes. Unless you know a lot about business income taxes, your accountant's fee is well justified. In order to save on accountant's fees, provide him or her with good records in good order. Remember that with incomplete records on your expenses you will have lower business deductions and will be paying higher taxes. And if you miss recording some of your events, you may have problems if you are ever audited.

16
Legality: As Necessary As Dishwashing

Most people considering a career in a small business venture don't have the vaguest idea of the complex legal and financial matters they are about to undertake. Businesses that are producing environmentally sensitive or potentially harmful products have additional difficulties. Most branches of the service industry are not in this category but they have the extra burden of governmental protection since they serve the public. The food industry, and specifically a catering service, is in this category.

When you are a consumer, you welcome such protection. When your business is the one the government inspector is assigned to protect the public from, your welcoming smile fades. Such protection of the public translates into numerous rigorous regulations and restrictions that you must comply with from the birth of your business until you close the door.

I suspect that if a potential entrepreneur was confronted with all the regulations he or she must conform with early on, the entrepreneurial enthusiasm would all but vanish. It really is a formidable list if you live in an area that takes regulations seriously. As difficult as conforming may be, it can be done if you accept the rules and go about acquiring permits and licenses step by step, swallowing your frustration, and attempting to enjoy the time you have to stand in line at the health department or waiting weeks for a needed certificate or

license to arrive. The problem comes when you already have catering events to run and a moneymaking business to conduct. The time needed to get your official and legal documents, generally during regular business hours only, is often long and can cut seriously into the time you need to plan and execute your events.

a. In the United States

Sometimes it is more fortunate to still be waiting for paying clients while getting the legal aspects settled. Let's review what a small catering business requires in terms of the many permits. The following outlines the situation in California, one of the most restrictive places in the United States in which to conduct business. If you live elsewhere, you may get off a little easier. Also, smaller municipalities generally have less restrictive regulations than larger ones, but the guidelines are often similar:

(a) Once you've made your decision about operating as a sole proprietor or incorporating your business, you act accordingly regarding legal matters. There is generally no additional legal requirement if you are a sole proprietor. If you incorporate, papers have to be filed, forms filled out, and fees paid and incorporation recorded, so it is best to use your lawyer to be certain that the procedure is legally correct and no step is left out. Partnerships are also legally

138

complex; legal advice or assistance is advisable.

(b) File for a fictitious business name; decide what name you want to use for your business. Visit the county recorder's office and search the files to determine if anyone else may have reserved the name. Both active and inactive files must be searched. If a name has not been actively used for a certain number of years, it is no longer reserved and you are free to use it. After finding that your chosen name is not being used by anyone else (by the way, never have business cards or brochures printed up until you know the name you've chosen is available) fill out forms and pay a fee to record it, then run a fictitious business name statement in a local, legally qualified newspaper for a certain length of time (generally four times in a weekly paper). If no one protests, the name is officially yours. At the county recorder's office, find out how long you can use the name without refiling. A fictitious name is not yours for eternity, even if you are actively using it. It must be re-recorded before the expiration date, which is usually several years.

(c) Get a federal tax number for your business (also called the employer identification number). For small businesses operating as sole proprietorships and with only occasional employees, your social security number may be sufficient, but check with the federal tax department.

(d) Resale license. This license is necessary to prove to your suppliers that you are in a legitimate business and have the right to purchase from a wholesaler. And since you are reselling, you will not be charged sales tax on products that are resold in your business. For example, you will be taxed on cleaning supplies but not on disposable plates. If foods, beverages, and services are taxable where you live, this resale number will authorize you to collect sales tax from your clients on behalf of the state. You pay the collected taxes to the state at regular intervals, either monthly or quarterly. You may have to leave a security deposit if you are a new business owner without previous history of collecting sales tax. The amount of the deposit is based on the expected annual gross, so make sure you expect a small figure for this to keep the deposit low. After a given period of time, if you pay your sales taxes faithfully, the state will return your deposit, but you may have to request this.

(e) Business tax. This is either a city or county tax and you pay it annually. It is based on your gross receipts. Call your local administration offices to get information on what this entails.

(f) County property tax. While city tax is paid simply because you are in business, the county assesses you for equipment, supplies, and property that you own. You file annually, list-

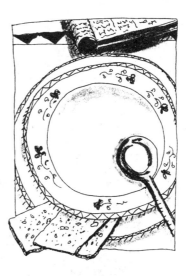

ing all your equipment or supplies, and any changes from the previous year. The amount of tax is determined by the total value you declare.

(g) Health department permit. Again, this is usually a county requirement. As explained previously, once your commercial kitchen has passed an inspection based on health department regulations, you can operate from the kitchen as a legitimate business provided all other permits and licenses are in order. However, a health inspector is likely to visit your facilities regularly without notice. If you are near the business district with many restaurants around, you can expect more frequent visits. If you are out of the main part of town, you will probably be visited less frequently or not at all. You will be sent an annual bill to cover the cost of the health inspector. The fee may seem unreasonably high, but you have no choice but to pay it.

(h) If you start from new kitchen facilities, you will also need the building inspector's approval before the health inspection can approve from his or her point of view.

(i) Workers' compensation insurance. If you have employees (even spo-

radic employment counts in California), you are required to enroll in the state insurance program for workers' compensation in case of job-related injury, illness, or disability. The premium is based on your annual payroll and you pay it once or twice a year. If you don't have a regular payroll, you will be charged a predetermined minimum premium.

(j) Social Security Insurance (FICA). Again, if you have employees, you must withhold the required percentage from each of your employees' paychecks for social security, and you must contribute your share as well. This is a federal law.

(k) Unemployment insurance. This is a state deduction, and it is paid entirely by the employer.

(l) State disability insurance. In some states you are required to have disability insurance. Inquire about the status of this in your location.

(m) Business insurance. Many caterers don't bother with any insurance coverage when they are just starting out, partly because they cannot afford the additional and very substantial cost, but mainly because no insurance company will insure an unlicensed caterer. Unless you live in a cardboard box and own only a shopping cart and its contents, it is very risky to do any business, especially catering, without proper business insurance coverage. You risk losing everything you own in these lawsuit-prone times. One guest bites into a missed olive pit, takes you to court, and demands replacement of not only his complete bridge, but also plastic surgery on his chin and cheeks, plus a million dollars for his pain. And he might even get away with it, or at least part of it.

If you are uninsured or work out of a unapproved kitchen, you are automatically in the wrong no matter how absurd the demand is. Each situation is different, but with an insurance agent and your expected income you can come up with a minimum insurance coverage necessary to operate safely.

Insurance will likely be your second highest overhead item after rent. The premium for business insurance is based on your estimated gross revenues and revised once you know the exact gross. If the gross is less than expected, you will get a refund that is applied to your next premium. If it is more, you will be charged the additional amounts of premium that you underpaid. Generally, the cost for adequate insurance for a year is about one to two percent of your annual total sales.

(n) Zoning laws. Whether you're renting or purchasing, make sure that the local zoning laws allow this type of operation on that location. You have to be absolutely certain or you will have big problems. Don't rely on what the landlord thinks might be true. If there are restaurants in the neighborhood, chances are that zoning regulations permit off-premise catering.

(o) Liquor laws. If you are planning to serve and sell liquor, you need to have a liquor license. If you are planning to serve and sell occasionally, you can get a license for one day only in most states. If you are planning to serve your clients' liquor but there is no exchange of money for it, you may not need a liquor license, but you still need liquor liability insurance. Find out all the local and state regulations for future reference and keep the information in your files.

No doubt, many municipalities will not require all the permits listed above, and some may require more. However, of one thing you can be certain: for each one there is a charge, often an annual charge, and you will be required to pay several sets of taxes every year in addition to your income tax.

b. *In Canada*

In Canada, each province has its own laws, codes, and regulations. Your business must comply with applicable federal, provincial, and municipal laws. Generally, each municipality has special health requirements and licenses for food service businesses.

(a) A business may operate as a sole proprietorship, a partnership, or a corporation. If your company name is an important part of your business, you might want to consider registering it as an official trademark. See *Register Your Trade-mark in Canada*, another title in the Self-Counsel Series, if you are interested in doing this.

(b) In Canada, businesses may apply to Revenue Canada for a provincial or federal tax number, which grants exemption from payment of tax on merchandise purchased for resale. Businesses also pay federal income tax.

If you own your own business property, you also pay property tax. If you rent, the tax is included in your rental payment.

(c) In Canada, businesses with gross revenue over $30,000 must charge 7% goods and services tax (GST) on the goods and services they provide. They must also pay GST on anything they buy. You can register with Revenue Canada for the GST, which allows you to recover any GST that you spend on business purchases.

Registration is mandatory for businesses with gross revenue over $30,000. Small traders (i.e., businesses with under $30,000 gross revenue), do not have to charge GST. For more information about the GST, see *The GST Handbook,* another title in the Self-Counsel Series.

(d) Employers must also pay unemployment insurance premiums and make Canada Pension Plan (CPP) contributions for each employee. Long-term disability insurance and business insurance are optional and are handled through private companies.

In some provinces, businesses of a certain size must contribute to a province-wide health plan for their employees. In other provinces, employees must make their own contributions.

These are just a few of the regulations that businesses in Canada must follow. Since licensing and operating requirements may differ from region to region, contact your local licensing authorities for specifics. For further discussion about the legal aspects of setting up a business in Canada, see also *Starting a Successful Business in Canada,* another title in the Self-Counsel Series.

17
Kitchen Hints For Caterers

The small caterer's kitchen is very different than any other commercial kitchen. The kitchens of large caterers function, to some extent, like standard restaurant kitchens with some predictability; most items are prepared repeatedly and diversion from standard menu items is not frequent. This is certainly true for low-end or even medium-quality catering. The high-end small catering business thrives on customized and unique menus. That changes the character of the kitchen.

In a small, high-end caterer's kitchen, most events are different. Individual and unique menus are exactly what makes smaller catering fun. The routine work lasts not much more than a few hours and something else takes its place. Because there is little routine, the number of food ingredients that should be available on the small caterer's shelf is very large. With a fixed menu, you can get away with ingredients that the standard menu items require. With a customized menu, you'll need items for a dozen different types of foreign cuisines, regional dishes, local ethnic specialties, and food style preferences of groups demanding out-of-the-ordinary cooking — vegetarian, heart-healthy, California light, or kosher, to mention just a few.

The other difference in your kitchen is its erratic use. For two days all machines are purring, refrigerators and freezers jammed to overflowing, the large collection of bowls, pots and pans seemingly not enough to keep up with the demand, and everyone is fighting for space on the prep tables. Then all of a sudden the event is over, and the kitchen is deadly quiet for days, even weeks. The only sound is of the overworked appliances and machines, now resting and sighing in relief.

Managing such a kitchen and running it with top efficiency is also somewhat different. The following hints may help you in running your own catering kitchen efficiently. Some tips apply to any kitchen, some to a caterer's kitchen, and some specifically to a small caterer's kitchen. Use what applies to your situation.

a. Spices, herbs, and flavorings

As discussed in chapter 14, the shelf-life of spices and herbs is not very long. The finer the grind and crushing, the quicker the essential oils escape. Whole seeds, by the way, preserve their flavor for a long time, perhaps years. Experiment for yourself.

The flavorings of spices and herbs are usually the essential oils that the plant material contain. Essential oil may be in the seed and the cavities between the cells both in leaves and stems, like those in the carrot family (caraway, coriander, cumin, dill, fennel, parsley). Or it may be in specialized hairlike oil glands, covering leaf and stem, like in the mint family (basil, marjoram, oregano, mint, rosemary, sage, thyme). Drying organic material reduces the chance of its spoiling. By breaking down the cell structure in the course of drying, it is easier to extract the essential oils when added to foods. It may surprise you that dry herbs can be much more potent than fresh ones, or at least more oil can be extracted from it during the cooking process.

In citrus fruit the volatile oils are in the skin in specialized oil glands. They volatilize (vaporize) fairly fast and in fresh form they should be used immediately after grating. Most essential oils are slightly volatile and slowly leave their host plant material. That's why you should buy them in small quantities and use reasonably fresh herbs and spices in your cooking.

You'll want a complete collection of all spices and herbs you may need to use in your kitchen. If your repertoire inclines toward relatively simple food and your menu is basic, then stock your spice and herb collection with only basic ones. But if you need some sophisticated items for the clients who want ethnic, regional, trendy, or unusual flavors, have a larger variety on hand. Anything you use frequently you can keep an extra supply in the freezer, if it is something that keeps well frozen. This is both for emergency and regular use. Examples are chopped parsley, dill, grated orange and lemon peel (you can chop them in the food processor with sugar), chopped garlic and ginger, and fresh lemon juice. There are certain herbs that don't keep their flavor very well in freezing, possibly because they loose their volatile oil after chopping. These include cilantro, oregano, and basil.

Garlic is best kept in two, or even three, different forms — chopped in the freezer, chopped in the refrigerator under oil, and fresh in cloves. The commercially available fresh-chopped garlic in oil, sold in jars, is not as flavorful and powerful as the garlic you chop fresh yourself.

You should stock the usual extracts like vanilla, lemon, orange, and almond. Extracts are in alcohol and probably have a very long shelf life so you are safe to buy them in large containers.

Finally, there is a little known form of many spices and herbs — the highly con-

centrated essential oils that you can buy in natural food stores. They come in tiny (generally half-ounce bottles) quantities and are very powerful. Most people would not be able to use them, or would not be able to resist using too much. Their dispensers are generally like eye droppers. In place of one teaspoonful of lemon extract, for example, you would use one to two drops of the essential oil of lemon. They give a wonderful flavor and are available for many spices and herbs. There is no general guide for them that I have found. Experiment with them yourself.

Try peppermint oil to start with. Prepare a gallon of good iced tea from real tea leaves or tea bags and add two drops of the essential oil of peppermint. You will have a prize winner peppermint iced tea.

b. Onions

You will find an endless number of advice on how to chop onions without tears. The only foolproof way I've found to chop onions without the powerful irritation to my eyes is to wear a pair of tight-fitting swimming goggles. Your staff will stop giggling after they've tried this method, too.

c. Breads

People love good bread almost more than anything else. You need a good source of bread for your events. You could bake it yourself, but it is time-consuming and you may not be equipped to bake breads and rolls for large groups. That's a bakery's job. However, there is no reason why you can't bake for a smaller gathering if you find time for it.

You should always take plenty of fresh bread to any event. For luncheons count on two to three average slices per person. For dinner, provide one and a half to two slices or about one and a half rolls per person. You will probably end up with extra bread and you should. You can use the leftovers in many things. If it is getting stale, dry it and use it for bread crumbs. Unsliced loaves go right into the freezer. Even if it has been sitting out for several hours, freeze it. When you need it again, remove it from the freezer several hours before an event, sprinkle it with water, and pop it into a hot oven for five minutes. It will be like fresh bread straight out of the oven. If it was frozen stale, instead of sprinkling it with water, give it a very quick shower under the running tap.

Never keep bread in the refrigerator. The staling of bread is a chemical reaction. This reaction is unusual in that it proceeds at a moderate pace at room temperature, very slowly below freezing and very quickly at around 40°F. That's the temperature inside your refrigerator. So bread will keep fine at room temperature and in the freezer, but stales rapidly in the refrigerator. Some commercial bread-baking companies considered putting a message on their bread wrappers, warning people not to store it in the refrigerator. I haven't seen that label yet.

d. Legumes

Dry legumes are a useful part of the catering business. They are inexpensive and when cooked fresh (instead of opening a can), they give a nice flavor and texture to all kinds of foods or can be used by themselves. They are wonderful in salads of almost any sort, and they give bulk at a low cost, especially in the winter when the fresh vegetable part of the salad is expensive and not very good. They are very easy to prepare. All my cookbooks say they need to be soaked overnight and their cooking takes hours.

This is all myth. You don't need to soak any legume overnight, or even for a few hours. And very few take more than one hour to cook, even if they are really old. Just take your beans, wash them well, boil enough water to have about four times the volume of beans, and add salt of about one tablespoon per gallon of water. When the

water is boiling, add the legumes, turn the burner down to simmer, and set your timer. Most beans are tender in 45 to 50 minutes. Lentils and split peas only take 20 to 25 minutes. Have a good store of legumes on your shelf, especially the pretty ones — black beans, red beans, and kidney beans. Depending on what color you need in your salad, select out the beans and add them at the approximate rate of 0.5 dry ounces per person.

One more hint about beans. All legumes cook only in neutral or slightly alkaline liquids. If you will be adding sauce to the beans, make sure they are fully cooked before the sauce is added. Most sauces, especially with tomato in them, are acidic. As soon as you add it to the beans, they stop cooking. Veteran chili makers know this. Once the beans are added to the chili sauce, they can cook it for hours and the beans will never be overcooked.

e. Stocks

Restaurant kitchens use stocks far more than catering kitchens. That's because soups are a daily menu item in restaurants while caterers don't provide soups very often because they are awkward to transport and serve.

Nevertheless, stocks are used in catering, and it is nice to have either ready-made stock or ingredients you can make

it with in your freezer. You can get a very full-flavored, wonderful stock from the parts you cut off. For vegetable stock, use the peelings and other vegetable parts that are discarded but have flavor. Make sure you wash the vegetable thoroughly before peeling. Any vegetable peels, leaves (like celery), pea pods, root parts (celery bottoms), unusable but still flavorful and healthy parts of scallion, the center part and outer peelings of onions, mushroom trimmings, tomato pieces, and parsley stems can be used. Don't include parts that have no flavor (taste it if you have doubts), like papery outer parts of onions, garlic, inner pith, seeds, and membranes of peppers. Anything you save for your stock should be perfectly healthy, so when preparing vegetables, the blemished and spoiled parts you are removing should go in a waste pile, not the stock pile. Keep all this good vegetable material in a plastic bag in the freezer, labelled for stock. When you have more peelings and trimmings, add them to the bag.

You cannot add every piece of vegetable to your stock. You have to control the flavor of the final product. Find a good stock recipe and collect material in the approximate proportion of what the recipe calls for. You need a lot of carrot, celery and onion parts, the basic ingredients of stock, and much smaller portions of any other vegetables. The stronger the flavor of the vegetable trimming, the less of it you want to add so the flavor won't overpower the stock. Some vegetables are so strong in flavor that you should avoid them all together, like cabbage and brussels sprouts. Others will give too much color, like beets.

Don't collect any more than you need. These trimmings take up too much space in your freezer. When you need a vegetable stock, pull the collection, dump it into a pot, cover with water, and add salt, peppercorns or other spices and herbs you like in your recipe. Bring it to a boil, simmer for a couple of hours, and you have a fresh vegetable broth. Vegetable stock needs only a short time to simmer because the vegetable cells break down fast in simmering and flavors are quickly extracted. Cool, strain, and store the broth. If you didn't use too much water, you get a rich stock, even a concentrate that you can dilute.

For chicken and meat stocks, the procedure is the same. Save the trimmings and bones. Many caterers use boneless chickens and meat. You cannot make a good stock from meat trimmings, but you can from chicken trimming, including the skins. When you're ready to make a chicken stock, add both vegetable and chicken trimmings to the pot. Go through the same procedure, but simmer it a little longer — three hours for chicken trimmings, four hours with bones — and you have a chicken stock. Once you have strained and cooled it, put the stock in the refrigerator so the fat collects on top and congeals. Then remove as much as you want. Remove it all for a fat-free stock, or leave just a little for flavor and appearance. Using chicken trimmings with no bones will give you virtually every bit as good and full-bodied a stock as if you used a whole stewing hen. Try making chicken stock both ways if you don't believe it.

For meat stock you need to use the bones, and that takes longer simmering, about six hours.

One more item about stocks. When you finish making your stock, it is recommended in cookbooks to chill it quickly to avoid bacterial contamination while cooling. If there is fat in the stock, this is unnecessary overkill in safety. The fat layer on top seals the stock from any access by bacteria from the air. Nothing penetrates it. You can let it sit out on top of the stove until cool, and it should be perfectly safe. To add an extra measure of safety, don't remove the lid after you turn off the stove. Stocks are almost always boiled again before using them in cooking, which is another safety factor.

Any stock or concentrate can be frozen or refrigerated. If frozen, don't freeze it in large volume unless you expect to use a lot at a time. It is better to package it in smaller units — one or two-quart containers, so you can defrost smaller volumes at a time. Ziplock bags are great for freezing stocks. They take minimal space in the freezer and there's nothing to wash after defrosting. When you need to add stock to a dish, you can even cut the plastic off the frozen chunk and dump it into the pot without defrosting.

f. Using your freezer

No matter how large a freezer you have, it's not big enough. Be judicious about what you fill the shelves with. A small quantity of often-used ingredients is nice to have at all times. My freezer usually holds chopped herbs (especially parsley), fresh lemon juice, yeast (in the freezer it will remain alive but dormant for a very long time), tomato paste (any part of the can you have not used) wrapped in plastic wrap so it is easy to cut part off while still frozen, lemon and orange zest, leftover egg white and egg yolk, bread and rolls, and pastry dough.

Leftover egg white is part of any kitchen. It freezes well and is worth saving in a jar. Whenever you need only the yolk, add the white to the rest already in the freezer. Compile a collection of recipes that use a lot of egg whites. The whites of seven large eggs fill one cup.

Occasionally you have extra egg yolks. Yolks freeze well, too, but they need to be stabilized either by gently stirring a little salt or sugar into them in the proportion of one tablespoon sugar (or honey) to three egg yolks, or just a dash of salt. Gentle stirring is to eliminate trapped air that would oxidize the yolk in the freezer. Freeze egg yolk in small batches; you won't need too much at a time. The plastic egg carton cups are good receptacles to freeze them in. After they are solid, you can re-pack them in a plastic bag. About 13 egg yolks make one cup. For short-term storage mix the yolk with a little water so it won't dry out; then keep it in the refrigerator.

Storing some vegetables in the freezer is a good idea, too. Not many are suitable however — the best are green peas and corn.

Keep a written inventory of the contents of your freezer unless you have a great memory. List items by shelves, remembering to cross out items you remove and adding items to your list when putting them in your freezer. It is much easier to study a list than to search through masses of frozen items. And needless to say, everything in your freezer should be labeled, dated, and well wrapped.

It is questionable whether it is better to have a large freezer or the equivalent volume in two smaller ones. It depends on your business and your personal preference. Two smaller freezers take more space than one larger one. But often you only need to run one for your daily use, turning on the second one only during peak periods, like the wedding months and holiday season. One smaller one is probably more efficient to run energy-wise than a large freezer. Another consideration is that if your freezer fails, you need to have a plan of action to protect the contents which represent a fairly substantial investment. You can use the second freezer as a backup, transferring everything into the working one. If you have only one large freezer, you've got a real problem.

g. Blanching

Blanching of many vegetables is a great idea in better class catering. It will produce a different vegetable than the guests usually expect. Blanching is also necessary before you marinate vegetables. Blanching definitely takes extra time and involves extra steps, but that's why you are justified in charging a little extra. It also stops enzyme action that otherwise continues to ripen and eventually overripen the vegetables, so blanched vegetables keep longer. It has two major benefits for a caterer: it produces more intense colors — deep orange in carrots, deep green in broccoli and snow peas, and it takes the raw taste away but still retains the crispness. Vegetables to be blanched should be cut to size first.

To blanch vegetables, you need a large pot of boiling salted water and a basket with a long handle in which you immerse the vegetables into the water. The more water, the faster it comes to a boil again, so don't blanch too much at a time. Figure out

your own guide. Carrots take about two minutes (depending on the size they were cut), for broccoli half a minute, for green beans four to six minutes, and for zucchini half a minute. Snow peas only take about 20 seconds.

Cookbooks say that after taking them out of the boiling water, the blanched vegetables should be quickly immersed into iced water. That is an unnecessary extra step. A large bowl of cold water is just fine.

Another possibility is to steam them. For that you need a large steamer with several vertical steaming compartments, like a Chinese three-story steamer. That allows you to do three batches of vegetables at the same time. The disadvantage is that they will take longer to steam than to blanch and you have to remove different vegetables at different times as they finish their respective limits. Once you calculate the correct steaming times for different vegetables, write them down on a chart and have several timers to remind you to stop steaming the various batches. In my experience steaming will never give you the same crisp, intensely bright, appetizing-looking vegetables as blanching does. Some chefs may know the secret of perfect steaming that will produce equally appealing vegetables than blanching.

h. Browning meat and chicken

Browning meat and chicken for a caterer is often a problem. Your limited budget allows limited space. You may not have large ranges either. To get around the problem, brown in the oven. It's far better when you need a hundred or even several hundred pieces of meat or chicken breasts. The results will not be identical but are perfectly acceptable. The difference in flavor of browning it in hot fat or in the oven will not be significant. The advantage is twofold. It's much faster and you add much less oil to your dish.

To oven brown, place your meat or chicken on oiled pans and brush the top with oil. Place the meat in a very hot oven (500° F conventional or 450° F convection oven) until it's brown on top. If you wish, turn to brown the other side.

This is an equally good method for browning large amounts of vegetables when frying is one of the steps (e.g., egg-plant slices for moussaka). You will have not even a quarter of the amount of oil soaked up by the eggplant compared to frying it.

i. Extra food

You will be returning from most events with a substantial amount of extra or left-over food. Eventually you will learn what can be used now or reused later. Fresh produce of any sort is often a loss. You and your staff can use it perhaps, but it has no further value to your business. Some salads hold well for several days, but it's not for reuse in your business. Whole fruits are fine, but cut-up fruits are not unless you are making a fruit salad the next day. Leftover salads can be chopped up fine in the food processor, mixed with mayonnaise or sour cream and served as dips.

Milk, cream, and half-and-half all freeze well. They can be used for cooking and baking after being defrosted, though de-frosted milk is perfectly wholesome for drinking or coffee. Cheeses can also be used in future preparations. They are best grated and frozen. Many recipes call for cheeses so these are rarely wasted. Most pastries, cookies, pies, and cakes freeze very well, and you can barely tell the dif-ference between fresh and defrosted prod-ucts. This includes savory pastries, too, like quiche. To make them even fresher tasting, heat them up just before serving. They will be perfectly good.

Bread and rolls, whether yeast or baking powder, freeze well, too, but you should freeze them before they get stale. Rolls can be baked without defrosting, directly from the freezer. If these yeast products were not very fresh when frozen or they have been in the freezer too long, sprinkle them with water before putting them into the hot oven so they regain their lost moisture.

j. Brand-name or generic products

Using brand-name versus generic prod-ucts is really debatable. Only experience will tell you when you should buy known brands and pay a little more and when the lower priced no-brand item will be just as good.

But you can never be sure that brand-names guarantee high quality. Food mag-azines and most cookbooks urge you to buy the high-priced alternative of a prod-uct, like imported durum wheat pastas and extra virgin olive oils to get the best tasting meals from your kitchen. I haven't always found this to be so. To give you a couple of examples, *Consumer Reports* magazine (May, 1992), tested pastas and gave high ratings to inexpensive domestic brand names and even house brand products not to the high-priced imports and even fresh pastas. I tested five different pastas the same way, from cheap to expensive. Then I asked guests to blind test and rate them.

They found no significant difference in flavor or consistency in any. Pasta is pasta.

While we are discussing Italian cuisine, let's talk about highly overrated olive oils. *Consumer Reports* found the extra virgin oils somewhat better in flavor than the pure (lowest-priced olive oil from the last extraction of olives), but possibly not as much better tasting to justify the price.

Little experiments like these are easy to do and even fun. I encourage you to do your own testing. It may save you money and it will certainly teach you a lot about food. It will show you how little you can trust the so-called food authorities.

k. Flavoring foods

Some cookbooks tell you that when preparing in large quantity, you don't increase herbs and spices in proportion to the increased quantities or the food will be overwhelmed by that flavor. Disregard the advice. Scale the recipe up in direct proportion, including all spices and herbs, and it will be just right. Test it for yourself, of course. Don't believe me anymore than anyone else.

The trend is for more spices and herbs, and stronger flavors in all foods. However, caterers are advised to increase spices and herbs even slightly more. Not to a degree that the food is overpowered by the flavorings but enough so that the guests notice it. The idea is to give their flavor buds a sudden kick. That's how they notice your food, and that's how they will remember that they ate something different. The common tossed green salad will gain several degrees when you add some chopped fresh herbs. Everyone with any life left in their tired old taste buds will notice that salad. Or a simple beef bourguignonne; give it some extra garlic and thyme, and your guests will definitely notice it if they have the slightest interest in what they are eating.

l. Defrosting

Defrosting requires planning ahead or quality will suffer, in some cases drastically so. You remember the rubber chicken breast they serve in hotel banquets? Do you know why it's so dry, chewy, and rubbery? When hotels have large functions, they very often get their supplies on the day of the event. (They don't have space to store three or four hundred chicken breasts.) The supplier delivers them in the morning, the food prep people open up the packages, put the breasts under running water for half an hour and the breasts are instantly defrosted. This method of defrosting is the worst, and quality suffers severely. Natural juices are lost from the cells, and the guests end up with the famous hotel banquet rubber chicken breasts.

The way to defrost meat to preserve the most meat juices, and preserve the highest quality is slowly in the refrigerator. To defrost 50 chicken breasts slowly will take several days in the refrigerator, so you must plan ahead when to pull them from the freezer. If you do it right, your chicken will be like fresh.

Some items can be defrosted fast without deterioration — milk, juices, breads, anything baked, and anything in general that does not release juices from the cells. It is still a good idea to plan ahead and place them in the refrigerator from the freezer well ahead of time instead of letting them sit out on the counter.

m. Exotic and rare ingredients

Today's cooking must be distinctive in order to appeal to catering clients who are usually sophisticated restaurant patrons. One way to do this is to use exotic or rare ingredients that are spelled out distinctly in the name of the food item, like sautéed fava beans with crushed garlic and thyme flowers. There are not many ways to get fresh thyme flowers. They have to be special ordered or picked from a garden. Will they give a distinctively different flavor to your fava beans? Absolutely not. Or do you think the shiitake mushrooms added to the soup will make it taste any different than adding ordinary garden-variety commercial ones? Not really, but the dish sounds better and you have to charge more for it because shiitake sells for about six or seven times more than the common mushroom.

Another way to have your dish exotic is to use readily available ingredients but be extravagant about the sheer number you use, like six-pepper fillet of pork with blue cheese. The flavor will be guaranteed to be indistinguishable, whether you use two or six peppers. But such little gimmicks make your catering menu different and distinctive from a simple hole-in-the-wall or neighborhood restaurant.

To be sure, exotic and rare ingredients are essential in truly ethnic cooking. However, an authentic ethnic dish, like a genuine Ceylon curry, would be quite difficult to swallow (literally) by almost anyone with an average western palate. It would be much too hot and much too spicy. Most ethnic restaurants, unless their clientele is almost exclusively from that ethnic background, alter and tone their authentic food down drastically to fit the local palate. Try the Italian food in Italy, the Greek food in Greece, or Thai food in Thailand. They are not for the average North American.

However, take a look at the produce selection of a large, well-stocked supermarket. Chances are they will have some unusual fruits and vegetables most people wouldn't be able to even name. Supermarkets will keep them not just for selling but as a relatively inexpensive way of making their display look lavish, elegant, and unusual. It attracts customers and they will remember that supermarket for its wonderful selection. Produce managers will throw most of those exotic things out once they look old and replace them with fresh ones. Just ask the produce people.

And this is another problem with exotic and rare ingredients you will run into — their freshness. They are expensive, there is a low demand for them, and their turn-around time on the shelf will be much slower. So even if they are available, they may have passed their peak when you need them.

Appendix 1
Cake cutting diagrams

Cutting Sheet Cakes

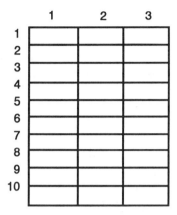

9 x 13 inches, 30 servings

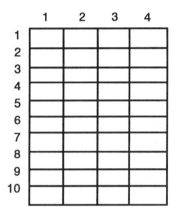

10 x 20 inches, 40 servings

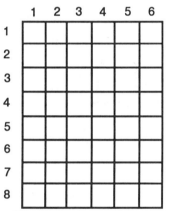

18 x 25 inches, 48 servings

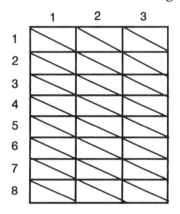

18 x 25 inches, 48 servings

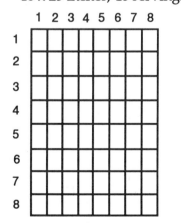

17 x 25 inches, 64 servings

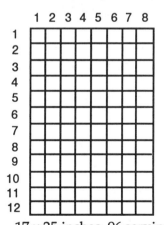

17 x 25 inches, 96 servings

Cutting Square Cakes

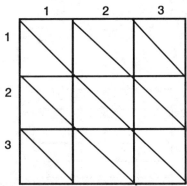

8 x 8 inches, 9 or 18 servings

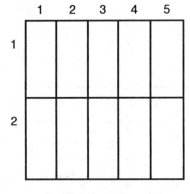

8 x 8 inches, 10 servings

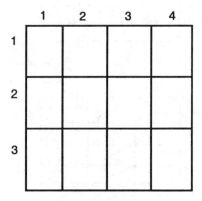

9 x 9 inches, 12 servings

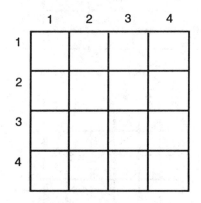

9 x 9 inches, 16 servings

Cutting Loaf Cakes

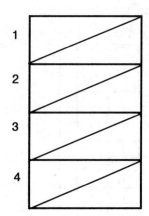 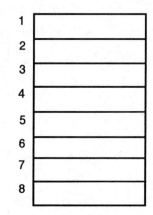 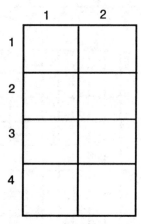

1 pound cakes, 8 servings

Cutting Two-Layer Cakes

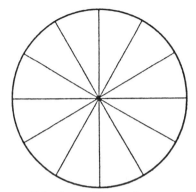

8 inches, 12 servings

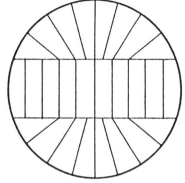

11 inches, 26 servings

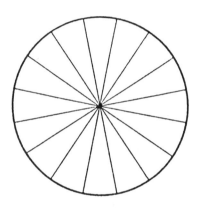

9 inches, 16 servings

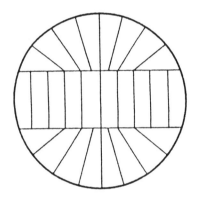

12 inches, 26 servings

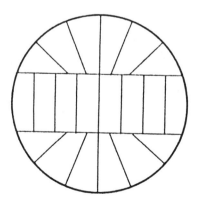

10 inches, 20 servings

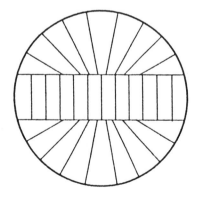

12 inches, 30 servings

Cutting Two-Layer Cakes

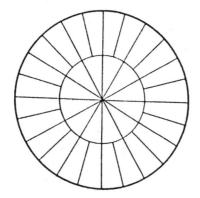

12 inches, 36 servings

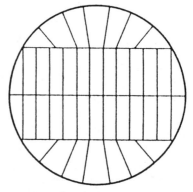

14 inches, 40 servings

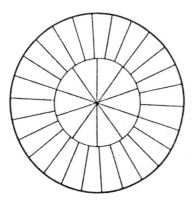

13 inches, 36 servings

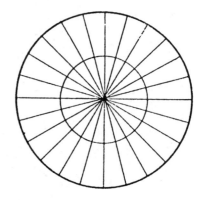

16 inches, 48 servings

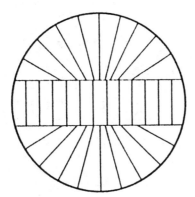

14 inches, 33 servings

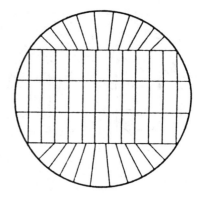

18 inches, 60 servings

Cutting Tier Cakes

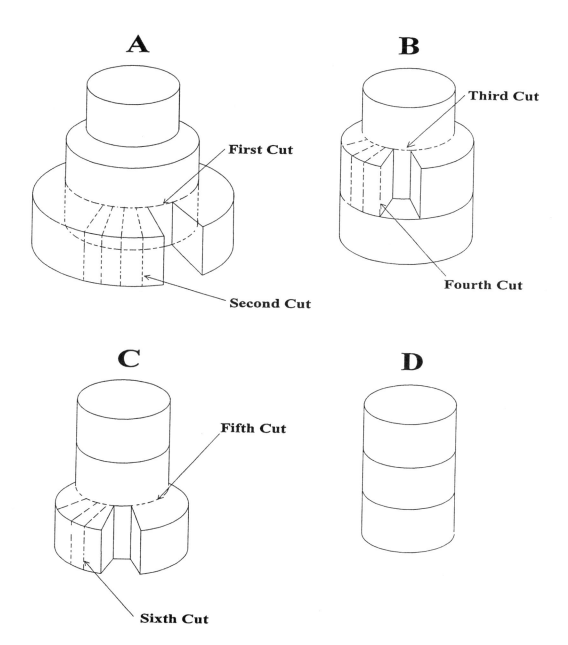

Appendix 2
Recipes for success

These recipes offer tasty ways to introduce something more adventurous into standard reception fare. Clients and guests are always pleased to discover new delicacies.

Calzone

Calzone is a very popular Italian stuffed yeast roll that is heavenly when fresh baked. Different fillings can be used to suit the client's preference, the budget, or the occasion. The ingredients are relatively inexpensive, but making it is labor intensive. It is versatile; it can be served for brunch, lunch, dinner, or as hors d'oeuvres. Calzone is like a sealed pizza with a sealed cover on top. Like pizza, calzone is loved by everyone. Here is an example of a vegetarian cheese calzone.

Dough for 20 – 22:

6 cups flour (may be part whole wheat)

1 tbsp. dry yeast	2 tsp. dry herbs (optional)
1 tbsp. salt	2 - 2¼ cups warm water
1 tbsp. sugar	¼ cup vegetable-olive oil blend

Filling for 22 – 28 calzones (depending on size):

2 lbs. spinach	4 oz. parmesan
4 oz. chopped onion	1½ tsp. salt
4 cloves minced garlic	1½ tsp. pepper
2 lbs. ricotta	2 tsp. dry herbs
12 oz. mozzarella	

To prepare dough, proceed as for yeast bread. Let dough rise once until doubled, punch it down and cut dough into 20 – 22 portions for medium-size calzone.

To prepare filling, cook spinach until nearly dry. Sauté onion and garlic. Mix into spinach with remaining ingredients.

To prepare calzone, shape each portion of dough into a ball and roll out into a circle. Put filling on one half of dough. Moisten edge of half the circle with water. Fold second half over filling to form a half-moon shape. Seal top half over bottom half by pressing dough along moistened edge. Press along same edge with the tines of a fork for additional sealing. Pierce top with tines of fork to let moisture escape while baking. Brush with egg wash.

Bake in 450°F oven for 12 – 14 minutes. Calzone freezes well after baking. To reheat, pop them into a hot oven for 5 minutes. Can be baked while frozen, but in this case, allow 10 minutes in the oven. ❦

Tortilla Roulade

Simple, inexpensive, and quick, yet much appreciated Tex-Mex style spicy hors d'oeuvres.

1 9½" flour tortilla

7 oz. cream cheese

1 oz. finely chopped pimento

1½ oz. finely chopped jalapeno

1 oz. finely chopped black olives

Warm cream cheese to room temperature. Mix in the pimentos, jalapenos, and black olives; you can do this easily by hand or with a food mixer. Spread the mix evenly on the flour tortilla with an icing spatula. Roll up the tortilla tightly. Cover loosely with waxed paper or towel; don't use plastic wrap or foil because the tortilla will become soggy. Chill.

Just before serving, slice roulade in to 20 – 25 pieces. You can vary the spiciness by blending hot and mild jalapeno to fit your guests' preference. Older people prefer it just barely spicy; younger ones don't mind the bite.❧

Baba Ghanouj

An unusual, highly spiced but not hot Middle Eastern spread or dip that guests either fall in love with or leave it alone. It has a strong garlic flavor. Serve it as hors d'oeuvres with french baguette or crackers or even as dip with vegetables. Serve this only for a more sophisticated crowd when it is one of many other items. It is fairly time consuming to prepare, but one pound serves 40 to 50 guests.

1 2½ lb. eggplant

2 oz. sesame tahini

1 oz. chopped garlic

2½ oz. lime juice

2 tsp. salt

½ tsp. pepper

2 tbsp. olive oil

¼ cup finely chopped cilantro

Punch holes in eggplant. Bake it whole in a 400° F oven for 50 minutes. While cooling, blend remaining ingredients. When eggplant is cool enough to handle, remove skin and puree in food processor. Blend with the tahini mixture. Chill.

This recipe makes two pounds and holds very well for a week to 10 days.❧

Layered Cheese Torta with Pesto

This dish is very popular and uses inexpensive ingredients; however, it does take time to prepare. It can be served alone or as part of a cheese display with french bread and crackers. Guests will ask you for this recipe. You can give it to them; they will never make it anyway since it is so tricky.

5½ oz. fresh pesto (your own recipe)

11 oz. cream cheese

5 oz. butter

Soften cream cheese and butter and blend in food mixer. Line a small, shallow loaf pan with cheese cloth. Divide the cream cheese and butter mixture into 6 portions and the pesto into 5 portions. Spread one portion of cream cheese and butter mixture evenly on bottom of the pan with a small wet spatula. Keep dipping the spatula into water so the mixture won't stick to it. Put pan in refrigerator to chill.

When hardened, spread a layer of pesto on top. Spread a second portion of the cream cheese and butter mixture very gently so as not to disturb the pesto layer. Chill. Continue in this fashion to build alternate layers. Chill for several hours.

Remove the cheese torta by lifting out with the cheese cloth. Peel off the cheese cloth.

Holds well for a week to 10 days; it can be prepared well in advance of an event. Guests tend to make a mess of the torta in short order, so when serving, don't put the whole torta out. Instead, cut it into smaller pieces in any shape you wish. Replace with fresh pieces as guests demolish them. You and your staff can nibble on the butchered first pieces. ❦

Hungarian Navy Bean Soup

A wonderful, hearty, inexpensive soup that is easy to prepare. Not only does it hold up well, but it tastes even better on the second day.

2 cups navy beans

8 cups water

1 tbsp. salt

1 ham bone or smoked bacon rind or
    smoked pork neck bone

1 bay leaf

2 carrots cut into rounds

1 parsnip cut into rounds

2 cups milk

¼ cup flour

2 tbsp. oil or butter

4 oz. chopped onion

1 clove chopped garlic

1½ tsp. vinegar

Cook washed beans in water with salt, bones or bacon rind, and bay leaf for 40 minutes. Add carrot and parsnip. Cook 10 more minutes or until vegetables and beans are tender.

Blend milk into flour gradually. Sauté onion in oil or butter. Add garlic and sauté for a few more minutes. Slowly add the blended milk and flour mixture to the onions and garlic, then add to the soup. Cook 15 minutes. Add vinegar.

May be served right away or can be held hot for hours. Serves 9 – 10. ❧

Malaysian Chicken Saté

A flavorful and attractive chicken suitable on the hors d'oeuvres table or as an entrée. The flavor is neither oriental nor Indian but a blend of the two, like much of Malaysia's cuisine. This is a popular dish and the ingredients are not expensive; however, it does take time to prepare. This dish is particularly low cost when you using chicken leg meat, which has more flavor than breast meat.

4 lbs. pure chicken meat, fully trimmed

2 green peppers

2 red peppers

80 bamboo skewers

To make the marinade:

1 cup soy sauce

¼ cup bourbon

2 tbsp. brown sugar

1 tsp. Worcestershire sauce

1 tbsp. sesame oil

1 tbsp. lemon juice

2 tsp. minced ginger

1 tbsp. chopped parsley

1 clove minced garlic

Mix marinade ingredients. Makes 1½ cups, enough for 4 lbs. chicken or meat.

Cut chicken into bite-size pieces. Make them small for light hors d'oeuvres; this will give you about 160 pieces. Marinate chicken for at least 4 hours. Marinating it longer will not harm it; it can be left in the marinade overnight.

Cut green and red peppers into small squares so you will have 80 squares of each. Skewer two pieces of chicken, one each of the green and red pepper squares alternately on the bamboo skewers, leaving them near the sharp end. Start with a green pepper and end with a chicken to prevent the green peppers from falling off the skewers after baking softens them. Bake skewers in 450°F oven for 20 – 25 minutes, turning them once. You can also broil the skewers, which takes about 8-10 minutes.

May be taken out of oven just before fully baked, transported to site and put back into oven to finish baking for about 5 minutes. Then they should be served hot. With several other dishes, 2 – 3 skewers will serve one person. For larger portions per person, cut the chicken into larger pieces. You'll have fewer skewers but more chicken on each. Or you can add more pieces of chicken on each skewer. ❧

Polenta Stufata

An authentic Italian meal that will be appreciated by everyone — from children to older guests used to traditional fare. Polenta is similar to lasagna but uses cornmeal instead of pasta. You can also make a vegetarian version. This dish is inexpensive but takes time to assemble. It holds well if the meal is delayed.

40 oz. cornmeal, preferably coarse
    ground (sold as polenta mix)

156 oz. water

1¼ tbsp. salt

1½ lbs. Italian sausage

7½ cups tomato sauce

9 oz. parmesan cheese

6 oz. cheddar or Jack cheese

8 oz. butter, melted

Mix cornmeal with some of the water until you have a thick, soupy mush. Bring the rest of the water to boil with the salt. Stir cornmeal mush into the boiling water and cook until quite thick, stirring often. Pour it into an oblong, lightly oiled dish, like a full-size hotel pan. When cold, turn it out on a large board.

Sauté sausage in a little oil, add tomato sauce, and cook for 10 minutes. Grate and blend the two cheeses.

To assemble, cut the polenta into thin horizontal layers; a wire cheese cutter is the best tool for doing this. Layer the ingredients like a lasagna: one-third polenta on bottom of a pan, then half of the sauce with sausage. Sprinkle with one-third of the cheeses and one-third of the butter. Add a second layer of polenta, top it with the rest of the sauce, another third of the cheeses, and one-third of the butter. Add the last layer of polenta and top with the remaining cheese and butter.

It is a good practice to reserve a little extra polenta to repair the top surface for an attractive, smooth presentation. To do this, put polenta and some water in a food processor and produce a smooth paste. Using a spatula, fill any gaps or imperfections on the top surface of the polenta already in the baking pan before adding the last layer of cheeses and butter.

Bake in a 375°F oven for 45 minutes or until uniformly brown. Let polenta set for 15 minutes before cutting. Serves 25 – 28. If you want to make a vegetarian polenta, omit sausage and increase cheeses by one pound.

Double Espresso Truffles

A classy but easily prepared dessert item that can be part of a dessert display this dessert is elegant and has an unusual flavor that will intrigue guests. It is moderately time consuming to make, but the ingredients are inexpensive. It also has a very long shelf life and can be prepared weeks or even months in advance.

1 cup strong espresso coffee

2¼ cups sugar

2½ cups walnuts, ground fine

5 tbsp. very finely ground coffee (espresso or Turkish ground)

5 tbsp. icing sugar

Combine espresso coffee and sugar and cook down until thick like honey. Stir in walnuts. Blend ground coffee and icing sugar. Using a spoon or a small scoop, form balls from the coffee-walnut mixture, roll each by hand into prefect spheres. Then roll them in the ground coffee and sugar mixture until coated. Place each ball into a tiny fluted bon bon or chocolate truffle cup. Makes 60 – 70 truffles.✨

Cream Cheese Tarts

These are delectable little bite-size tarts that look irresistible on the table. They are rich English tarts, also called tassies, that may be served as the full dessert or as part of a variety of sweet items. The tarts are time consuming to make but have a very long shelf life, so they can be made far in advance. Depending on the filling you choose, they can be inexpensive to moderately expensive.

Use tiny muffin pans for bite-size tarts or regular muffin pans for full-sized tarts.

Pastry:

6 oz. cream cheese

8 oz. butter

2 cups flour

Filling:

2 eggs	2 tsp. vanilla extract
1½ cup brown sugar	⅛ tsp. salt
2 tbsp. melted butter	1⅓ cups coarsely chopped walnuts

To make the pastry, combine cold butter and cream cheese in a food processor. Pulse repeatedly until dough begins to form. Don't over-process. When the dough almost starts to form, dump contents of bowl on table and manipulate by hand until uniform dough is produced. Chill. Divide into 48 portions for tiny tarts, 24 portions for regular tarts. Place each portion in an ungreased muffin pan and press to bottom and part way up the sides to form tartlets. Work dough while it is still cold.

Mix the filling ingredients, except nuts. Divide filling among muffin cups. Sprinkle the walnuts over the filling.

Bake in 350°F oven for 25 minutes or until pastry is beginning to brown. Remove from pan when cool with the help of a small knife. Makes 48 small or 24 regular tarts.✨

Strawberry Fool

Fool is an English fruit dessert. It is similar to the more familiar mousse but softer and thinner in consistency because it does not have gelatin or other congealing agent to set the fruit purée. Fools are very easy to make and inexpensive if you can use fruit that is in season. Add a small freshly baked cookie to individual servings, an elegant touch.

40 oz. fresh strawberries, crushed

1¼ cups sugar

½ tsp. lemon juice

2½ cups heavy cream

Combine strawberries, sugar, and lemon juice. Taste for sweetness. Depending on the ripeness of strawberries you may need more sugar. Stir vigorously until all sugar is dissolved. Fold in whipped cream. Serve individually in 5 – 6 oz. containers. Serves 12 – 16. ❧

OTHER TITLES IN THE SELF-COUNSEL BUSINESS SERIES

EFFECTIVE SPEAKING FOR BUSINESS SUCCESS
Making presentations, using audio-visuals, and more
by Jacqueline Dunckel and Elizabeth Parnham

Give dynamic speeches, presentations, and media interviews. When you are called upon to speak in front of your business colleagues, or asked to represent your company in front of the media, do you communicate your thoughts effectively? Or do you become tongue-tied, nervous, and worried about misrepresenting yourself and your business?

Effective communication has always been the key to business success, and this book provides a straightforward approach to developing techniques to improve your on-the-job speaking skills. This book is as easy to pick up and use as a quick reference for a specific problem as it is to read from cover to cover. Whether you want to know how to deal with the media, when to use visual aids in a presentation, or how to prepare for chairing a meeting, this book will answer your questions and help you regain your confidence. $8.95

Contents include:

- Preparing your presentation
- When and where will you speak?
- Let's look at visual aids
- Let's hear what you have to say: rehearsing
- How do you sound?

PREPARING A SUCCESSFUL BUSINESS PLAN
A practical guide for small business
by Rodger Touchie, B.Comm., M.B.A.

At some time, every business needs a formal business plan. Whether considering a new business venture or rethinking an existing one, an effective plan is essential to success. From start to finish, this working guide outlines how to prepare a plan that will win potential investors and help achieve business goals.

Using worksheets and a sample plan, readers learn how to create an effective plan, establish planning and maintenance methods, and update their strategy in response to actual business conditions. $14.95

Contents include:

- The basic elements of business planning
- The company and its product
- The marketing plan
- The financial plan
- The team
- Concluding remarks and appendixes
- The executive summary
- Presenting an impressive document
- Common misconceptions in business planning
- Your business plan as a tangible asset

MARKETING YOUR SERVICE BUSINESS
Plan a winning strategy
by Jean Withers, M.B.A. and
Carol Vipperman, B.A.

To effectively sell the service you offer, you must let people know that you exist and that you are better than your competition. This book explains what is necessary to develop a marketing plan that will work for service businesses ranging from law firms and dental practices to hair salons and auto repair shops. Whether your service is consulting or running a restaurant, you will profit from expanding your market.

The authors, consultants to service businesses, have provided 32 worksheets for you to develop your own specific marketing plan based on the procedures they describe. $12.95

The book answers the following questions and more:

- How does marketing a service differ from marketing a product?
- How do you prepare for marketing?
- Where can you find information about potential clients?
- What should you know about your competition?
- How do you establish goals that are desirable and realistic?
- What strategies for pricing and promotion will work best for you?
- How do you develop and implement an action plan for marketing?

RELATIONSHIP SELLING
Building trust to sell your service
by Karen Johnston, M.A., and
Jean Withers, M.B.A.

This skills-oriented book is designed for professionals, business owners, and administrators—in fact anyone in the business community. It provides a step-by-step system for selling your service in a way that you can feel comfortable with.

Selling services requires new skills and challenges, and in this book the authors combine their nearly 30 years' experience to bring together the information you need to help you be more profitable and successful.

Diagrams, figures, and samples help illustrate the skills discussed, and 23 worksheets are provided for you to work out your own selling strategy. $12.95

These are just some of the topics discussed:

- How selling a service is different from selling a product
- What relationship selling is and why it is important for selling a service
- How to sell when you are not a salesperson
- Understanding your feelings of resistance to selling and overcoming them
- Asking for what you're worth
- How to talk about and promote your service business

BASIC ACCOUNTING FOR THE SMALL BUSINESS
Simple, foolproof techniques for keeping your books straight and staying out of trouble
by Clive Cornish, C.G.A.

Having bookkeeping problems? Do you feel you should know more about book-keeping, but simply don't have time for a course? Do you wish that the paperwork in your business could be improved, but you don't know where or how to start?

This book is a down-to-earth manual on how to save your accountant's time and your time and money. Written in clear, everyday English, not in accounting jargon, this guide will help you and your office staff keep better records.

Inside you will find illustrations of sample forms and instructions on how to prepare all the records you will need to keep, including:

- Daily cash sheet
- Cash summary
- Statement ledger
- Payables journal
- Synoptic journal
- Payroll book
- Income statement
- Trial balance
- Columnar work sheet

U.S. ed. $7.95
Canadian ed. $8.95

KEEPING CUSTOMERS HAPPY
Strategies for success
by Jacqueline Dunckel and Brian Taylor
Customer satisfaction is your company's best asset!

Consumers today demand personal attention from businesses before they spend their money. So, customer service is moving up the priority list in dynamic companies and it is consuming more of their time and budgets; businesses that ignore customer relations do so at their peril.

You need good service to attract customers and keep them coming back, and this book provides plans and programs that have been proven successful by other businesses. No matter what kind of business you are in, this book will help increase profits through improved customer relations. $8.95

Contents include:

- Customer service — what it is and what it is not
- The "why" of customer relations
- The value of service
- Developing a profitable customer relations program
- Setting goals for your business
- Putting your plan together
- Communicating your customer relations program to your employees
- Training employees
- Bringing it all together

THE ADVERTISING HANDBOOK
*Make a big impact with a small
business budget*
Dell Dennison and Linda Tobey

If you want more bang from your
advertising dollar, this book is for you.
It explains, step by step, what advertising
is, how it works, and, most important,
what will work best for *your* small
business. Worksheets, samples, and
diagrams are used to explain advertising
concepts and help you d̶ ̶ ̶ ̶ ̶an
effective campaign. $̶

Some of the ̶ ̶ ̶ ̶ ̶ ̶ ̶ ̶clude:

- The im̶ ̶ ̶ ̶ ̶ ̶ ̶ ̶ ̶ ̶ing
- Hov̶ ̶ ̶ ̶ ̶ ̶er
  to̶ ̶ ̶ ̶ ̶ ̶ ̶-y
  ̶ ̶ ̶ ̶ ̶ ̶ ̶ own
  low-cost research
- Effective copywriting and
  design techniques
- When and how to use radio,
  television, print, and other
  types of media
- How to write a press release

ORDER FORM

All prices are subject to change without
notice. Books are available in book, department, and stationery stores. If you cannot
buy the book through a store, please use this
order form. (Please print)

Name_____

Address_____

_____

Charge to: ❏ Visa   ❏ MasterCard

Account Number_____

Validation Date _____

Expiry Date _____

Signature _____

❏ **Check here for a free catalogue.**

IN CANADA
Please send your order to the nearest
location:

Self-Counsel Press
1481 Charlotte Road
North Vancouver, B. C.
V7J 1H1

Self-Counsel Press
8-2283 Argentia Road
Mississauga, Ontario
L5N 5Z2

IN THE U.S.A.
Please send your order to:

Self-Counsel Press Inc.
1704 N. State Street
Bellingham, WA 98225

YES, please send me:

_____copies of **Effective Speaking for
Business Success** $8.95

_____copies of **Preparing a Successful
Business Plan,** $14.95

_____copies of **Marketing Your Service
Business,** $12.95

_____copies of **Relationship Selling,**
$12.95

_____copies of **Basic Accounting for the
Small Business** U.S. $7.95
Canadian, $8.95

_____copies of **Keeping Customers
Happy,** $8.95

_____copies of **The Advertising
Handbook,** $8.95

Please add $2.50 for postage & handling.

Canadian residents, please add 7% GST
to your order.
WA residents, please add 7.8% sales tax.